STORY

Katie Egan Cunningham

STORY

Still the Heart of
Literacy Learning

Foreword by Linda Rief

Stenhouse Publishers

Portland, Maine

Stenhouse Publishers   www.stenhouse.com

Library of Congress Cataloging-in-Publication Data

Names: Cunningham, Katie Egan, 1978- author.
Title: Story : still the heart of literacy learning / Katie Egan Cunningham ;
 foreword by Linda Rief.
Description: Portland, Maine : Stenhouse Publishers, 2016. | Includes
 bibliographical references and index.
Identifiers: LCCN 2015022555| ISBN 9781625310248 (pbk. : alk. paper) | ISBN
 9781625310699 (ebook)
Subjects: LCSH: Language arts (Elementary) | Literacy--Study and teaching
 (Elementary) | Storytelling.
Classification: LCC LB1576 .C8548 2016 | DDC 372.6--dc23 LC record available at http://lccn.loc.gov/2015022555

Credits

Page 8, Figure 1.1: Reprinted with permission of Lee and Low Books.

Pages 24 and 25, Walter Dean Myers quotes: From *The New York Times*, March 16, 2014 © 2014 The New York Times. All rights reserved. Used by permission and protected by the Copyright Laws of the United States. The printing, copying, redistribution, or retransmission of this Content without express written permission is prohibited.

Pages 57–58, Garth Stein extract: From *The Art Of Racing In The Rain* by Garth Stein. Copyright © 2008 By Bright White Light, LLC. Reprinted by permission of Harper Collins Publishers.

Page 59, "Marbles" by Valerie Worth: From *All The Small Poems And Fourteen More* © 1994 by Valerie Worth. Reprinted by permission of Farrar, Straus, and Giroux, LLC. All Rights Reserved.

Page 66, "Blackbird" by the Beatles: *Blackbird* Written by John Lennon & Paul McCartney. © 1968 Sony/ATV Music Publishing LLC. All rights administered by Sony/ATV Music Publishing LLC, 424 Church Street, Suite 1200, Nashville, TN 37219. All rights reserved. Used by permission.

Pages 115–116, Hemingway extract: Reprinted with the permission of Scribner, a division of Simon & Schuster, Inc. from *The Old Man And The Sea* by Ernest Hemingway. Copyright © 1952 by Ernest Hemingway. Copyright renewed © 1980 by Mary Hemingway. All rights reserved.

Pages 117, Figure 5.5 book covers:

The One and Only Ivan **by Katherine Applegate:** Cover Copyright © 2012 by Patricia Castelao. Used by permission of HarperCollins Publishers.

Walk Two Moons **by Sharon Creech:** Cover Art Copyright © 1994 By Lisa Desimini. Cover Copyright © 1996 By HarperCollins Publishers. Used by permission of HarperCollins Publishers.

A Long Walk to Water **by Linda Sue Park:** Copyright © 2010 by Linda Sue Park. Reprinted by permission of Clarion Books, an imprint of Houghton Mifflin Harcourt Publishing Company. All rights reserved.

The Red Kayak **by Priscilla Cummings:** Used by permission of Penguin Random House LLC. All rights reserved.

The City of Ember **by Jeanne DuPrau:** Used by permission of Penguin Random House LLC. All rights reserved.

Cover and interior design by Lucian Burg, Lu Design Studios, Portland, ME www.ludesignstudios.com

Manufactured in the United States of America

PRINTED ON 30% PCW
RECYCLED PAPER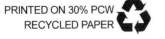

20 19 18 17 16 15   9 8 7 6 5 4 3 2 1

To Jack and Matthew

May you know
that your story matters,
and may you love
the story of your life.

CONTENTS

Foreword by Linda Rief   ix

Acknowledgments   xiii

Introduction
Stories Make Us Human   1

Chapter 1
Why Stories Matter   5

Chapter 2
Whose Stories Count?   21

Chapter 3
Where Do Stories Live?   51

Chapter 4
How Can Stories Come to Life?   79

Chapter 5
How Do We Build Stories?   107

Chapter 6
How Do We Talk About Stories?   129

Chapter 7
Why This Work Takes Courage   141

Appendix: Annotated Bibliography of Suggested Resources   149

References   163

Index   177

Foreword

[T]he minds we use to comprehend are veritable narrative machines—
we dream in stories, remember in stories, create our identities,
individual and collective, through stories.

Narrative is not . . . merely a type of writing. . . . It is a property of
mind, an innate and indispensible form of understanding, as instinctive
as our fear of falling, as our need for human company. Good writers
know that and construct plots—itches to be scratched—that sustain us
as readers. We are always asking, "What's the story?"

—Thomas Newkirk, *Minds Made for Stories*

*S*everal years ago, Savitri, permanently brain damaged and physically injured from an auto accident, limped into my eighth-grade classroom, dropped her backpack on the floor, and sat in the empty chair at a table with three other girls. One by one, each of those girls stood up and moved to other tables.

I shot those girls horrified looks. Each gave me an excuse: "The sun was too hot there," "I couldn't see the board," "My back was to you."

At the end of class, on her way out the door, Savitri leaned toward me and said, "It's okay, Mrs. Rief. But I know it wasn't from the sun."

Several days later I handed the book *This Same Sky* (1992), a collection of poetry compiled by Naomi Shihab Nye, to Savitri, hoping she would find a poem she liked, a poem that would speak to her. What this eighth grader found was far more than a poem. "Home" by Nasima Aziz, an Indian poet, spoke so personally to her that when she chose to read the poem aloud, a bridge was built not only between the writer and his reader but also between this young woman and her classmates—two bridges that told her she was not alone in her longing.

Savitri longed to be "normal." When she read aloud the lines "Grief grips my throat. I must go on/Over the vanished years, into the empty room,/Come back, come back, come back," every fourteen-year-old in that room knew it wasn't only India that Savi was longing for. It was her whole being—who she used to be and who she knew she would never be again. In the silence, Rachael—one of the three girls who had moved from that table—asked sincerely, "Would you read that again?"

With the voice, the timing, and the confidence of a poet, Savitri breathed life into Aziz's words. Amid the spontaneous burst of applause that followed her reading, she smiled.

In their lives, those students will never hear a more beautiful, passionate, or powerful reading of a poem. The breathtaking words of a poet from India, translated scrupulously in Nye's collection, published by a perceptive editor in a skyscraper in New York, touched a child's life. An entire classroom of peers understood in that moment what her life was like, and how painful her longing was.

That poem and her reading led her to writing her own poetry: observations, thoughts, and feelings that helped her see the richness in life. She began to share the small moments of India—the little things that mattered deeply to her—with us. And her classmates listened.

Savitri spoke several languages before the accident. She was an accomplished runner. After the accident her long-term memory was intact—she could still speak English, German, Italian, and several Indian dialects. She remembered people and places from her earliest years. But she could not remember where her classrooms were, which locker was hers, or how to get to the cafeteria. She knew she would never run again. And she often wondered aloud if she would ever make it back to India—*home.*

I have told this story over and over again, because story matters. This story in particular matters for all it teaches us. Those girls made a mistake—a cruel, thoughtless gesture—when they stood and moved away from Savitri. They did not realize it until she read "Home." In that profound moment of understanding, all she longed for and would never again have became clear to those young women, and to the entire class. They felt something for her.

Story is what makes us human. Story connects our students to one another in the classroom and to the world. And that is precisely what Katie Cunningham is demonstrating for us in this book. The stories we tell matter. The stories we give our students to read matter. Cunningham asks us to reconsider the stories we share with students. Can students find themselves in these stories? She cites a poignant example from Walter Dean Myers, who left school precisely because he could not connect in any way with the reading expected of him. "Where am I, who am I?" he asked, in the literature offered to him as a high school student. Cunningham shows us how to do so much better for our students, with numerous examples of diverse topics, themes, genres, and media.

She offers open-ended questions that students bring to their reading, questions that energize them intellectually and emotionally, stories and questions that move their thinking forward. Cunningham asks these questions of herself as a reader and writer. She steps into the literature and the multimedia approaches she offers to her students in order to understand how she can deepen her own reading.

In an example from *The Art of Racing in the Rain* by Garth Stein, Cunningham gives us insight into her reading and thinking process as she looks closely at the way this story is crafted in a way to touch her, a way that deepens her understanding of self as well as others. She then asks, after sharing with students, "When has reading felt good [like this] for you?"

Through technology, the world is at our fingertips. Cunningham makes it even easier for the reader to find and access movies and art, informational writing and poetry, and helpful websites and blogs. She weaves technology seamlessly into her personal and classroom stories, introducing us to new ways of looking at story. As I read her book I stopped frequently to do just as she suggests: "Make your way there immediately." I looked at the photo blog by Brandon Stanton, *Humans of New York*, a site that has known incredible success because of its simple assertion that "we all have stories to tell and when asked the right questions (Can I take your photo? What's been your greatest accomplishment? What was the happiest moment of your life? Do you remember the saddest moment of your life?) we may be brave enough to share them with the world." As Cunningham reiterates, even in our classrooms, the simplest questions might help our students reveal their most important stories.

Cunningham introduces us to a plethora of helpful blogs, including *The Classroom Bookshelf* (a blog written by Cunningham and several other literacy specialists from Lesley University) and *BookDragon* (a Smithsonian site)—both of which I bookmarked instantly.

Stories live in literature, poetry, music, art, illustration, multimedia, and play. Cunningham shows us how choices made by writers and artists deepen our understanding of their stories and ourselves. She provides many fine examples of the power of the visual arts and surprises us with extraordinary literary techniques such as "mash-ups" (where artists and storytellers select existing material, combine selections, and make something completely new from the material) that engage readers in new ways.

In collaboration with her husband, a middle school principal, Cunningham has assembled a comprehensive list of text set considerations—grouped by themes (empathy and compassion, adversity and resilience, etc.) and relevant for grades 5–8—that include far more than novels.

This is a wonderful book: generous in its ideas, rich in its examples, and humble in the simplicity of its approach. It is a trustworthy addition to the field of literacy precisely because it values story to enrich and deepen the lives of our students.

Our work is to build bridges, bringing literacy to our students for life. When our students are immersed in the kind of reading that helps their development of wonder and vision, as Cunningham suggests and so astutely shows here, their writing and reading change.

Cunningham's book is the story of her learning and teaching. She shows us explicitly that, "As teachers, we have the incredible power of bringing stories to life. When we select thought-provoking and powerful books, images, and multimedia, our students want to hold these stories inside themselves. They want to linger in the story, enter its world, and roam around for a while." This is what you will want to do—enter her world, linger in her story, roam around for a while—as you reclaim the central place of story in your own classrooms.

Linda Rief, author of *Read Write Teach: Choice and Challenge in the Reading-Writing Workshop* (Heinemann, 2014) and *Inside the Writer's-Reader's Notebook* (Heinemann, 2007)

Acknowledgments

$\mathcal{T}$his book represents two years of weekends, stolen hours, and encouragement by so many people in my life. But, really this book is thirty-six years in the making. I am indebted and grateful for all of the influences on this book along the way. My first debt of gratitude is to my parents, Jim and Karin Egan, who dropped me off at the library on Sundays, gave me my treasured copies of *Little Women* and *Anne of Green Gables*, and let me escape to my room and burrow under the covers with a story long after bedtime. You had on your hands a girl eager to hit the card catalogue and microfilm. Not only did you inspire a love of stories and research early in my life, but you continue to be the greatest forces in my children's lives. Watching you interact with Jack and Matthew, I have learned about the power of closely and carefully observing young people. You give your whole hearts to the people you love and demonstrate an endless bounty of love and care. Thank you is not enough.

To my sister, Kristin, and her amazing three children—Alex, Lena, and Owen—you are living one incredible story and I am in awe of you. To my brother, Jimmy, you remind us that we each have different strengths and different journeys to take as our stories unfold.

When I was in graduate school, I had the great fortune of being in Maureen Barbieri's literacy course. She welcomed us each evening with a pile of poems, and shared her own story as a teacher and mother, and I instantly knew . . . I want to be like Maureen. Maureen, you were my first mentor in this great field and I have been in awe of your compassionate leadership, mastery of the art of teaching, and knowledge of the power of story ever since. Thank you thank you thank you for seeing a writer in me and for reaching out about the possibility of this work. You have helped shape this book from the beginning. Your reviews of each chapter were the light I needed to complete this work, and your patience, balanced perspective, and guidance have been essential at every step of the way to produce this book. How fortunate I am to have an editor who has been a mentor and friend.

I am forever indebted to the gifted and talented editorial and production staff at Stenhouse Publishers who transformed my ideas into something meaningful for teachers. Louisa Irele, you have been an enormous support making this book come to fruition. I am incredibly grateful for your guidance with sources, references, and permissions. Chris Downey, thank you for shepherding the manuscript through all of the stages of production. Your clear communication and heartfelt support made the process so seamless. Jay Kilburn, wow, wow, wow. I got goosebumps each time I opened a new file that had your brilliant design vision enclosed. You understood from the beginning that an abstract cover would capture the goals I had with this book—that stories are interconnected and everywhere. Each of your choices truly make this book shine. Chandra Lowe, your warm welcome to the Stenhouse family meant the world. Thank you for all things conference and author-engagement related. Chuck Lerch, thank you for capturing the essence of this book so succinctly to create the back cover and for your marketing vision. Toby Gordon, thank you for your editorial eye. Finally, thank you, Dan Tobin, for believing in this book and giving it a home in the Stenhouse family. I am forever grateful.

Special thanks to Linda Rief for your beautiful foreword. It's a huge honor to have your name alongside mine. You have greatly influenced my thinking about choice, true engagement, and the need to nurture our students as readers, writers, and young people making their way in the world. Thank you to Kelly Gallagher for the back-cover blurb. *Readicide* and *In the Best Interest of Students*, among your other works, continue to guide my thinking about what really matters most in our classrooms. Thank you both!

I am fortunate to be part of several professional groups of inspiring educators that shape my thinking on a daily basis. Grace Enriquez, Mary Ann Cappiello, and Erika Thulin Dawes—thank you for inviting me to join *The Classroom Bookshelf*. Every week when one of your drafts for book reviews comes in, I am amazed at the ways you read and interpret stories. You make our work in children's and young adult literature matter and remind me of the possibility of stories and the power of teaching invitations to invigorate young people to read, write, and create. I want to go back in time and be in each of your classrooms as a student!

When I was looking for a change in life, I was fortunate to join the LitLife team. Pam Allyn, your influence on my work (and life, really) has been oceanic. You have challenged and shaped my thinking in countless ways. Our shared love of *Little Women* and *Anne of Green Gables* was one of the first ways I knew LitLife would feel like a professional home, and I have felt that way ever since. Patty Vitale-Riley, you have been a cheerleader for me and this work, and I thank you for the phone calls, kind words, and belief in me. Jennifer Scoggin, you are one powerful literacy leader modeling the ways we can successfully lead, teach, and parent, always placing students first.

Maya Roth, Katie Armstrong, Gravity Goldberg, and Jaime Quackenbush, you continue to amaze me in all that you do in schools with teachers and young people. I don't know how many people get such strong and lifelong friendships out of C&T 5000, but I am forever grateful that I did. Our shared story has had such an enormous impact on the ways I think about our field across all settings and age groups.

My department colleagues at Manhattanville College are nothing short of inspiring. Kristin Rainville and Courtney Kelly—I remember our first meet-up at Panera Bread with our little boys in tow. Jack, Jack, and Joey started it all. Your depth of knowledge about literacy teaching and learning, culturally and linguistically diverse learners, and the politics of higher education have informed my thinking and teaching in countless ways. Thank you for supporting me in both big and small ways. Sandwiches, cupcakes, and camaraderie have defined our department meetings and have made the intellectual pursuits we engage in less daunting and oh so joyful.

I've had the wonderful fortune of working in great schools that supported me to place students' stories at the heart of my work. Alona Scott and Franny Thorndike, you are masters of your craft and handed me my first copies of Nancie Atwell's *In the Middle* and Howard Zinn's *The People's History of the United States*. You led by example and continue to be the model of great teaching in my mind. Elaine Natalichhi, your leadership of the Lower School at The Dwight School made us a community of engaged intellectuals. You encouraged us to continue to grow as professionals, reading and sharing journal articles with one another. You supported the ways I taught my fourth graders to think about stories, architecture, poetry, and art. Thank you for being the kind of literacy leader I wanted to be. Kim Davidson, you taught me endless lessons about understanding young boys. Your warmth and understanding are unparalleled in schools, and I am grateful you always understood the ways I supported my students as storytellers.

Suzanne Farrell Smith, you are a one-of-a-kind teacher, writer, mother, and friend. The best year a teacher could have was sharing a grade level with you. The only thing that would have made our teaching partnership better is if we were in the same room! Our shared love of the power of stories to transform lives, including our own, has been the fuel that's propelled our friendship long after we roamed the same halls. Anna-Bain Reynolds, your understanding of each student in your care amazes me still. You define what it is to teach with heart and vulnerability. You took risks to share stories you knew mattered. You gave up your own time for your students. May my boys and all students be lucky to have teachers like both of you.

Thank you to Jason Low, Jonathan Harris, and Aaron Mace for sharing your perspectives on stories with me and for all of the work you do in the world to make stories matter.

Thank you, Francesca DeLio, for your *Let's Talk About Race* read-aloud plan to use as a model. Observing your read-aloud and hearing your powerful voice bring this critical text to life was a joy. You will change the lives of countless students in the years to come.

So many schools have been welcoming places for me as a consultant. How fortunate I've been to be received with open doors, minds, and hearts. Mary Shannon, Anthony Lombardi, and the P.S. 49 team gave me the space to explore what close reading could look like beyond the printed page. Your innovations in redefining shared reading as a place for shared music, art, and poetry are an inspiration, and I hope other schools adopt your methods for redefining what counts as text. Karen Brenneke, Anne Bilko, and the team at Sarah Noble Intermediate School, I am grateful that you gave me the opportunity to dig deeply into the power of language. Analyzing and interpreting the stories you love helped me rethink the boundaries between narrative and informational text. You lead a model school where children know they matter, where their smiles and engagement reveal what's most important in classrooms, and you represent the powerful teaching all children should have. Thank you, Mary Lavoie and the team at Schaghticoke Middle School, for welcoming me into your classrooms to think about and try techniques together to truly center student engagement through reading and writing. Jodi Falk and the team at Saint Joseph's School for the Deaf, you have challenged me to rethink what it means to be a reader and writer. Your innovative work on American Sign Language poetry, fairy tales, and the power of asking questions—to name a few of your wondrous units—is truly remarkable. You are driven by the power of story and the right all children have to see themselves as storytellers. Thank you for welcoming me and for teaching me so much I didn't know. Sue Ostrofsky, thank you for cheering for me in a crowd and for truly meaning it! You lead a model school that accepts nothing short of authentic, engaged, inquiry. To the teachers at Mount Kisco Elementary, thank you for sharing your classrooms and students with me. You give your whole selves everyday to transform the literacy lives of your students. Maria Flores, Ivan Tolentino, and the teachers at Thomas Edison Elementary School, it has been a great privilege to be a part of your school the last five years. Monday afternoons with your students are a highlight of my week, every week, and I am grateful for learning alongside them. To the literacy coaches and leaders of Milford, Connecticut—Kelley O'Brien, Julie Aliberti, Patti Cavanna, Melissa Prompovitch, Danielle Montini, Megan Schumann, Donna Coulombe, Mary-Rita Killelea, and Jennifer Sinal—thank you for your collaboration around curriculum that bridges powerful texts with purposeful strategy instruction. You are redefining what it means to be a reader and writer for thousands of children each year.

And, thank you to the teachers and leaders of the Wooster School: Stephanie Bell, Liz Higgins, Elyse Felicione, Heidi Ryan, John Zahner, Jaime Greco, Ted Krupman, Caitlin Bellagamba, Stacey Koenig, Kelly Mohr, Melissa Munk, and Catherine Plummer. You have created a culture of learning and compassion that all children should experience in school. Learning alongside you has been a great professional and personal privilege.

I am incredibly grateful that my own children have had kind-hearted, talented teachers who let each child know that he or she matters in every possible way. Pam Ely, Maureen Thresher, Sara Tansille, Elise DiCorato, Meg Post, Cathy Ugarte, Carol Dubrowski, Stephanie McNamara, Lauren Toris, and Carol Maxwell—thank you for supporting my boys to live their stories, to become the characters they love, and to see themselves as readers and writers. I have had the chance to learn from you every time I am in your classrooms and every time Jack and Matthew come home with something to share.

Words are not enough when it comes to thanking my husband and children, but I'm going to try anyway. Chris, you understood completely when I needed time away on Saturdays and Sundays to work on this book project. Like our wedding song, you are "here, there, and everywhere" in this book. Thank you for reading aloud to me in college. For being the kind of dad that I learn from endlessly. For being a thoughtful school leader. For being a great man. I am forever grateful that our stories have been intertwined for the last fifteen years and that our lives together have endless stories ahead. Finally, I am especially indebted to Jack and Matthew for constantly reminding me about the beauty and challenges of childhood and the power of story to make every day meaningful. How lucky I am to be your mom and that your story is the center of my story.

Introduction

Stories Make Us Human

> *'Cause it's a long road to wisdom, but a short one to being ignored.*
>
> –The Lumineers, "Flowers in Your Hair"

*W*e live in a world of stories. When I turn on my phone the first thing I see is a story—a picture of my two boys, Jack and Matthew, sitting on pumpkins one recent fall day. I swipe my finger across the screen and click on the photo icon and I'm taken to hundreds if not thousands more stories. When I dip into Facebook (too many times a day some days) I do so because I'm drawn to stories. Each day heartfelt stories fill my news feed in the shape of photos, videos, hyperlinks, and anecdotal tidbits. I've seen the stories of dozens of my friends' babies born, of their parents passing away, of the successes and failures in their work lives and personal lives, of the battles they engage in for their children and the children of others. Beyond words and images, I have access to all kinds of soundtracks that make me feel like my story is shared. At home and at work, I tune in to the streaming stories that sites like *Songza*, *Pandora*, and *Spotify* provide me, allowing me to tailor my song choice to the story I want my day to unfold into. Whatever mood I'm in, whatever activities I'm doing, aha . . . there's a soundtrack to match the story I'm living right now. And others are tapping into the same streaming stories simultaneously. Imagine that.

We live in a time where stories exist where they always have: inside the walls of our homes, outside our front doors, in our backyards, on our playgrounds, in the pages of books, in the brushstrokes on canvas, in the imaginative play of children, and in the lyrics and rhythms of songs. Yet, today we are also free to tap into and curate stories in new ways. The premise of this book is that the free-flowing, streaming power of stories can be replicated or heightened in our classrooms.

As teachers, we have a lot of responsibilities. We greet students at the door with a smile. We write beautifully sequenced unit plans. We align our curriculum to the standards. We arm students with strategies to break the code of print. We support them with habits of good readers. We cultivate writers with care. We model. We guide. We watch. We listen. We respond. We read beautiful stories. We share our own. We create our own stories with them every day.

When I meet with teachers early in the school year and ask them "Tell me about your students," I expect to hear about funny things that have happened so far in the year along with successful and less successful teaching moments, the stories their students have taken to, and what kinds of stories they tell. These days I'm often met instead with a list of their students' reading levels and concerns about how much lower the levels this year seem to be. This makes sense given the pressures teachers face to have students reach benchmarks by the end of the year. Because I am a literacy consultant, teachers instinctively and immediately share the reading level spread in their class as a call for help. I understand this. I empathize. I lie awake at night and strategize. Yet, I can't help but problematize the framing of "Tell me about your students" with the automatic response of reading levels. Instead, tell me about the authors your students are drawn to. What stories had the class laughing out loud? What moments in stories made them all gasp or fight off tears or give high-fives to their neighbors on the carpet? Tell me about how Jack embodies the stories he loves, meshing fact and fiction following his TV idols Chris and Martin Kratt—better known as the Wild Kratts. Tell me about Lillie's voracious story-writing, shown by the scraps of paper that collect in her pencil tray. Tell me about breakthrough moments for students as writers and what inspired them to take to the page.

As a teacher, researcher, and parent, I wanted to write this book to reclaim the central place of stories in our classrooms and our curriculum. As our classrooms and our society become increasingly diverse, I wanted to encourage teachers to look carefully and critically at the stories they share and whether they represent the children in their classrooms. I wanted to offer tools and invitations to center both traditional and emerging forms of story as the heart of language arts classrooms. Finally, I wanted to help teachers to have the courage to place story at the center of their teaching, to be fearless in their beliefs about story as the heart of literacy teaching and learning, and to be confident that when we allow ourselves and our students to express vulnerability—to feel things through story—we are creating pathways for learning.

Kate DiCamillo, the beloved author of *Because of Winn-Dixie* and the National Ambassador for Young People's Literature, reminds us that "story is what makes us human" (Brown 2014). In an educational landscape that is undergoing sweeping changes, and where the daily pressures can at times feel insurmountable, returning to story as the heart of our language arts classrooms can human-ize our teaching. I believe in the power of inquiry, and this book is centered around questions that first guided my work as an elementary school classroom teacher, then literacy specialist and coach, and now consultant and teacher of teachers: Whose stories count? Where do stories live? How can stories come to life? How do stories grow? and How do we talk about stories? Bookends to these questions are statements, or calls to action: why stories matter, and why this work takes courage.

Chapter 1, "Why Stories Matter," will provide some context on the powerful ways that stories can transform our classrooms and our students. Chapter 2, "Whose Stories Count?" takes an in-depth look at honoring students' identities and interests through story selection, with a particular emphasis on closing the diversity gap in our classroom text selections. Chapter 3, "Where Do Stories Live?" looks at literature, poetry, music, art, multimedia, and play as sources for stories, concluding with considerations for building thematic and multicultural text sets. Chapter 4, "How Can Stories Come to Life?" discusses the methods we use and how to make them stronger. Chapter 5, "How Do We Build Stories?" provides a new way of thinking about our student writers as architects building on the stories they love. Chapter 6, "How Do We Talk About Stories?" is designed to support you with examples and tools for engaging students in complex conversations about the stories they read, view, compose, and experience in life. Chapter 7, "Why This Work Takes Courage," is written to empower you to take action in your own classroom, making the reading, writing, and sharing of sto-ries the heart of your teaching and your students' learning. There has never been a more important time for children to become storytellers, and there have never been so many ways for them to share their stories.

Chapter 1

Why Stories Matter

After nourishment, shelter, and companionship, stories are the thing we need most in the world.

–Philip Pullman

As someone who has the privilege of being a small part of many different schools, I tend to immediately notice school spaces that are centered on story. I hear teachers sharing their own stories and wonderings, students leaning in to well-chosen read-alouds, a culture of story being built. I also tend to immediately notice school spaces devoid of story. In these spaces I see students disconnected, doodling away, hands down, voices missing. In all these classrooms, I see well-intentioned teachers, but along the way some classrooms have lost story as their core and have replaced it with an overemphasis on skill or strategy. In this chapter, I want to remind us why stories matter, what they give us as teachers, and what they give our students that nothing else can.

What Stories Give Us

There are stories we hear that we remember forever. There are stories we tell ourselves that we know are not true. There are stories we wish we did not remember. There are stories that bring us closer to others and stories that drive us apart. Is there any greater human invention than the all-powerful story? In my work as a classroom teacher, literacy specialist, teacher of teachers, and consultant, I have found that above all, stories have the power to give us *mirrors* and *windows* as readers, *inky courage* as writers, and *wide-awakeness* as speakers, listeners, and participants in the world. In this section,

I use these concepts to explore the powerful ways stories nurture us and help our students to grow as readers, writers, and young people. Kathy Short (2013) calls story "the landscape of knowing." Story moves us, informs us, confirms or expands our memories and identities, and calls us to action.

Mirrors and Windows

Some of the biggest questions that we spend a lifetime trying to answer include *Who am I?* and *Where am I from?* When we dig into stories we seek answers to these lifelong questions and in many ways pose further questions about the world and our place in it: Who do I believe I can be? Where are others from? Is this story my story? Is it someone else's? On my bookshelf at home, I have a treasured copy of *Little Women* (Alcott 1880) beautifully bound and made with paper with crinkled edges to make it look antique. As a girl, I loved entering the worlds of Jo, Beth, Amy, and Meg March. I found myself drawn to their stories when I was searching for the girl I wanted to be. Also on my bookshelf is a copy of *Bringing Up Bebe: One American Mother Discovers the Wisdom of French Parenting* by Pamela Druckerman (2014). I devoured this book as a new mother, wondering what kind of parent I wanted to be. As the author shared her story, her voice urged me to value play and the countless ways our children strive to be independent. I marked up passages, read, and reread. I embodied what it means to read closely—parenthood was on the line! I was finding my voice as a mother through the voice of Druckerman.

Dr. Rudine Sims Bishop (1990) used the terms *mirror* and *window* books to describe how we both see ourselves and see others when we read literature. The girls in *Little Women* and the voice of Pamela Druckerman helped me see myself and learn from the experiences of others. As white, middle-class boys in suburban America, my sons often find mirrors in the books they read: they find their life experiences reflected in the social context of the stories and see children who look like them in the illustrations. Children from dominant social groups have always found mirrors in books. Yet for many children, books do not offer mirrors where their life story is shared. In my graduate school courses, I often have students in their 20s and 30s who share with me that they never saw themselves in a book until college. In an interview for the blog site *Mr. Schu Reads*, 2015 Newbery Medal winner Kwame Alexander used the term *literacy lifeline* to describe the impact he hoped his book *The Cross-over* (2014) and the twelve-year-old African American, basketball-loving main character, Josh, had on readers. When discussing what the Newbery meant to him as a writer he stated, "I think it means that my daughter, and your son, and all of our children will have widespread access to, and maybe even find themselves inside what many reviewers and librarians have called an 'accessible literary tale'" (Schumacher 2015).

America's classrooms are increasingly diverse in terms of race, class, religion, language, and family and home life, not just in urban districts but throughout suburbs as well. In 2014, our classrooms had a milestone moment—the overall number of Latino, African American, Native American, and Asian students in public kindergarten through twelfth-grade classrooms was projected to exceed the number of non-Hispanic white students. The National Center for Education Statistics (2014) projected a new collective majority of students of color at 50.3% of the nation's student population, and the new majority is expected to grow. However, our classroom libraries and the texts we center in our classrooms do not reflect this great diversity. Not yet. The multicultural children's book press Lee and Low Books has conducted a series of studies on the diversity gap in America, including a study of children's books. According to their research using census data and the Cooperative Children's Book Center's statistics, the population has continued to become increasingly diverse, but the number of children's books that center characters from diverse backgrounds has not changed much in the last twenty years (see Figure 1.1).

This raises significant questions for all of us who want to center stories in ways that will provide both mirrors and windows for all of the students in our classrooms. Students from dominant social groups need to learn about life experiences different from their own, and children from minority social groups must see their stories reflected on the page. The year 2014 can give us some hope. Perhaps we are on our way to recognizing society's diversity in children's and young adult literature. We see some change reflected in Kwame Alexander's *The Crossover* (2014) winning the Newbery Award and Jacqueline Woodson winning the National Book Award, a Newbery Honor, and the Coretta Scott King Award for *Brown Girl Dreaming* (2014).

So, how do we provide mirror and window books for all of our students? We begin by taking an inventory of our classroom libraries and the books we read aloud throughout the year. Not only should we be looking for greater balance between fiction and nonfiction, more imperatively, we need to be looking for books that provide both mirrors and windows for students from all backgrounds. When we see ourselves in stories we feel like we belong and we often gain courage to take on our own obstacles in life. When we see others' life experiences we gain inspiration and often build an ethic of understanding.

And, of course, most of the best stories provide mirrors and windows simultaneously. As Rudine Sims Bishop (1990) wrote, "When lighting conditions are just right . . . a window can also become a mirror" (ix). When I read *Charlotte's Web* (White 1952) aloud with students in New York City I hope they experience both mirror and window moments. They look through a window when they gain knowledge of Fern's life on a farm. And my hope is that they see themselves or the people they want to be when she stands up for what she believes in and says in defense of Wilbur "This is the most terrible case of injustice I ever heard of" (3). When I choose to read aloud from *Charlotte's Web* I

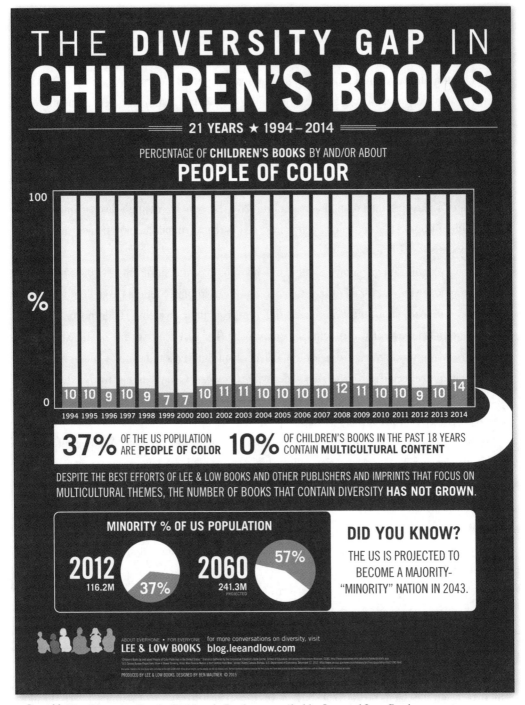

Figure 1.1 The Diversity Gap in Children's Books, compiled by Lee and Low Books

think about Fern's strengths and about other characters who share her quest for justice and her raw courage, and I build text sets that give students mirror and window possibilities. Fern shares her strengths with many other fictional characters, including the children in C. S. Lewis's (1950) *The Lion, the Witch and the Wardrobe,* who take on the White Witch to reclaim Narnia; Grace in Mary Hoffman's (1991) *Amazing Grace,* who auditions for Peter Pan, overcoming racial and social expectations; the boy in Ken Mochizuki's (1993) *Baseball Saved Us,* who steps up to the plate to counter the internment camp guards who glare at him from towers; and August, who braves school and the world, in R. J. Palacio's *Wonder* (2012). When I read across these stories I build in more mirror and window possibilities, considering the ways characters give us a parallel universe to place ourselves in. There are also many biographies, or life stories, that I turn to that represent courage with characters from diverse cultural and social backgrounds. They include *Sixteen Years in Sixteen Seconds: The Sammy Lee Story* by Paula Yoo (2005), about the first Asian American gold medalist, who was banned from pools due to discrimination, and *Silent Star: The Story of Deaf Major Leaguer William Hoy* by Bill Wise and Adam Gustavson (2012), about a player who made history but certainly faced resistance and stigma. There are countless stories, fictional and biographical, that offer our students mirror and window moments, where especially children from non-dominant cultural backgrounds can see themselves represented and where all children can draw strength and reflect on their own experiences.

Inky Courage

The life questions *Who am I?* and *Where am I from?* often guide our reading lives and the selections we make as readers. They are also some of the most important reasons why we write—to share who we are and where we are from with others. The writer Brenda Miller (2011) used the term *inky courage* in her essay on the value and importance of form in writing. I use the term more liberally as a way of thinking about the courage one draws upon simply to make a mark on the page. In an article I co-wrote with my friend, colleague, and confidant, Suzanne Farrell Smith, about the power of memoir, we draw comparisons between the inky courage we engage in as writers and the memories many of us have of the first time we performed a "trust fall." We wrote,

> *Surrounded by summer camp buddies or fellow classmates on an orientation trip, we volunteered to stand stiff, close our eyes, cross our arms in front of our hard-beating hearts, and fall back. We wondered: What if they can't catch me? Worse, what if they won't? When we are at our most vulnerable, we most need to trust those around us.*
> (Cunningham and Smith 2013, 132)

As a classroom teacher, I wanted to create spaces for students to share their stories, starting small—to share who they were and the many places they were from. I decided to have my second-grade students write personal statements based on "I" statements and be prepared to share them with each other (I like it when _____ / I worry about _____ / I believe that _____ / I get angry when _____ / I am happiest when _____). Quiet and reserved, Andy got up to share his statements. One of them read "I like it when I get high-fives." On the way back to his seat, all of his classmates gave him a high-five. Henry then got up and shared, "I worry about my grandmother in heaven." Diana shared, "I worry about my reading." Henry shared, "I believe that I can be a better friend." This was where it all started. We were at the beginning of understanding each other's stories. These statements were short and quick, but we were getting to the heart of each other's thoughts and building a community of storytellers willing to take risks and share ourselves. The trust falls were happening. I needed them to have the inky courage to tell these small stories of themselves and know they would be listened to and valued.

We have long acknowledged in education that the first step in connecting our students' lives outside school to their lives in school is to get to know them as individuals through their stories. We ask our youngest students to have the courage to write about what has impacted their lives—the beloved pet or even a relative who passed away, the fear of sleeping with the light out, the bravery of getting back up when you skinned your knee—and to share their creations. As teachers, I believe we can center story in small ways to encourage students to keep trusting in each other and in themselves and to have the inky courage to keep sharing. We can offer "I" statements for students to write from, like the following:

- I am happy when _____.
- I love it when _____.
- I remember when _____.
- I am sad when _____.
- I am angry when _____.
- I am frustrated by _____.
- I am scared of _____.
- I worry about _____.
- I want to shout from the rooftops "_____!"
- I want everyone to know _____.
- I hide from _____.
- I imagine that _____.

These are the kinds of writing territories that students of all ages have access to. We all feel things and can use our feelings to tap into some of the most important stories we want to share.

Beyond "I" statements we can encourage students to have inky courage by using Georgia Heard's (1998) heart mapping technique and pairing it with dream mapping. Giving students the opportunity to create heart maps as fuel for writing allows them to tap into the people, places, memories, objects, and feelings that center their hearts (see Figures 1.2 and 1.3).

Figure 1.2 (above), Figure 1.3 (below) Students create heart maps with various materials.

By extending this to dream maps we allow students to imagine lives different from their own. Lisa dreamed of talking with her dad, whom she hadn't spoken to in two years. Michelle dreamed that she would go back home to Mexico where her mom and dad lived. Ed dreamed that he would be a writer

Figure 1.4 A student's abstract watercolor painting

like R. L. Stine. David dreamed that he would stay in America instead of being deported next month. Their dreams became the source of poetry, watercolors, stories, and songs (see Figures 1.4 and 1.5). Not limited by genre or topic, they each had things to share and things to say. They each found inky courage to take to the page and keep writing, often starting with abstract images and using those as a springboard for writing.

In my work with preservice teachers, I ask my students to share themselves and draw on their inky courage to write a series of six-word memoirs inspired by *SMITH* magazine's six-word movement. The boundary of six words creates a safety net for students to try. It lets them take to the page. They can change their ideas of their writing from "I'm not creative enough" to "Look what I created."

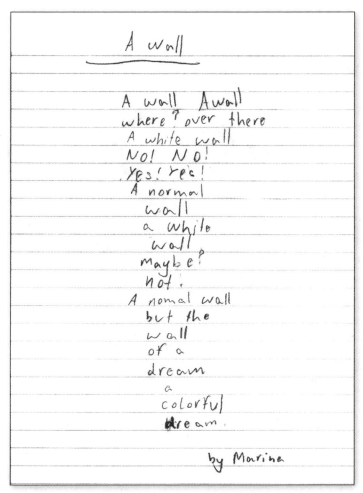

Figure 1.5 Watercolor-inspired poem by a fourth-grade English language learner

They write about an embarrassing shoe addiction, fears about whether they will ever get pregnant when they have been trying for so long, and the heartache and betrayal of divorce. They also write pieces about their breakthroughs as early career teachers and leaps of faith they've taken.

Invitations to draw on inky courage can be small. Sometimes, the smaller the better. In Peter Reynolds's (2003) book *The Dot*, Vashti stares at her blank paper in art class, convinced she is not an artist. Her teacher simply smiles at her and says, "Just make a mark and see where it takes you." Like Vashti's teacher, when we stoke inky courage in our students, we witness transformation. Our students shift from discomfort to comfort, willing to fall with trust that our smiles, words, and the community we have built will catch them.

Wide-Awakeness

When we center stories in our classrooms, we encourage students to be wide awake. In his Second Inaugural Address (2013), President Obama emphasized the legacy of Martin Luther King Jr. when he said, "Our individual freedom is inextricably bound to the freedom of every soul on Earth." Stories can help our students realize this. Maxine Greene (1998) believes that teaching from a wide-awake perspective offers teachers and students opportunities "to create situations that allow for many modes of meaning-making, many modes of 'seeing' and 'saying,' moving outward from self-interest and individualism onto a wider moral, political, and social domain" (xxvi). Much of the work towards wide-awakeness is about how we talk with students around stories—both the talk we plan and the talk that is unexpected.

Like me, Sam and Mike were teaching in New York City on September 11, 2001. They tried all day to shield their students from the events on the other side of the East River from their Brooklyn classrooms. They closed the blinds and carried on with their day, only to have a student come back from the water fountain with important questions about what she heard from a third grader in the hall about a big tower that fell. Sam and Mike had a decision to make. Engage or disengage. The magnitude of that day in our teaching lives is rare, but the decisions we have to make about which topics to support through discussion and which to shut down are often centered by stories that we either permit in our classrooms or dismiss.

Some of these decisions are planned and are rooted in text selection that encourages wide-awakeness. When we share stories where characters' lives are complex, where struggles feel real, and where characters demonstrate care for one another, we offer a value system that interrogates injustice, but also one that emphasizes our collective humanity. In this way, we do more than provide strategies for reading. We provide strategies for successful life practices inside and outside the classroom. We talk and we listen. This starts with planning questions that ask students to closely consider the meaning within and beyond the story, for example:

- What are defining moments for the characters?
- How do the characters demonstrate care for one another?
- How does the main character share his or her voice with the world?
- Who supports the main character throughout the story? Why?
- How do the characters show pride?
- How do the characters set high expectations for themselves?
- What do the characters overcome in life? Why do they persist despite challenges?
- Reflect on the characters' journey. What can we learn from their lives that relates to our own lives? What specific moments in the text can you refer to in support of your ideas?

- What do you disagree with in the story?
- How is your story different?
- Who is powerful in the story and who is not? How do you know? How do you feel about this?
- What would you change in this story and why?

In my research on read-alouds across different school settings, one of my dearest friends and colleagues read aloud the controversial picture book *And Tango Makes Three* by Justin Richardson and Peter Parnell (2005). Consistently one of the most banned books in the country, *And Tango Makes Three* is based on the true story of two male penguins, Roy and Silo, who hatched and raised a penguin egg in the Central Park Zoo. This story of a nontraditional family has raised controversy since its publication in 2005. My friend Anna-Bain had reasons for reading this book. In her own childhood, she found that books had been her saviors and she hoped this book would open up conversations about family with her students. She wasn't naïve about the risk of controversy or the undertones of the story. She expected most students to support Roy and Silo, especially since the egg would not have survived without their care. She didn't expect one student to declare, "I think it's wrong." While many teachers might have shut down the conversation right there, Anna-Bain didn't. She respected the boy's opinion and asked him to explain what he meant. Then, she stepped away. The students followed her respectful tone and shared their ideas, countering one another and explaining their thinking with personal accounts of relatives and friends who had two moms or two dads. The conversation was not easy, but it was critical.

Some of our decisions are unplanned, made on the spot based on what students bring to the discussion. Sometimes we encourage conversation through our teaching techniques. At other times we discourage critical conversation without even realizing it. While our politics and our comfort levels about the stories we share in our classrooms may differ, some of the ways we can focus our teaching towards wide-awakeness across stories and topics are as follows:

- Acknowledge that every story has mirror and window possibilities.
- Emphasize that we live in a diverse society.
- Arm students with stories where their background is represented in a positive light and where their life experiences are validated.
- Discuss themes in stories to unpack mirror possibilities for all children.
- Read aloud stories that represent the human spirit and where characters rally together for collective action.
- Be open to discussions of inequality in society that you see in stories and in life.
- Discuss with children a vision for a better world.

Closely Reading Our Students and Their Stories

The stories we choose to center in our classrooms give our students the power to see themselves and others in stories, the power to put their stories on the page, and the power to be wide awake to stories and complexities around them. But there is also the power of the stories right in front of us. Aristotle is said to have stated, "We are what we repeatedly do. Excellence, then, is not an act but a habit." To center story requires closely reading students and interpreting their stories—those that they share and those they hide. We must make this a habit. The Common Core State Standards have sparked debate about what close reading looks like in classrooms. I want to argue that we do not sufficiently emphasize what close reading of students looks like. I believe we can hone our skills as close readers of students to better understand their stories. Our students' stories provide us with indispensable information about who they are, what they value, and how they best learn. Consider the classroom teacher who makes it a habit to closely read students, not just their work but their actions, gestures, and words. Isn't this data that matters just as much as a test score, a reading level, or a rubric score?

There is great beauty and strength in the students who fill our lives. Stories we read and the stories we observe in our classrooms can remind us of just how beautiful, powerful, and courageous young people are. Stories can celebrate the simple acts of care people bestow on one another. Stories can, in turn, inspire acts of kindness. While more and more autonomy is being taken away from classroom teachers as scripted curriculum sweeps the country, we still have some choice about what stories we share, and we certainly have a choice about which stories about our students we will adopt. During a school day, students are constantly negotiating social and school expectations and defining themselves in reaction to multiple discourses at work in their classrooms, within their own social networks, and within societal systems. The words they use, the actions they take, and the identities they adopt shift from hallway to classroom to school bus to home life. And we need to consider it all to understand their stories.

I had the chance one winter at the National Council of Teachers of English Assembly for Research Conference to hear some of the student poetry teams who compete in the "Louder Than a Bomb" competitions each year in urban Chicago. Organized as afterschool poetry teams, they construct stories through words, rhythm, repetition, and sound. On stage, the eleventh and twelfth graders I saw spoke of oppression, making links between gang violence in their neighborhood and "massa" mentality, equating guns with the whips and chains of slavery. They spoke with fervor and passion and pushed us as an audience to take notice. After the performance, they slipped into other selves and became more soft-spoken and reserved in their responses to questions from the audience of teachers and teacher educators. I asked a few of them over post-performance cheese and crackers what message they had for teachers. In a word one boy said–*listen*. Then a girl followed up with, "When you have a student who refuses to take pencil to paper or puts her head down on the desk, what story do you see? Do you ask 'How's it going?' and 'Are you okay?' or 'What are you thinking about?' You don't know what she went through that morning before school or what she's worried about." Every conference we have with a student is an opportunity to listen, notice, wonder, and consider the story in front of us.

To closely read children requires mindfulness. It also requires us to know what to look for and what to do with the stories we notice. Many of us are close readers of children wherever we go. When I'm on the playground with my own two children, I notice the child crying in the playhouse and the two girls whispering to each other at the top of the slide. I notice the other parents and caregivers, and the ways they talk to their children, and the effects of that conversation. I notice my own children pretending, inventing, and imagining as they run, slide, and skip across the landscape of childhood.

As a teacher, I notice students who enter the classroom with their heads held down. I notice the ones who remain silent as they take their seats. I notice who is chatting and about what. I notice which students open their books with zeal, eager to get to the next chapter. I notice who comes to the rug leaning in to the story I'm going to share. I notice who takes to paper right away, scribbling away, believing his story is worth sharing. I equally notice who wrestles with books, who asks to go the bathroom every day during reading, and whose pencil remains parked until I come to her side.

As a consultant in schools, I notice hallways of childhood chatter and the sounds and sights of learning. I notice bulletin boards that showcase authentic student work with pride. I notice which classrooms have pulled students into learning through the stories teachers tell, the hooks they create, their guiding questions, and their support. I also notice when students have their backs to each other, when they answer but do not ask questions, and when they appear lost in their own thoughts, passively making their way through school.

All of this noticing leads me to wonder. I wonder about the backstory of the child who is crying or has her head down or dismisses the books before him. I wonder what makes some students doubt themselves and others believe. I wonder about how to best help every child to see him- or herself as a reader and a writer. I wonder about how I can best reach teachers and administrators when the classrooms need an overhaul and how to share the successes of those who have the power to inspire. When I look at student data, I wonder about the story the numbers tell me. I wonder about the magic behind big gains and the story behind backslides. I wonder where I fit into the story and how I can best support the school leaders, teachers, and students doing the difficult work of teaching and learning.

In the past few years, much of my work in schools has been focused on small-group instruction, modeling for teachers how I approach guided reading and strategy instruction. A teacher told me that I make each student feel comfortable and that time seems to stand still in my small groups. I let the students know that during our time together they are the most important thing in the world. I learned this by watching my own parents, who let my boys know each time they are with them that they are seen and heard and loved. When we are close readers of students we employ particular habits of mind that guide our thinking, particularly when we are struggling with how to reach a student as a reader or writer, or struggling to connect with a student to build a path for learning. Habits of mind are dispositions that are skillfully and mindfully taken up by successful problem-solvers, especially when solutions are not immediately apparent (Costa and Kallick 2009). In my observations of classrooms there are seven habits of mind central to teachers who consistently read students closely:

- Notice the story before you.
- Wonder about actions, thoughts, and words.
- Listen with understanding and empathy.
- Respond with wonderment and awe.
- Create, imagine, and innovate.
- Persist through guided support.
- Remain open to continuous learning.

All of these are relevant to effective teachers, particularly when we are struggling to reach a student; when a student's learning has plateaued; or when we are trying to understand the story behind a student's actions, words, feelings, or postures. Being planned and purposeful in our teaching is essential, but equally so is flexibility and attentiveness.

Is Story in Danger?

In an age of accountability, in which testable skills have become the measure of literacy success, we may feel that stories have become secondary to the mastery of discrete skills. As Nieto, Gordon, and Yearwood (2002) write, "evidence is mounting that the testing frenzy—a direct result of the call for standardization—is limiting the kinds of pedagogical approaches teachers use, as well as constricting curriculum, especially in classrooms serving low-income and minority students" (342). Yet, I know of no better way to encourage the children in our lives to become empathetic, caring people and more committed learners right now than through the sharing of stories.

When I see students who have rich reading and writing lives on Facebook and Instagram but can't access or share those lives in their classrooms, I worry that story is in danger. When we no longer see centers and areas of engaged play in kindergarten classrooms, I worry that story is in danger. When I see city-wide benchmark assessments devoid of narrative, I worry that story is in danger. Yet, the power of story is everywhere and more accessible than ever. Bomer and Bomer (2001) remind educators, "We frame what counts in the human community we construct with students" (13). Across schools and classrooms, teachers often remain the gatekeepers of the stories that are read aloud, displayed, and permissible. The text choices teachers make and the encouragement we give students to shape stories have great implications for what learning takes place. Kelly Gallagher (2009) argues that we are facing "readicide" in many of our classrooms where reading is routinely killed through rote practice exercises and skills work devoid of context, interest, or meaning for our students. Throughout this book, I position story as alive and vital to the work we do with young people for them to read and keep reading stories in print and digital spaces, to engage in trust falls again and again and find their inky courage, and to be wide awake to the stories and issues around them. I will highlight the value of different genres to shape our students' understandings of story and to counter the artificial separation of literary and informational texts that currently pervades the discourse within the field. I will emphasize the power of narrative to encourage our students to lean in, take notice, wonder, dream, and come to new ideas about who they are, where they are from, and who they want to be. In this way, I aim to encourage you to reframe what counts in your classroom and in the human community you create with your students.

Chapter 2

Whose Stories Count?

We were the people who were not in the papers. We lived in the blank white spaces at the edges of print. It gave us more freedom. We lived in the gaps between the stories.

—Margaret Atwood, *The Handmaid's Tale*

I am indebted to a student of mine who introduced me to *Humans of New York*, a photoblog dedicated to capturing the people of New York City, one story at a time. When I began to write this book in the summer of 2014, *Humans of New York* had over 7.7 million likes on Facebook. Only six months later as I kept writing and finalizing, over 5 million more people liked the site. That means that as I write this, over 12 million of us scroll through our newsfeeds and see intimate stories told by people in New York every day. The incredible success of the site lies in its simplicity—that we all have stories to tell and, when asked the right questions, we may be brave enough to share them with the world. Created by Brandon Stanton, the site (www.humansofnewyork.com) features portraits of people on New York City streets followed by their words from brief interviews by Stanton. "Can I take your photo?" "What's been your greatest accomplishment?" "What was the happiest moment of your life?" "Do you remember the saddest moment of your life?" The collective portraits remind viewers of how incredibly singular but seemingly universal our personal stories can be. As I scroll down my newsfeed I meet a father, the manager of his fourteen-year-old's heavy metal band; a former bank robber; a mom who says she wants to be present for her son; a man in a turban who says he's seen as an outsider first; a construction worker who believes his best asset is his body. I see every shade of skin, every level of income, every social location told through faces, gestures, postures, and words. What's more, thousands of comments and hundreds of thousands of likes accompany each portrait—the stories are heard, debated, and valued.

Humans of New York is a reminder to the world that every story counts. So what is the educational significance of *Humans of New York*? It is that every story must count in our classrooms, too. As Stanton's work reveals, often it is through the simplest questions we ask our students that we hear the most important stories.

Changing Times

There is a reason for the expression "change is the only constant." I remember walking into a patisserie in Brooklyn in 2008 pushing a stroller as a new and confused mom yearning for a coffee and a chocolate croissant when I saw my first iPhone. I was amazed at the screen, the maps, the music, and the messages, all on one device that could fit in the palm of your hand. I thought to myself—"It will be years before I have one of those." Now wherever I go I see people using these incredible devices: on playgrounds, at school pick-up, on line at the grocery store, walking down the street. Only a few short years after my first iPhone sighting, data from the Pew Research Internet Project (Madden et al. 2013) shows that one in four teens are "cell-mostly" Internet users and that 78% of teens ages twelve to seventeen have cell phones, almost half of which are smartphones. Another study by Common Sense Media (Rideout 2012) found that almost a quarter of teenagers access social media sites at least ten times a day, and more than half use social media once a day. These figures alone indicate rapidly changing times.

Think of it. We can now type in almost any address in the world and, thanks to Google Earth, instantly zoom in to see a satellite image in real time. We can Skype or Google Hangout anyone from anywhere and talk to friends, colleagues, or clients across the ocean from the comfort of our beds (business on top, pajamas on bottom). Marina Keegan, the young writer from Yale who suddenly and tragically died shortly after her graduation, wrote in her collection of essays and stories *The Opposite of Loneliness* (2014):

> *We have the Internet. Millions and billions of doors we can open and shut, posting ourselves into profiles and digital scrapbooks. Suddenly and totally, we're threaded together in a network so terrifyingly colossal that we can finally see our terrifyingly tiny place in it.* (205)

Think of a day when you did not check e-mail, pick up your cell phone, or check social media, and contemplate your own place within the digital landscape. The time when we weren't guided by our devices and social media feels like a distant memory.

Even social media itself has changed as sites like Instagram gain in popularity, with over 90 million users on Instagram each month. Visual literacy may have trumped print in the world of social media. Teachers and principals across school contexts continue to tell me that their students are not Facebook users. Rather, they are Instagram and Snapchat users seeking visual spaces for sharing their stories. These transformative spaces have educational significance—young people increasingly have access to information and storytelling tools; they have had adult models of how to use, navigate, and connect through personal devices throughout their childhoods; they often learn how to scroll through touch screens before they learn to ride a bike or tie their shoes; and they may prefer visual storytelling tools to print-dominated ones. Students will likely continue to find new spaces for telling stories that have the power to amaze and inspire us, and outside of school, students continue to find ways for their stories to count.

What's more, these countless stories are everywhere. According to BBC News, "Back in 2010 Google chief executive Eric Schmidt noted that the amount of data collected since the dawn of humanity until 2003 was the equivalent to the volume we now produce every two days" (Wakefield 2013, 1). Big data is everywhere. Using that data to uncover stories is a new method analysts are employing to measure things like the health and happiness of cities and nations. Through digital sensors and cameras, we have now created smart cities that have made digital maps of our physical world and our interactions within it. We are constantly leaving digital footprints of who we are, where we are from, what we believe, and how we feel. A friend and fellow educator, Seth Fleischauer of the Banyan Global Learning group, has created an imaginative twist on the concept of big data for our classrooms. With his team at Banyan, Seth has created the BigDayta Project (Banyan Global Learning 2015). This project asks students around the world to use a Google form to record what happens every hour on a given school day. The participants use data from children around the world to answer meaningful, real-life questions they have about how similar or different their days may be—unraveling the story behind the data. What if our classrooms began to take on the same analytical approach, and to center everything as a potential story?

Changing Classrooms

While many of our classrooms have steadfast traditional structures—teacher at the front of the room; students at desks; and pencils, pens, and notebooks as our primary tools for writing—it is hard not to notice the changes in classrooms today since my first classroom. Everything from SmartBoards to document cameras to electronic tablets to the nature of research itself has changed. Undoubtedly, our classrooms are changing according to the technologies we have access to and the ways we use them to teach, to learn, and to share stories.

But our classrooms are changing in other ways. In the country's 67 largest school districts, the population is already nearly 79% nonwhite, with no single ethnic group making up more than 40% of the school population (Council of the Great City Schools 2010). And this is not just occurring in urban schools. In addition to racial and ethnic diversity, America's classrooms have increasing linguistically diverse populations of students, with 20% of preschool–grade 12 students coming from homes where native languages other than English are spoken (United States Bureau of the Census 2000). Our students come from many countries, speak many languages, and have many shades of skin color and many levels of access and privilege.

And, of course, this is in addition to the changes teachers have experienced in the last few years with new standards through the Common Core in 2012, new teacher evaluation measures in many states, new teacher certification requirements across the vast majority of the country, and a new testing regime fueled by the two consortiums PARCC and Smarter Balanced. So, with all of these changes, what are the stories students have to tell? How do we give voice to their diverse experiences? How do we find our own voice in a sea of change?

Unchanging Texts

Despite changes to the ways we live, the ways we interact with one another, the ways we teach and learn, and the diversity of students themselves, the texts our students have access to within the four walls of our classrooms are incredibly unchanged. When I walk into classrooms in the districts I partner with, I try to look at classroom libraries through children's eyes. I look at the social locations of the children. I often wonder—do the students in this room see themselves in these stories?

In a *New York Times* article titled "Where Are the People of Color in Children's Books?" the author and former National Ambassador of Children's Literature Walter Dean Myers (2014) wrote about his own love of reading and how he abandoned reading when the white-dominated landscape of literature began to take its toll. He wrote,

> As I discovered who I was, a black teenager in a white-dominated world, I saw that these characters, these lives, were not mine. I didn't want to become the "black" representative, or some shining example of diversity. What I wanted, needed really, was to become an integral and valued part of the mosaic that I saw around me. Books did not become my enemies. They were more like friends with whom I no longer felt comfortable. I stopped reading. I stopped going to school. (SR1)

For many young people, the power of a single book can change everything. Walter Dean Myers found such a book, and the world of literature is forever grateful. He writes,

Then I read a story by James Baldwin: "Sonny's Blues." I didn't love the story, but I was
lifted by it, for it took place in Harlem, and it was a story concerned with black people like
those I knew. By humanizing the people who were like me, Baldwin's story also human-
ized me. The story gave me a permission that I didn't know I needed, the permission to
write about my own landscape, my own map. (SR1)

If books transmit values and provide a pathway for our shared humanity, what does that mean for children who aren't represented by the books on our shelves?

Each year the Cooperative Children's Book Center at the University of Wisconsin catalogues the children's books published that year. They found that of the 3,500 children's books published in 2014 that they received, just 179 were about African Americans. In the same *New York Times* issue as his father's article, Christopher Myers (2014) refers to this as the apartheid of children's literature, in which characters of color "are never given a pass card to traverse the lands of adventure, curiosity, imagination or personal growth" (SR1). My friend and colleague Jane Gangi (2008) writes about this as the "unbearable whiteness" of children's literature. She found in her study of children's literature that it is not only the literature itself that privileges whiteness but that reading lists, awards, school book fairs, book order forms, and children's literature textbooks all, perhaps not surprisingly, diminish opportunities for children of color to see themselves in books. This in turn diminishes their ability to make critical text-to-self connections and develop reading proficiency with complex texts. We have changing times, changing classrooms, but unchanged texts. So, what are we going to do about it?

Jason Low, a publisher with the independent multicultural children's and young adult literature press Lee and Low Books, hopes for the world of children's literature to move beyond the Diversity 101 story. That story simply acknowledges that there is a fundamental gap in children's and young adult literature—that the cartography created by children's book publishing has not supported every child to see him- or herself through literature. Jason hopes that a Diversity 102 story will emerge. The Diversity 102 story is when we take action and change the landscape of books for all children. As teachers we need to survey the literature in our classrooms, and partner with school and local librarians, the community, and the families of our students to spotlight literature that provides a mirror, a window, *and* a map for our students. In personal correspondence with Jason, he described the Diversity 102 story to me:

It means buying and supporting diverse books that are new and backlist. It is about
being consistent in thinking of diversity as not just special books relegated to an ethnic
observance month (e.g., Black History Month) but incorporating diverse titles into curric-

*ula and collections all year long. It is also about being vigilant and active and looking
at annual recommendation lists like summer reading lists and gauging whether these
lists are diverse or not—and, if not, taking the initiative to contact the organizers and
recommend great diverse books for the list. Even personally looking at our own reading
habits and seeing if we are reading diversely for our own pleasure and, if not, making a
concerted effort to do so.*

So how do we begin to write the Diversity 102 story? It takes knowing and valuing who our
students are, where they are from, and what their diverse life experiences have been, and critically
rethinking our read-aloud texts, our shared texts, our suggestions for independent reading, and our
own reading lives. I have long believed that all teachers of reading must love reading themselves. Now
is the time for us to lead the way in the campaign for diverse books. We cannot wait while thousands
of children every day say "Books are not for me. Reading is not for me. I'm not here."

One way to participate is to follow the Twitter and Tumblr #weneeddiversebooks movement and
get involved. The #WNDB movement began at the 2014 BookCon annual convention held in New
York City. The campaign emerged out of the initial all-white author line-up the publishing convention scheduled. #WNDB presented a panel of authors advocating for diverse literature for all young
people. They also announced the planning of the first Children's Literature Diversity Festival, to be
held in Washington, DC, in the summer of 2016. I can hardly wait! Is it 2016 yet? Excellent ways to
learn about diverse children's literature are to visit the sites of independent children's book publishers, to follow bloggers who write about children's literature in the now formalized *KidLitosphere*,
and to read and highlight award winners that represent high-quality children's literature with diverse
authors and subjects (see Figure 2.1). Search for topics, levels, and stories of interest. It's time to
change the landscape. We are the cartographers.

Coming to Know Students' Identities and Interests

Becoming familiar with and falling in love with literature that represents a diverse society is an essential step and one we can often take alone in the comfort of our homes on summer and winter breaks
or when our children have fallen asleep. An equally imperative step is one that involves our relationships with our students—coming to know their interests and multiple identities.

In my first year of teaching I taught in an all-girls school where my fifth graders constantly challenged definitions of what it means to be a girl. They organized relay races at lunch through rain,
sleet, and snow. They loved science and math. They made connections to characters and authors of
all genders and backgrounds, from *Anne of Green Gables* (Montgomery 1908) to *Johnny Tremain*

PUBLISHERS	CONTENT
Lee and Low Books	Diverse books for young readers featuring multicultural content
BeBop Collection	Early reader collection from Lee and Low based on Fountas and Pinnell and DRA levels
Tu Books	An imprint of Lee and Low focused on fantasy and science fiction for middle grades
Children's Book Press	An imprint of Lee and Low focused on English/Spanish picture books
Shen's Books	An imprint of Lee and Low focused on Asian and Asian American content
Cinco Punto Press	Children's and adult books featuring multicultural and bilingual books
Just Us Book	Multicultural books featuring black interest for children and young adults
Roadrunner Press	Fiction and nonfiction books for young readers featuring American West and America's Native Nations
Piñata Books, an imprint of Arte Público	Juvenile and young adult books focused on Hispanic culture and by US Hispanic authors
Barefoot Books	Books for young readers that feature social, cultural, and ecological diversity
BLOGS TO FOLLOW	CONTENT
The Classroom Bookshelf www.classroombookshelf.blogspot.com/	Written by four leaders in children's literature, and features weekly a recently released work of children's literature, a book review, teaching invitations, and text sets
The Open Book http://blog.leeandlow.com/	Lee and Low Books blog site that includes multicultural content, posts by authors, and strategies for working with culturally and linguistically diverse students
Living Barefoot Blog http://blog.barefootbooks.com/	Barefoot Books blog site written by the two founders of Barefoot Books as they reflect on childhood, the impact of stories, and strategies for extending learning through hands-on engagement
Colorín Colorado http://www.colorincolorado.org/	Features diverse books, particularly bilingual books, and strategies for working with linguistically diverse students
The Brown Bookshelf http://thebrownbookshelf.com/	Features African American voices writing for young readers
Diversity in YA http://diversityinya.tumblr.com/	A Tumblr site dedicated to diversity in young adult literature
Rich in Color http://richincolor.com/	Reviews and promotes young adult fiction starring people of color or written by people of color
American Indians in Children's Lit http://americanindiansinchildrensliterature.blogspot.com/	Critical perspectives and analysis of indigenous peoples in children's and young adult books, the school curriculum, popular culture, and society

Figure 2.1 Where to Find Children's Literature That Features Diverse Stories and Content

Latinos in KidLit http://latinosinkidlit.com/	Explores the world of Latino/a children's literature, young adult literature, and middle grades literature
BookDragon http://smithsonianapa.org/bookdragon/	The Smithsonian Asian Pacific American Center's recommendations
Interesting Nonfiction for Kids (I.N.K.) http://inkrethink.blogspot.com/	Focused on the craft of nonfiction for young readers
The Children's Book Cooperative http://ccblogc.blogspot.com/	Observations about books for children and teens from the Cooperative Children's Book Center
AWARDS	**CONTENT**
John Newbery Medal	American Library Association (ALA) award for most outstanding contribution to children's literature
Randolph Caldecott Medal	ALA award for most distinguished American picture book for children
Michael L. Printz Award	ALA award for excellence in literature written for young adults
Coretta Scott King Book Award (Author and Illustrator Awards)	ALA award for African American author and illustrator of outstanding books for children and young adults
Pura Belpré Award (Author and Illustrator Awards)	ALA award for a Latino author and illustrator whose children's books best portray, affirm, and celebrate the Latino cultural experience
Robert F. Sibert Informational Book Award	ALA award for most distinguished informational book for children
Stonewall Book Award–Mike Morgan & Larry Romans Children's & Young Adult Literature Award	ALA award for a book of exceptional merit for children or teens relating to the gay, lesbian, bisexual, and transgender experience
Schneider Family Book Award	ALA award for books that embody an artistic expression of the disability experience
Andrew Carnegie Medal	ALA award for excellence in children's video
Asian/Pacific American Award for Literature	Honors and recognizes individual work about Asian/Pacific Americans and their heritage
Middle East Book Award	Honors and recognizes individual work about Middle East heritage
American Indian Youth Literature Award	Honors and recognizes individual work about American Indians and their heritage
South Asia Book Award	Honors and recognizes individual work about South Asian heritage
Rainbow Project Reading List	Honors and recognizes LGBT books
Notable Books for a Global Society	Honors and recognizes books that promote understanding across lines of culture, race, sexual orientation, values, and ethnicity

Figure 2.1 (*continued*)

(Forbes 1943) to the poetry of Langston Hughes. For years afterwards, I taught at an all-boys school where I was constantly challenged to rethink my own assumptions about what it means to be a boy—having never been one myself. Nearly all of my second- and third-grade boys loved art and music, thanks to brilliant and engaging teachers who positioned these subjects as essentials. The boys studied the work of Matisse, Van Gogh, Mozart, and Beethoven, but also the work of Georgia O'Keeffe, Sammy Davis Jr., and Miles Davis. Being a boy meant many different things. My first year there I made the mistake of assuming that all boys like baseball and began the spring with a writing prompt about, you guessed it, baseball—which was wrong on two counts. First, they didn't need my prompt to have interesting things to write about. Second, there were several boys in my class who cared little about baseball and would have much rather written about the rollercoaster they were making out of popsicle sticks, or the bug collection they were starting, or their dreams of being musicians, painters, or anything else but baseball players. I learned from my students that what it means to be a boy or a girl is never simple, universal, or singular (see Figure 2.2). The identities and interests of students are their own.

For a few years I had the privilege of teaching at an international school where the languages and cultures of children did not mirror my own. I had to constantly consider who my students were, the values and beliefs of their families, and how I could harness the power of story to build connections when English was not a common denominator for so many of my students. I turned to the subjects and stories I loved to build a foundation, to share my love of books and words, and to tap into the students' curiosity. It was here that I began to think about the importance of story coupled with strategies to support students on a path toward independence. Strategies alone would never build a community of readers, writers, speakers, and listeners in a classroom as racially, linguistically, and socioeconomically diverse as mine. I needed the power of stories. While I was still learning about my students, I started to share my own identities and interests with them. Before my career in education, I studied architecture. My students and I all lived in New York City, so we began our collective story with a study of the place we lived (see, for example, Figures 2.3 and 2.4). I read aloud *The Cricket in Times Square* (Selden 1960) and *From the Mixed-Up Files of Mrs. Basil E. Frankweiler* (Konigsburg 1967). We went on photo walks. We sketched buildings along the reservoir in Central Park. We learned about homes around the world. We visited the Metropolitan Museum of Art and the Guggenheim.

We interviewed the man who ran the coffee cart outside of school, the pizza shop owner, and our family members. We started to tell our own New York City stories influenced by the places we loved, the people we spent our days with, and the things that amazed us in our hometown. We built models, made labels, wrote reports, and conducted presentations with honored guests from other classrooms and our homes. Students studied architects and monuments from the places they were from—Christ the Redeemer in Rio de Janeiro, Tiananmen Square in Beijing. By starting with our shared identity as New York City dwellers, and an openness towards inquiry, I could begin to learn about their interests and identities and begin to build our class story.

Figure 2.2 A student-created comic book cover featuring the characters BookBoy and BookGirl. The role of "comic book creator" became a central identity for this student for several years.

Figure 2.3 Student collage and watercolor painting of the New York City skyline

Understanding the multiple identities of your students is complex work, particularly when your students come from a different race, ethnicity, home language, or gender from yourself. When I'm not sure if my interests and our shared identity works as a starting place, I do my best to look for a range of literature from a range of authors that represents our diverse society. At other times, I look for significant and somewhat obvious gaps. For example, when I walk into a school where nearly 99% of the children are from Latino/a backgrounds and I can't find a book with a Latino/a character or by a Latino/a author, I know what I need to do first. I need to comb my bookshelves and those of the libraries I visit. I start with Pura Belpré Award winners. I look for poets like Pat Mora and Pablo Neruda. I look for bilingual books like *My Colors, My World/Mis Colores, Mi Mundo* by Maya Christina

Gonzalez (2007). And I start reading. I am not a native Spanish speaker and often need to ask children to be my guide when I'm reading a bilingual text. It doesn't stop me. It can't. I love the moments when I turn a book over to a fifth grader to conduct the read-aloud when his reading will be more fluent and understandable than mine. I love the moments when I read aloud from *Confetti* by Pat Mora (1996) and the children want to hear more and more of her Spanish and English poems. I love when students recognize that their language, heritage, and identities are valued, that their stories count.

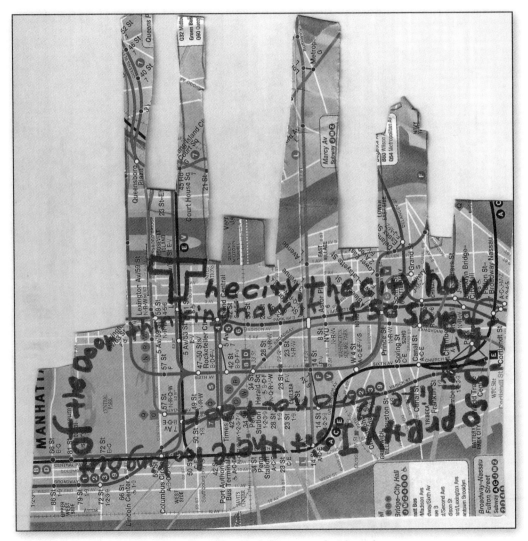

Figure 2.4 A student's shape poem about New York City created with a subway map

To build a foundation in your classroom based on the identities and interests of your students requires a couple of things. First, it requires a willingness to share your own interests and identities: to share what you love to read, write, and learn about. Next, it requires looking closely at your students. To go beyond the surface, we need to become story sleuths. As I described in Chapter 1, techniques such as heart mapping and dream mapping have always been ways I've begun to better understand my students and what matters to them. The stories slowly drip and then pour out as I lean in to ask students about a drawing here or a word there. But I often need more data to deeply understand who my students are, what they're interested in, and the multiple places they come from. I have a series of surveys I ask my students to complete to better understand who they are and where they are from. Many of the questions are like Brandon Stanton's in *Humans of New York*. I ask about moments when they felt something strongly, which evokes memories of people and places they love. Inspired by my friend and colleague Pam Allyn, I ask about their reading and writing preferences, beginning with when reading and writing have felt good for them (Figure 2.5) and when they haven't, and I share similar experiences from my own life.

I also ask my students' families to share some of their thoughts on family stories and moments that they hold on to. The toolkit at the end of the chapter includes a sample student survey and family survey to consider for your own classroom.

Once I have more student and family data rooted in story, I turn to building text sets that not only will support my students in gaining proficiency and independence as readers, but will give them opportunities to see that their stories count in the world of literature, art, song, and multimedia.

Creating Thematic and Issues-Based Text Sets

When I have a sense of my students' interests and their multiple identities, I start to build a catalogue of stories and themes in my head to match them both individually and collectively. Why do I think we need to do both? Students need to be supported with rich, powerful stories to read independently and with access to shared stories through read-alouds, shared reading, and small-group instruction that helps build a community around stories. Having a love of words and of children's and young adult literature are essential to building a world of story in your classroom. Yet, we need to move beyond a simple books-based approach and create multigenre, multimodal text sets to build interest, momentum, and connections across text types, stories, and topics.

So, what is a multigenre, multimodal text set? In their informative and important book *Teaching with Text Sets,* Mary Ann Cappiello and Erika Thulin Dawes (2013) explain that *multigenre* means all traditional genres of literature, as well as purpose-driven types of writing, from blog entries to recipes. *Multimodal* means texts that vary in modality—visual texts, such as photographs, illustrations, and visual art; audio

INTRODUCTION	
Connect previous teaching, capture students' attention and interest, or activate prior knowledge.	*When I think about myself as a reader, I know there are times that reading feels good to me. I just finished a book called* The Art of Racing in the Rain *(Stein 2009). I was struggling all fall to find a book at home that I could really connect to and then my husband, the biggest reader I know, recommended this for me and he proved he really knows me. From the first few pages, I was hooked. Even though the story was so moving that I cried sometimes, this book felt good for me to read because I couldn't put it down. I wanted to talk with everyone I saw about it. I wanted to pass it on to my friends and family and I couldn't stop thinking about the characters and events.* *Leading up to finding this amazing book, I picked up a few others this fall that didn't feel quite right. Either I was bored by the story or I felt lost by vocabulary words I didn't know. I wasn't feeling good about my reading.* *Luckily, I can build off of reading* The Art of Racing in the Rain *and look for more books that have characters I can relate to and stories that grab me by this author or authors like him.*
TEACHING	
Teach one thing. Choose the way to teach. Try and model as much as you can.	*Today I want you to think about times when reading has felt good for you. And when it has not. Think to yourself for a moment about a book you've recently read that you liked, where you were, and what about the reading made it feel good. Then think about a time when reading hasn't felt so good . . . why?*
GUIDED PRACTICE	
Engage students with a quick opportunity to rehearse their ideas, such as through a turn and talk, stop and jot, stop and act, or brief discussion.	*Turn and talk to someone sitting next to you about those experiences. Remember to focus on when reading has felt good for you and when it hasn't.* After a few minutes, have students share with the class and create a class chart.
CLOSURE	
Restate the teaching point and connect it to ongoing student work.	*When you are reading today in your independent reading books, I want you to ask yourself "Is this reading feeling good for me (why?) or is it feeling not so good (why?)." Your teachers and I will be conferencing with you, asking about how your reading is going and offering some teaching points that can help you make choices as a reader to find yourself reading in ways that feel good.*
INDEPENDENT PRACTICE	
Students will be reading independently and thinking about what about this reading is making it feel good or not so good and trying to articulate that in our conferences.	
WRAP-UP	
Have students return to the rug to share what about their reading today felt good and/or what didn't feel good.	

Figure 2.5 Mini-Lesson: When Has Reading Felt Good?

recordings such as music, podcasts, and radio broadcasts; and digital texts that are multimodal in their construction. Mary Ann and Erika suggest starting with content, building a text set of high-quality print and digital resources, organizing the texts, and then helping students to read and respond within and across the texts. When I start to build a text set, I usually start with a theme that will capture my students' interests individually or collectively, based on what I have learned about them. I then search across children's and young adult literature using my school and local library; awards lists, notably the American Library Association annual awards; and professional blogs. I also search for children's and young adult magazines, particularly for science texts and current events. I then move into multimodal sources connected to the themes, notably TED Talks, YouTube videos, CNN news clips, audio stories from sites such as NPR's The Moth, and essays read aloud at sites such as This I Believe. Finally, I search for visual texts such as photographs, paintings, and artifacts. It is truly a process I enjoy from the start.

Another way to build a text set is to start with a core text. I am fortunate to be part of a blogging community at *The Classroom Bookshelf* (Cappiello et al. 2010–2015) founded by Mary Ann, Erika, and our friend Grace Enriquez. Every week one of us selects a recent work of children's or young adult literature, and as coauthors we build a text set related to the themes within the book. We think widely. We compile suggested reading and writing invitations, and we connect the core text to several other texts within and beyond the genre. We find digital sources. We think about multiple grade levels. We strive to support teachers in building classroom bookshelves that harness the power of story and that honor the diverse interests and identities of children and young adults. We believe that great teaching starts with a community that values and loves stories that are told well, stories that move us, and stories that make us wonder.

Following blogs about children's literature, reading, and writing is an important way of staying connected to what is happening in the field. Blogs are written from many different perspectives. I find that the voices I follow often ring true to me but also challenge me to rethink my assumptions and beliefs about teaching and learning. Some bloggers are teachers, and others are parents or librarians. Bloggers on children's literature have now formed a society called *The KidLitosphere,* where you can find many different perspectives and positions on children's literature and the power of story. The *School Library Journal* (www.slj.com) and the *Cooperative Children's Book Center* (ccbc.education. wisc.edu), two sites that feature books of the week, will help you follow trends in children's and young adult literature.

Taking Note of Genre and Format

As you begin to consider the children's and young adult literature that guides your teaching, think about the genres and formats (such as picture books) you privilege throughout the year and whether there is a balance in the types of texts you read aloud and offer in your classroom library. It is also essential to consider how to diversify the selections you make within genres to more closely resemble the diverse society we live in.

Traditional stories are some of my family's favorites. My husband is a master storyteller, and my boys often want to hear before bed the stories of Hercules, Theseus and the Minotaur, Johnny Appleseed, and the Anansi tales. Even the youngest of children are interested in these characters and their quests. For your classroom, consider using traditional stories that may open up connections between home and school. Invite families to share their favorite traditional stories. Consider holding text clubs during or after school, where students study a type of traditional story from one part of the world and groups share their findings to notice similarities and differences in how traditional stories have been told.

Realistic fiction is often a favorite genre of upper elementary students as it provides them with stories of growing up, facing adversity, and the complexity of navigating their way through child-hood. Yet, have you noticed that the vast majority of realistic fiction represents white children in middle-class suburban settings? Look for realistic fiction that provides representations of diversity, so your selections more closely resemble our whole society. Examples include *The Chalkbox Kid* by Clyde Robert Bulla (1987), *The Janitor's Boy* by Andrew Clements (2001), *Monster* by Walter Dean Myers (2004), and *American Born Chinese* by Gene Luen Yang (2008). These stories explore growing up alongside issues of class, race, ethnicity, and belonging.

The Harry Potter and the Twilight series are testaments to the enormous popularity of fantasy. We learn to love the characters as they engage in their quests, and we wonder about how our world could be different. As Pam Allyn (2015) wrote for Scholastic's edublog, "The Harry Potter series offers rich-ly diverse characters in all their human complexity. They are diverse because they are humanly diverse. In fact, it is not clear what color Hermione's skin is by reading the series. She is described by the movie image of her as being white, but this is not at all defined by the words in the series itself." Many characters from fantasy and science fiction stories are represented as white and suburban, like those represented by realistic fiction. Lee and Low Books has an imprint focused on fantasy and science fic-tion, Tu Books, that features characters from a range of sociocultural backgrounds that maintain the integrity of the genre. Encourage students to interrogate the ways book covers and films often portray characters as white when the text itself gives no indication of race or ethnicity.

Nonfiction literature creates endless possibilities for connections to science and social studies topics. Consider topic choice when supporting students with nonfiction literature, and look for a range of text structures including nonfiction texts that use a narrative structure. Some of the best writers weave information purposefully and powerfully. Thomas Newkirk (2014) in *Minds Made for*

Stories: How We Really Read and Write Informational and Persuasive Texts argues that there is a need to question the ways in which the lines are being drawn between "informational" and "narrative" reading. He further argues that the best writing always includes a narrative structure and that we often read narrative texts to extract information and, in fact, prefer to learn in this way. (Learn more about the authors of nonfiction literature, such as the iNK [Interesting Nonfiction for Kids] collaborative that includes authors Vicki Cobb, Andrea Warren, and Alex Siy. Their website [http://inkthinktank.com] includes the Nonfiction Minute—short, well-written pieces by esteemed nonfiction writers. The Nonfiction Minute is a powerful, purposeful, and accessible way of bringing nonfiction writing into your classroom.) Reading texts that use a narrative structure to convey information serves as a model for students to write in the same way. Figure 2.6 provides an example of a fourth grader's culminating writing piece following independent research on the topic of sea slugs during a biodiversity integrated unit.

Biographies, autobiographies, and memoirs are a specific type of nonfiction literature that beg us to consider the question "Just who will I be?" When we read about the lives of others, it often gives us an opportunity to reflect on our own lives. I like to look for stories that are often untold and that demonstrate diverse backgrounds and life goals. I often turn to picture books that vividly describe people's passions and stories of adversity, including *Honda: The Boy Who Dreamed of Cars* by Mark Weston (2014), *Baby Flo: Florence Mills Lights Up the Stage* by Alan Schroeder (2012), *Brave Girl: Clara and the Shirtwaist Makers' Strike of 1909* by Michelle Markel (2013), *Who Says Women Can't Be Doctors? The Story of Elizabeth Blackwell* by Tanya Lee Stone (2013), and *On a Beam of Light: A Story of Albert Einstein* by Jennifer Berne (2013). For middle schoolers I use longer works, including *The Circuit: Stories from the Life of a Migrant Child* by Francisco Jiménez (1997) and *Bad Boy: A Memoir* by Walter Dean Myers (2002). Learning about history through story has always been my go-to method for teaching social studies. Consider the time periods and diversity of characters that are represented in your selections.

The world of poetry is rich and diverse both in terms of the sociocultural backgrounds of well-known poets and in terms of the themes and topics they write about. Consider highlighting poets who come from the same as well as different sociocultural backgrounds than your students. Vary the length and type of poetry you share. Make poetry a daily or weekly endeavor rather than something reserved for April's poetry month. Share the work of Emily Dickinson and Robert Frost alongside Langston Hughes, Pablo Neruda, Pat Mora, and Naomi Shihab Nye.

What's a classroom without picture books? We often assume that upper elementary school students are beyond picture books, but the story lines, both in print and in the illustrations, often provide complex themes, vocabulary, and syntax for students to read and reread. In 2010, the *New York*

A SEA CREATURE

Hi! I'm…. (I'll give you three guesses). All right, all right I'm a sea slug. But you can settle me as Kathy.

Most sea slugs leave their mum when we hatch but our family always stayed together. But sometimes I do wish my brother had gone away (he is such a pest).

If you are French you may think "Oh, slugs. Tasty, yum, yum." But that is where you'd be wrong. I (or we) taste horrible - absolutely disgusting. Good thing too or I can't tell you everything before I'm eaten. Mum says I'm also poison, like her. I'm not so sure if I am or not because no one has eaten me yet. So "Na, na, na" to the sharks that live near us.

I can zap you too. I know that because I tried it once on my brother, who was sadly asleep when I did my hardest one. Not that it was feeble, but all he did was turn over (so lazy).

My brother can't zap anything but if he wanted to he can leave a very thick goo behind him. When other fish taste it they feel sick and leave him alone. (Even Mum doesn't want it in the house.)

We have new neighbors called lemon slugs and you can guess how they got that name.

I wish you could see Dad because he never failed to surprise me because he has so many frills and he is a master of hiding. See? Sea slugs aren't so boring and we aren't just brown like boring old normal slugs but we are also pink, purple, orange and rainbow yellow and every other color you can imagine.

Have to stop now. It's dinner and……mmmm my favorite: seaweed with small zapped fish.

Bye bye from Kathy.

P.s. Did I tell you the time I meddled a shark?

Figure 2.6 Student writing that uses a narrative structure to convey information learned from research on sea slugs

Times ran an urgent article on the demise of the picture book, "Picture Books No Longer a Staple for Children" (Bosman), which described a drop in picture book sales and a drop in the number of picture books from the top-selling publishers, despite librarians' and teachers' recognition that picture books are often more complex than early chapter books. Yet, it is precisely by reading picture books that our imaginations work to fill in missing themes. Picture books offer students far beyond early childhood opportunities for critical thinking, inference building, and engagement with complex social issues. In the summer of 2014, the *New York Times* ran a series of essays in their Room for Debate section on whether books for children, largely picture books, should be political—that is, should they deal with issues of diversity, including race and sexual orientation, or should they keep story lines politically neutral. Opinions ranged from "Beware of Propaganda" to "Children Need a Political Primer." Several of the essays argued that picture books continually and historically break new boundaries and that they serve as a democratic art form, encouraging readers of all ages to ask questions and make observations about the story and the world.

As you consider which genres and formats are privileged in your own classroom and whether the texts you draw from represent our diverse society, consider the value of multigenre and multimodal texts sets. To build a multigenre text set requires moving from a single text approach to thinking of themes, essential questions, or topics that are compelling and found across genres and text types. To think of the human experience. To build a multimodal text set is to go one step further and to value not only print-based texts, but visual, multimedia, and audio texts as well. The next section highlights some ways to build multigenre and multimodal text sets that close the story gap, encouraging all students to affirm their interests and identities across texts.

Moving to Multigenre and Multimodal Text Sets with Students in Mind

To become a cartographer in the classroom, to change the literary maps that have traditionally been given to many children from many different backgrounds, is to make a pledge to ensure that all of your students have access to interesting, engaging texts that honor who they are, where they are from, and who they want to be. It also means getting current and moving beyond a solely book-based approach. Diverse voices and stories are everywhere. As you build multigenre and multimodal text sets, consider a range of text types to offer greater diversity in the types of stories shared and voices heard. There is no magic formula or prescription for creating text sets, but Figure 2.7 will help you select from different genres as you blend print, visual, multimedia, and student-created texts into your thematic or issues-based sets.

Recently, I've partnered with my husband, a middle school principal, to build thematic text sets for a series of courses he developed for his middle schoolers called "Reason and Rhetoric." Starting in fifth grade, students learn about the roots of philosophical arguments. They consider logical reasoning and critique their own thinking as well as the thinking of others. They learn how to argue their point of view in writing and in speaking. Their learning is guided by inquiry and story. They read, listen to, and view not only narratives but also essays, speeches, and videos. They view artwork and listen to musical selections that tell stories but that also persuade us, inform us, and teach us about fundamental human experiences and ideas. The individual works they study serve more than one purpose. By starting with compelling themes, the texts hook students to learn new ideas and ways of thinking.

A BALANCE OF GENRES AND FORMATS	CHOOSING WITHIN THIS GENRE OR FORMAT
Traditional Stories: folklore including fables, folktales, myths, legends, and fairy tales	Consider the cultural backgrounds of your students, and support teachers with traditional stories that represent different cultural backgrounds and originate from different parts of the world.
Realistic Fiction	Center characters from the same sociocultural backgrounds as the students in your school and provide representations of diversity that more closely resemble society at large.
Historical Fiction	Look for historically accurate representations and for characters with a range of diverse historical, cultural, social, and geographical backgrounds.
Fantasy and Science Fiction	Fantasy and science fiction stories often lack diversity in terms of the sociocultural backgrounds of the characters, both in print and in film versions of stories. Look for books that feature characters from a range of sociocultural backgrounds and maintain the integrity of the genre.
Biographies, Autobiographies, and Memoirs	Include stories of people from sociocultural backgrounds similar to your students, which can be featured during a biography unit or throughout the year in particular grade levels. Feature stories of figures that are often omitted.
Other Nonfiction Literature	A strong nonfiction literature collection—including nonfiction books, magazines, newspapers, and online sources—supports students with important science and social studies content. Classroom library collections should include an array of informational text types and topics. When possible, connect to science and social studies units of study, but also appeal to a wide range of diverse interests.
Poetry	Make poetry more than a singular unit of study by building daily or weekly poetry rituals. Feature the work of poets from diverse backgrounds. Share your favorite poems and poets. Listen to the poetry read aloud using sites such as Poetry Out Loud (www.poetryoutloud.org).
Picture Books	Look closely at the covers and illustrations of picture books to choose books with diverse representations, particularly of children.
Comic Books and Graphic Novels	Comic books and graphic novels are an opportunity to support students with inference-building and high-level themes than are often not found in lower-level texts. They are especially appealing to upper elementary students and to English learners as well as native speakers of all reading levels.

Figure 2.7 Multigenre and Multimodal Text Set Considerations

FEATURING VISUAL TEXTS	
Captioned Photographs, Images, and Artwork	Consider photographs of the authors and poets that are featured in the classroom library. Consider displays of famous works of art by a range of artists from diverse sociocultural backgrounds. Consider a rotating visual prompt that encourages reflective writing.
INCORPORATING MULTIMEDIA TEXTS	
YouTube and Vimeo Clips	Search YouTube and Vimeo for themes and topics connected to units of study. Search for authors' videos as well as book trailers of core texts read aloud.
News Clips	Search children's and young adult news sources as well as sites such as CNN to find relevant, engaging, and newsworthy clips tied to themes of study.
Podcasts	Search for online audio files such as NPR's *This I Believe* project and *The Moth*'s stories.
STUDENT-CREATED TEXTS	
Writing	Consider incorporating student narratives, poetry, and informational and argumentative texts into text sets to enhance motivation and interest.
Digital Stories	Incorporate student-created digital stories and videos as they connect to the themes and topics of study to enhance motivation and interest.
Student Podcasts	Incorporate student audio files, book reviews, and podcasts as they connect to the themes and topics of study to enhance motivation and interest.

Figure 2.7 (*continued*)

The table in Figure 2.8 represents the progression of themes and text sets we created for grades 5-8. We started with the themes and moved to thinking about diverse texts that shared each theme. We wanted students to have opportunities to write and speak about what they noticed within and across the texts and to compare their points of view with those of the authors and artists. We are building skills, particularly the skills of close reading and writing about reading, through purposeful study with specific goals in mind. We have taken into account the social locations of students, all of whom are African American or Caribbean American. Many of the students come from low-income homes. About 75% of the student population receive reduced or free lunch. Every lesson every day is an opportunity to empower students to disrupt the status quo, to consider issues of historical importance, identity, and social justice, and to closely read across texts to form their own conclusions rooted in evidence and reason.

GRADE 5			
Themes	**Guiding Questions**	**Texts**	**Text Types**
Responsibility and Interdependency	How do we depend on one another? What responsibilities do we have to each other? How do we depend on our environment? How does our environment shape who we become?	• *Marshfield Dreams* by Ralph Fletcher • *Seedfolks* by Paul Fleischman • *Everybody Needs a Rock* by Byrd Baylor • *Those Shoes* by Maribeth Boelts • Ying Ying Yu's *This I Believe* essay, "A Duty to Family, Heritage, and Culture" • Excerpts from "Self-Reliance" by Ralph Waldo Emerson • "I Think We All Need a Pep Talk" from Kid President • Excerpts from Mr. Rogers's Commencement Address, Dartmouth College, 2002 • "Where We Are Shapes Who We Are" by Adam Alter • *The City*, painting by Fernand Leger • "Google and Twitter Help Track Influenza Outbreaks" by Helen Thompson • "New York's Looming Food Disaster" by Siddhartha Mahanta • "Material Remains: The Perpetual Challenge of Garbage" by Robin Nagle • "The Case for Reviving Extinct Species" by Stewart Brand • "Water Quality: An Ignored Global Crisis" by Cecilia Tortajada and Asit K. Biswas	• Autobiography • Poetry • Essay • Short film • Speech • Painting • Informational texts • Opinion writing
Friendship and Belonging	What is a true friend? How do you know? What responsibilities do I have to my friends? Do I need to be friends with everyone? Can friends get into conflicts? In what ways?	• *Enemy Pie* by Derek Munson • *The Name Jar* by Yangsook Choi • *Pink and Say* by Patricia Polacco • *Freak the Mighty* by Rodman Philbrick • *Love That Dog* by Sharon Creech • "Belonging," short film by Jesse Filimon from Screen It 2012 Competition • "Can Hailing a Ride Really Be About Making Friends Again?" by Christine Grimaldi • "What Are Friends For? A Longer Life" by Tara Parker-Pope	• Picture books • Historical fiction picture book • Realistic fiction novel • Poetry within realistic fiction novel • Short film • Informational text

Figure 2.8 A Beyond Books Approach Through Multigenre and Multimodal Text Sets (With special thanks to Chris Cunningham)

GRADE 5			
Themes	**Guiding Questions**	**Texts**	**Text Types**
Resolving Conflicts	What causes conflict between people? What are some ways to resolve conflicts? Can a person be in conflict with themselves? Can conflict be a good thing?	• Various myths • *Click, Clack, Moo: Cows That Type* by Doreen Cronin • *King for a Day* by Rukhsana Khan • *Smoky Night* by Eve Bunting • Excerpts from "Lessons from the Lab: How to Make Group Projects Successful" by Annie Murphy Paul • *Guernica*, painting by Pablo Picasso	• Myths • Picture book • Short story • Painting • Informational text

GRADE 6			
Themes	**Guiding Questions**	**Texts**	**Text Types**
Social Structures and Institutions	What is the impact of leadership on society? What is the government's responsibility to the general welfare?	• *The Breadwinner* by Deborah Ellis • Scenes from *A Midsummer Night's Dream* by William Shakespeare • TEDx Talks: "Why Good Leaders Make You Feel Safe" and "How Great Leaders Inspire Action" by Simon Sinek • TED Talk: "Why We Have Too Few Women Leaders" by Sheryl Sandberg • President Obama's Commencement Speech, University of Michigan, 2010 • "Why Does China Not Have Famines Anymore?" by Brian Palmer	• Realistic fiction novel • Play • Video from live talk • Speech • Informational text
Courage	What is courage? Can individuals make a difference? How do I know when I should be courageous?	• *Wringer* by Jerry Spinelli • *The Boy Who Dared* by Susan Campbell Bartoletti • *Homeless Bird* by Gloria Whelan • *Crispin: The Cross of Lead* by Avi • *Brave*, music video by Sara Bareilles • Muhammad Ali's *This I Believe* essay, "I Am Still the Greatest"	• Realistic fiction novel • Historical fiction novel • Music video • Essay

Figure 2.8 (*continued*)

GRADE 6			
Themes	**Guiding Questions**	**Texts**	**Text Types**
Adversity and Resilience	How do human beings best deal with adversity? Can I change my thoughts? How can I learn from my mistakes?	• *Knots in My Yo-Yo String* by Jerry Spinelli • *Junebug* by Alice Mead • "They Shut Me Up in Prose" by Emily Dickinson • *Bird* by Zetta Elliot • *Baseball Saved Us* by Ken Mochizuki • *The Arrival* by Shaun Tan • *The Steerage,* photograph by Alfred Stieglitz • *Bully*, film directed by Lee Hirsh • TED Talk: "Success, Failure, and the Drive to Keep Creating" by Elizabeth Gilbert • JK Rowling, Commencement Address, Harvard University, 2008 • Brian Grazer's *This I Believe* essay, "Disrupting My Comfort Zone" • "How Your Moral Decisions Are Shaped by a Bad Mood" by Travis Riddle	• Autobiography • Poem • Picture book • Wordless picture book • Painting • Full-length film • Video from live talk • Speech • Essay • Informational text
Empathy and Compassion	How well can you ever "know" another person? What do we all share as members of the human race? Is empathy possible when there are differences between people?	• *Wonder* by R.J. Palacio • *Mockingbird* by Kathryn Erskine • *Migrant Mother*, photograph by Dorothea Lange • *The Power of Empathy,* short film by Royal Society for the Encouragement of Arts and Brené Brown, directed by Katy Davis	• Realistic fiction novel • Autobiographical stories • Photograph • Animated short film

Figure 2.8 (*continued*)

GRADE 7			
Themes	**Guiding Questions**	**Texts**	**Text Types**
Identities (Personal identity and cultural diversity)	What is race? How does it impact who we are? What is gender? How does it impact who we are? What makes you *you*? Can you have multiple selves? Is there such a thing as a real you?	• *Walk Two Moons* by Sharon Creech • "Song of Myself" by Walt Whitman • Poems from *Bronx Masquerade* by Nikki Grimes • Scenes from *Twelfth Night* by William Shakespeare • Will Thomas's *This I Believe* essay, "The Birthright of Human Dignity" • Phyllis Allen's *This I Believe* essay, "Leaving Identity Issues to Other Folks" • Kamaal Majeed's *This I Believe* essay, "Being Content with Myself" • "A Teen Confronts Her iPhone Addiction" by Shane Achenbach • "More Women, but Not Nearly Enough" by Tali Mendelberg and Christopher F. Karpowitz • TED Talk: "The Danger of a Single Story" by Chimamanda Ngozi Adichie • Lupita Nyong'o's "Black Women in Hollywood" Acceptance Speech • Lee and Low Books diversity infographics • *Girl Before a Mirror*, painting by Pablo Picasso • *The Scream*, painting by Edward Munch • *Girl with a Pearl Earring* and *Girl Reading a Letter at An Open Window*, paintings by Johannes Vermeer	• Realistic fiction • Autobiographical essay • Essay • Informational text • Poetry • Play • Video from live talk • Infographic • Painting
Wellness	What is health? Physical? Mental? Who decides and how do they know? Can a society be healthy? A world? How?	• Doodle4Google 2014, "If I Could Invent One Thing to Make the World a Better Place" • TED Talk: "The Paradox of Choice" by Barry Schwartz • TED Talk: "Teach Every Child About Food" by Jamie Oliver • TED Talk: "Choice, Happiness, and Spaghetti Sauce" by Malcolm Gladwell • "Science Can Help Us Live Longer, but How Long Is Too Long?" by Randy Rieland • "Does Your Diet Influence How Well You Sleep?" by Alexandra Sifferlin	• Google doodles • Videos from live talk • Informational articles

Figure 2.8 (*continued*)

GRADE 7			
Themes	**Guiding Questions**	**Texts**	**Text Types**
Freedom	Why did slavery exist? Why did it last for so long in the United States? How does justice relate to freedom? Historically, why has there been a struggle between security and liberty? What rights should children have? Is freedom ever free?	• The Declaration of Independence • Declaration of the Rights of the Child (UN Commission on Human Rights) • Andrew Sullivan's *This I Believe* essay, "Life, Liberty and the Pursuit of Happiness" • *Chains* by Laurie Halse Anderson • "Caged Bird" by Maya Angelou • Rosa Parks's *This I Believe* essay, "Standing Up to Injustice" • "I Have a Dream" by Martin Luther King Jr. • "50 Feet from MLK" by Mortimer B. Zuckerman • "I, Too" by Langston Hughes • "I Got Myself Arrested So I Could Look Inside the Justice System" by Bobby Constantino • "A Back-to-School Fight over the Right to Classroom Prayer" by Adam Cohen • *The Migration of the Negro*, painting by Jacob Lawrence • Paul Revere's etching of Boston Massacre titled *The Bloody Massacre in King Street* • *El Tres de Mayo*, painting by Francisco Goya	• Historical primary source • Essay • Historical fiction novel • Short story • Poetry • Painting

GRADE 8			
Themes	**Guiding Questions**	**Texts**	**Text Types**
Transitions	How can I deal with challenges ahead if I don't know what they'll be? What new responsibilities may I have in the future? How is the world changing? What do I need to know about these changes?	• "Alone" by Maya Angelou • "If" by Rudyard Kipling • "A Network to Build a Dream On" by John Horgan • "These 5 Foods Will Be Harder to Grow in a Warmer World" by Chris Woolston • "No More Night? The Meaning of the Loss of Darkness" by Brandon Kiem	• Poetry • Book review • Informational text

Figure 2.8 (*continued*)

GRADE 8			
Themes	**Guiding Questions**	**Texts**	**Text Types**
Coming of Age	What is the difference between an adult, a child, and an adolescent? Who decides? Does age matter? Should we change age restrictions in this country?	• "Letter to a Person on Their First Day Here" by Kid President • "Modern Families: Chips Off The Old Block" by Paul Wallich • *Growing Up* by Russell Baker • "On Turning Ten" by Billy Collins • "Father and Son" by Cat Stevens • "Forever Young" by Bob Dylan • "When I'm Sixty Four" by the Beatles • TED Talk: "How to Live Before You Die" by Steve Jobs	• Video • Poetry • Song • Speech
Humanity	What defines humanity? Why are humans capable of great compassion and great terror towards one another? What can we learn about others and ourselves when we believe in humanity?	• *Humans of New York* photoblog by Brandon Stanton • Jay Frankston's *This I Believe* essay, "Speak Up" • "The Bitterness of Sugar" by Peter Singer • "What Makes Us Human? Cooking, Study Says" by Nicholas Mott • "Theme for English B" by Langston Hughes • "So Much Happiness" by Naomi Shihab Nye	• Photoblog • Essay • Poetry • Informational articles

Figure 2.8 (*continued*)

We began with themes central to the human experience, purposefully organized to increase in complexity through the years. Each grade level has guiding questions and core texts central to the thematic study. From there we selected short texts, multimedia pieces, and works of art and music to dig deeper into the themes and to support students in considering the multiple dimensions of each theme from a range of diverse viewpoints. We included journalistic pieces that represent various text structures not only to support the thematic study but to provide inspiration for students' own expository responses.

Final Thoughts

In titling this chapter "Whose Stories Count?" I have intentionally called into question how we as a field have traditionally underrepresented or misrepresented the diverse students in our class-rooms through the children's and young adult literature selections we make. I hope I have made a compelling argument that many of our students are left out of the majority of children's and young adult literature, but that we have the resources to change that—to center stories that represent our diverse society and to do so not only through written literature but also through visual, audio, and multimedia stories. The next chapter focuses on where stories live and will offer more details about ways to invite students to wonder about the great stories in literature, poetry, music, art, and multimedia. As you continue to consider whether the students in your classroom are repre-sented in the stories you share and whether your classroom bookshelves represent our diverse society, Chapter 3 will offer specific guidance for how to read for story across text types. You are the cartographer, and you have the capacity to change the literacy landscape and write the Diver-sity 102 story.

 TOOLKIT Student Survey and Family Survey

STUDENT SURVEY

Some of the questions I ask students include the kinds of things that Brandon Stanton asks in his photoblog, *Humans of New York*. To tap in to stories is to first assume that everyone has a world of stories to tell and that every story has value and is worthy of telling. Here are some of the questions I ask students to respond to whether they are in second grade or in graduate school:

1. What is a time when you remember being really happy?
2. Describe a time you were really excited.
3. Describe a time you were nervous.
4. What is a time that you remember being sad?
5. What makes you angry or frustrated?
6. What are some of the things you are most proud of yourself for?
7. What are some of the things you most love about yourself? What are some of the things you think your friends or family love most about you?
8. What are some things about yourself you would like to change?
9. What do you imagine yourself doing in five years?
10. Who are some of the people you look up to? Why?
11. If you could do one thing all day long what would it be? If you could learn one subject all day long what would it be?
12. How much do you like school, on a scale of 1 to 5?

| 1 | 2 | 3 | 4 | 5 |

(School is ok)   (School is awesome!)

I also ask about reading and writing preferences:

1. When has reading felt good for you?
2. When has reading not felt good for you?
3. When has writing felt good for you?
4. When has writing not felt good for you?
5. Do you like to read books of your own choosing?
6. Do you like to have someone to talk to about the things you're reading?
7. If you are reading a book or books right now, what are the titles?
8. My favorite time to read for pleasure is: _____
9. Do you have a favorite author or authors? Who is it? _____
10. What are some of your favorite types of books to read?
11. Do you read in other ways beyond books? With an e-book or tablet? On your phone? What are the kinds of things you like to read beyond books?
12. What are the kinds of things you like to write or that you are proud to share with others?

13.   How much do you like reading, on a scale of 1 to 5?

1   2   3   4   5

(I avoid reading)   (Reading is awesome!)

Tell me more about your choice:

14.   How much do you like writing, on a scale of 1 to 5?

1   2   3   4   5

(I avoid writing)   (Writing is awesome!)

Tell me more about your choice:

FAMILY SURVEY

I also firmly believe in the power of home and school partnerships and that homes are full of important and revealing stories. The following is a story inventory I send home to families to learn more about my students and the stories they have lived and shared at home.

1.   When you think of your child's happiest moments what do you picture in your mind?

2.   What are some of the things about your child that you are especially proud of him or her for?

3.   In what ways do you notice your child being especially independent, carefree, or confident?

4.   What are some things your child likes to do at home? What are some things you like to do together?

5.   Do you have favorite stories you share with your child? Would you like to share one of these with the class?

6.   What do you hope the "story" of this school year will be for your child?

Chapter 3

Where Do Stories Live?

Even the silence

has a story to tell you.

Just listen. Listen.

—Jacqueline Woodson, *Brown Girl Dreaming*

*I*n the short film *16: Moments* by National Public Radio's program *Radiolab* (2009), we see a stream of everyday moments that we often ignore. Putting a sticky note on a computer and having it quickly fall off. Noticing a young boy grasping a balloon string only to watch it slip between his fingers. A hand turning the pages of a book. A guitar string breaking. A boy kicking a ball and hearing his friends cheer for him. A bird flying from a tree branch. The footprint of a baby imprinted on pink paper. A man shoveling a pile of dirt into a grave, amplified by the sound of the shovel scraping and lifting. The film eloquently captures these everyday stories and reminds us as teachers what we tell our students—that stories live everywhere.

If you visit We Feel Fine (www.wefeelfine.org), you will witness an ever-growing, always-changing catalog of human stories. The site was designed to capture the stories that people share through blog pages using the phrase "I feel" or "I am feeling." Since its launch in August 2005, We Feel Fine has shared the heartbeat of the world at any given second—as stated in the site's mission, "human emotion on a global scale." The site collects between 15,000 and 20,000 new entries each day. To open the page, you click on a large heart with the phrase "We Feel Fine" in its center. What the creators, Jonathan Harris and Sep Kamvar, have done is program a site that will not only mine for and capture stories but also transform those stories into various forms of data that they call movements.

Each pixel represents a feeling—its size, color, shape, and opacity tell us more of the story that lies behind it. The site's founders describe it on their "mission" page:

> At its core, We Feel Fine is an artwork authored by everyone. It will grow and change as we grow and change, reflecting what's on our blogs, what's in our hearts, what's in our minds. We hope it makes the world seem a little smaller, and we hope it helps people see beauty in the everyday ups and downs of life. (Harris and Kamvar 2015)

Jonathan Harris went on to create new digital platforms for stories. Perhaps his best-known site is Cowbird, (www.cowbird.com). If you haven't already visited it to consider new pathways for story in your classroom, make your way there immediately. Described as a "public library of human experience," the site provides a place to share your stories within a community through vignettes composed of text, photos, and sound. It is pointedly not a social network. There are no buttons for making comments and there is no messaging system. Instead, the site provides a simpler means of telling meaningful stories that can stand on their own and provides pathways for connecting those stories. Rooted in the ideals of equality and inclusiveness, Cowbird is designed to be less about authorship and more about the stories themselves and the interconnectedness of stories that defines us as humans. To inspire and encourage the storyteller in all of us, the site created "Retellings," or opportunities to build on an existing story, and "Collections," handpicked assortments of stories which are the equivalent of mix tapes in the Cowbird world. The site does not have ads or sponsors. It is independent and free, and home to tens of thousands of storytellers around the world sharing in real time.

In a personal correspondence, Jonathan shared with me his perception of where stories live and why they are important to our lives. Jonathan wrote:

> Stories are containers for wisdom — they're the best technology we've invented for packaging insights in a format that allows them to travel, so they can move through the world and transform other people. An insight delivered on its own (an inspiring quote, a principle, a law) will never resonate as deeply as a story, because stories deliver the experience of Illumination, not only its outcome.

Stories have always had this power. Today, stories have the capacity to immediately influence people we will never meet in person, and they are now shared in new ways—online, through snapped images, through seconds-long videos that replay continuously, through audio recordings—the shouts and murmurs of today are not limited to print on the page.

As teachers, we tend to glorify print. We discuss at faculty meetings whether penmanship is a lost art. We put our heads together and strategize when we think that a student isn't giving it his all or reaching his full potential, based on what he has shown on the page. As teachers and parents, we give in to these pressures. It's time our classrooms caught up to the outside world. To rethink where stories live and how we can give students access to new and engaging storytelling tools. To share your story, in the medium of your choosing, should be a fundamental human right. To know that your story is heard is in many ways to know you are loved.

This chapter is designed to help teachers as they consider where stories live in literature, in poetry, in music, in art and illustration, in multimedia, and in play. A student in your classroom may be drawn to one medium over another as a reader and as a writer. Supporting students with the language of each medium and providing mentor texts that build deeper understandings of stories can foster the storyteller in each of your students. Throughout this chapter, I will provide examples of mentor texts as well as instructional language that can support early childhood and elementary students as well as middle and high schoolers. These examples are meant as guideposts. Knowing your students' interests and identities should guide your own decision-making about what stories, in all forms, will spark your students to more deeply understand and interpret a variety of stories and, in turn, become more inspired storytellers themselves.

In Literature

For many of us, literature is an old friend. We have homes and classrooms chock-full of books. We scavenge at library book sales and treasure our finds. We love the feeling of turning the pages. We give book talks to our students that probably go on for too long—we can't help ourselves. We love what's within those pages and we imagine the possibilities for how our students will come to know themselves and others just a little bit better thanks to our beloved authors. We know that it is through the pages of books that we often realize that we are not alone. As a reader, you discover, as F. Scott Fitzgerald once stated, "that your longings are universal longings, that you're not lonely and isolated from anyone. You belong." And we want to share that feeling with our students.

In literature, powerful stories lie in authentic characters that feel like they could be our childhood friends, or our sister-in-law, or that quirky neighbor down the street. In powerful stories events happen that are compelling and keep us wondering what's going to happen next. Powerful stories are composed of small scenes with big themes. While I sometimes over-taught the structure of a story—well-intentioned as I was—I would have better encouraged my students to make meaning from literature by focusing on what we know and can learn from deeper study of authentic characters, compelling events, and the impact of small scenes to better understand universal, human themes.

Authentic Characters

As a second-grade teacher, I often turned to characters that I felt could provide both mirrors and windows for my students and moments when windows become mirrors. I hoped for that effect when we read *The Chalkbox Kid* by Clyde Robert Bulla (1987). My students were in many ways socially and economically privileged. So, Gregory's experiences as a working class boy did not initially provide a mirror for many of them. But his struggle to make friends and find his voice through his chalk drawings resonated. I wondered, year after year, why so many of the boys in my class connected with Gregory. What made him "authentic" so that they connected with him?

Authenticity is a complex term, and many argue that there is no such thing as an authentic self— that we are all actually multiple selves. I agree. Yet, when we are looking for characters that feel authentic, we mean that they come to life for us as readers. They live beyond the words of the page and share space with us at our desks, on the rug, and in our bedrooms: they feel things. They experience challenges that we all face. They are influenced by the words, actions, and ideas of others, and they may change because of those things. They represent multiple selves, just as we do. And they act differently and speak differently depending on to whom they are talking.

Authentic characters share certain qualities and capacities that we often notice about people in our lives who live whole-heartedly (more on that in Chapter 7). Brené Brown (2010, 2012) found in her research on social work that those who live whole-heartedly share

- the courage to be imperfect;
- the compassion to be kind to ourselves and others;
- connections as a result of authenticity; and
- a full embrace of vulnerability.

After following Brown's work for the last few years, I've started to wonder: if we can better understand each other through these lenses, can we better understand characters in literature in the same way?

Think of the characters in literature that you love, that feel authentic to you. Now think of Brown's research on whole-hearted people. Ask yourself, in what ways do these characters demonstrate courage? Did they show compassion as you would expect people in your own life to? Do they build connections? In what ways? And do they recognize that sometimes in life we get hurt, that there are risks, but that the rewards are often greater?

I wanted to hold some of my favorite characters up to this test of whole-heartedness as a marker of authenticity. So, I started with what is quickly becoming a children's literature classic, the Knuffle

Bunny picture book trilogy by Mo Willems. In book one, *Knuffle Bunny: A Cautionary Tale* (2004), we see Trixie courageously wailing full-force as she goes "boneless" on city streets to wordlessly explain to her father how she left her bunny behind at the laundromat. In book two, *Knuffle Bunny Too: A Case of Mistaken Identity* (2007), preschooler Trixie is full of scorn, a natural human emotion, when she realizes Sonja, her classmate, has the same bunny. By the end of this book, we see the connection she forms with Sonja through their shared bunnies, and we are left to ponder the complexity of friendship in all of its forms. In the final book, *Knuffle Bunny Free: An Unexpected Diversion* (2010), we see Trixie as a young girl as she loses her beloved bunny on an airplane only to find it in her seatback pocket on her return flight home. We see her compassionately give her bunny away to a crying baby on the flight. We see her demonstrating vulnerability—that the time has come for her to give up something she loves for someone who needs it more. Throughout the trilogy, we see Trixie as a model of early childhood whole-hearted living.

To consider whether characters I loved for upper elementary and middle school readers passed the whole-heartedness test, I turned to *Brown Girl Dreaming* (2014), a memoir told in verse, by Jacqueline Woodson. Throughout the story, we feel the growing pains Jacqueline experienced as a girl of color born in the North, raised in the South, and transported to Brooklyn, New York. We feel the anguish of the loss of her grandfather, and we sit with her on the Brooklyn stoop as she thinks about how her family life is different from her Latina best friend's. We read how she had the courage to be imperfect in comparison to her overachieving sister. We come to understand why she is her granddaddy's favorite for her compassion towards others. We understand the connections she has to her uncle especially when he returns from prison. Throughout the memoir, we come to realize that she embraces the uncertain and recognizes that many things unfold in life simply because. She embraces vulnerability and, in turn, we embrace her.

It is these and other authentic characters that make stories come alive. But, of course, stories are memorable not only for their characters but also for what happens to them over the course of the story.

Compelling Events

When I finally got my hands on a copy of the 2015 Newbery Award–winning book, *The Crossover* (Alexander 2014), I sat down in a comfy chair in our local library, and I did not get up until I reached the last page. Electric and heartfelt, Kwame Alexander's language in this novel-in-verse is lyrical and rhythmic, like the sounds of a basketball being drilled down court. Yet, what kept me glued to my chair were the compelling events that happen to twelve-year-old Josh, on and off the basketball court. The events in Josh's life drive us to read on, furiously turning pages even if we know little or nothing of the game. When his twin brother, JB, cuts Josh's dreadlocks after a bet, my jaw dropped. When Josh's anger bubbles up and he throws a basketball, breaking his brother's nose, I was on the edge of my seat. When I read the news of Josh and JB's father, my heart sank.

How did Alexander do this as a writer? First, the events rang true to my perception as a reader of the struggles of adolescence, family dramas, preteen romance, team dynamics, and the importance of one's hair, shoes, and other markers of identity. Next, Alexander organized the events so that the reader comes to know the main character right away, in the section of the book titled "Warm Up." He chunks the text to mirror the flow of a basketball game, moving from "Warm Up" to "First Quarter," "Second Quarter," "Third Quarter," "Fourth Quarter," and "Overtime." This sectioning of the text allows us to synthesize the life events of the characters before reading on. Finally, he uses language that encourages us to read more closely, with lines like "Happy is a huge river right now and I've forgotten how to swim"(2014, 207). I read that line over and over, drawing connections to my own life and imagining the ache in Josh's heart. To help your students to notice compelling events, consider creating character lifelines as a class or in partnerships. Look for ways to section or chunk text into logical groupings that support synthesis. Finally, look for language that encourages students to read more closely to help them understand both the events and the feelings characters have in those compelling moments.

Small Scenes/Big Themes

To see a play live, whether it's in a black box theater, on a Broadway stage, or in an elementary school classroom, is to see stories come to life. From the simplest reader's theater kindergarten production to the impromptu playground dramatists to the professional teams of Manhattan's theaters, each actor works to create a small scene and to convey something about the human experience that is about much more than that scene.

Consider the smallness of Shakespeare's Hamlet speaking to Ophelia: a brother speaking to his sister. Two people engaged in dialogue. Compare that to the magnitude of his quandary: a young man considering life and death, wondering if the dream that endless sleep provides is worth it:

> To be, or not to be, that is the question:
> Whether 'tis nobler in the mind to suffer
> The slings and arrows of outrageous fortune,
> Or to take arms against a sea of troubles
> And by opposing end them. To die – to sleep,
> No more; and by a sleep to say we end

The heart-ache and the thousand natural shocks

That flesh is heir to: 'tis a consummation

Devoutly to be wish'd. To die, to sleep;

To sleep, perchance to dream – ay, there's the rub. (1992, Act III, scene i)

Shakespeare was a master at weaving small scenes to create themes universal to human experience. We all experience crossroads—seas of trouble—rubs. This is why we remember the scene, understand references to it, and connect it to our own lived experiences. Writers of other narrative texts borrow techniques from drama to make their scenes come to life for us as readers.

In Chapter 2, I shared a lesson I wrote to encourage students to talk and write about times when reading felt good for them and when it felt hard. In this lesson, I shared my own reading life, using the example of *The Art of Racing in the Rain* by Garth Stein (2009). As an adult reader, this book grabbed hold of me. It has characters I could connect to and who felt authentic to me, but it was the collection of small scenes that had resonating themes that struck me page after page. Told from a dog's point of view, events unfold from Enzo's perspective as he struggles to make sense of what's human, all of the good along with all of the bad. Each scene is from Enzo's eyes and ears. Alternating description with dialogue, each scene feels as though it is happening right in front of you. Consider this scene from the first chapter:

"Enzo?"

I hear his footsteps, the concern in his voice. He finds me and looks down. I lift my head, wag my tail feebly so it taps against the floor. I play the part.

He shakes his head and runs his hand through his hair, sets down the plastic bag from the grocery that has his dinner in it. I can smell roast chicken through the plastic. Tonight he's having roast chicken and an iceberg lettuce salad.

"Oh, Enz," he says.

He reaches down to me, crouches, touches my head like he does, along the crease behind the ear, and I lift my head and lick at his forearm.

"What happened, kid?" he asks.

Gestures can't explain.

"Can you get up?"

I try, and I scramble. My heart takes off, lunges ahead because no, I can't. I panic. I thought I was just acting, but I really can't get up. Shit. Life imitating art.

"Take it easy, kid," he says, pressing down on my chest to calm me. "I've got you." (2009, 3)

This is a small scene, but it has significance for a larger human theme of the agony of growing older, as told from Enzo's point of view. We can encourage students in their own reading to notice how writers compose small scenes that draw us in and make us think more deeply about ourselves and the world. To help students to notice small scenes with big themes in literature, consider drawing their attention to the following:

- Dialogue alternating with description
- Incorporation of sensory images to show feelings
- Internal thinking
- A variety of sentence structures including simple, compound, and complex sentences
- A variety of sentence lengths
- Powerful and purposeful use of "I"

It is in the collection of these small scenes that big themes emerge, including what is good and what is hard about being human, or being a boy, or being a girl, or being a kid; what is good, hard, and complicated about friendship; what we can learn from challenges characters overcome; what we can learn about noticing the feelings of characters and how they relate to our own; and what we can learn from what characters wonder about, hope for, or dream about. Writers use their craft to make scenes emerge before us as if they were on a stage. Imagining the scenes before us allows us to connect with them and make meaning far beyond each small scene. It is in these scenes that we begin to care about the characters and, in turn, consider the ways we care for others in our own lives.

In Poetry

As a new teacher in New York City, I had the great fortune of often visiting the many great museums New York has to offer. I frequented museums with my students and often visited them alone after school. In many ways, the halls of the Met, the Frick, and the Guggenheim were my refuge. As a country dweller these days, I know how incredibly fortunate I was to have these experiences in my history. On a spring afternoon in my first year as a teacher, my head swimming with masterpieces, I met a poet outside the Metropolitan Museum of Art. He was throwing his poems into the wind, shouting "poetry in motion!" I was amazed at him, his performance, and also the passersby who didn't take notice of this man shouting and throwing scraps of paper into the streets. What a paradox, really, that poets closely study the world—observers of the smallest details—and no one on Fifth Avenue was taking notice of the grandest of performances in the name of poetry. I stopped and asked him about his poetry. We talked about our shared love of the poet Mary Oliver. I talked about Mrs. Danish, my high school English teacher, who inspired a love of nature and writing in me and gave me a sense of wide-awakeness to notice the beauty of small things and the inspiration of small acts of courage much like his own on New York's streets. He handed me some of his poems on golden paper. One hangs in my office today, as a reminder of the stories that live in poems themselves and the stories that are created through the sharing of poetry for all who will stop and listen.

Every year I celebrated poetry with my students. We read. We wrote. We hit the streets and the gardens. And we shared. I wanted my students to notice and have the academic language to discuss the sounds and structures that help us as readers to make meaning and imagine the story that a poem shares. I often started with Valerie Worth's (1996) *All the Small Poems and Fourteen More*. For early elementary students, I thought her poems had the closest connection to Mary Oliver, whose work drew me in to poetry—poems about grass, marbles, caterpillars, and coat hangers. Starting with these everyday objects we could start to see the world anew and imagine new places where poetry lived. In our pencil trays. Along the four sides of a sticky note. Under our shoes. On the doorknob. Oh, if that doorknob could talk—what would it say? We looked at structure, language, and the sound of poetry that helped tell the poet's story.

Marbles

Marbles picked up
Heavy by the handful
And held, weighed,
Hard, glossy,
Glassy, cold,
Then poured clicking,
Water-smooth, back
To their bag, seem
Treasure: round jewels,
Slithering gold. (Worth 1996, 23)

In the preceding poem, "Marbles," for example, we noticed structural elements:

- Short lines evident from white space on the right-hand side of the page
- Each line beginning with a capital letter
- Line breaks designed to give additional pauses

We also noticed Worth's language choices:

- Powerful verbs are used to help us imagine the weight of the marbles in our hands
- Adjectives are included in a series one after the other like marbles rolling around on the floor

And we noticed the sound elements:

- What our voices did when we hit each comma so that the adjectives sounded like a series of staccato notes in music
- How our voices paused after the colon to indicate the importance of the word *treasure*
- How Worth used a series of words that started with "h" to build alliteration: *heavy*, *handful*, *held*, *hard*

From Valerie Worth, we turned to Pablo Neruda (2013) and his "Ode to Fried Potatoes" and "Ode to a Sock." We noticed how Valerie Worth also wrote odes but didn't call her poems by that name. We read Eve Merriam's (1964) "How to Eat a Poem" and noticed her choices to make the experience of reading a poem feel like the experience of biting into a juicy apple, but an apple that we never had to finish eating. The stories that live inside of poems became a resounding heartbeat of our reading and writing lives.

To encourage your students to notice where stories live in poetry, consider the poems that you love and that remind you of the beauty and significance of everyday life. Share poets like Valerie Worth who specifically write with young audiences in mind, but stretch your students to consider other poets, such as Pablo Neruda, Mary Oliver, Langston Hughes, Maya Angelou, and Billy Collins. Start with poems about things your students know, and continue to help them to notice what they know as poems become more linguistically and structurally complex. As with any complex text, start with the known to build towards understanding of the unknown.

Set up a collection of poetry books and sticky notes and encourage students to browse for poems that speak to them. Post a monthly sign-up sheet for students to share their favorite finds at the start of class each day. Sharing the works of both well-known and lesser-known poets will continue conversations about poetry throughout the year, supporting students as they notice the language, sound, and structural choices poets make. Watch as your students start to sign up to share the poems they write in between classes, on the school bus, or in their bedrooms.

While the close reading of poetry can support students to feel more comfortable with complex texts, it is the wide reading of poetry that may ultimately fuel deeper appreciation of poetry and the stories that poets share with us. Browse the poems catalogued by the Poetry Foundation online. Listen to poets read their work, from Shel Silverstein to Naomi Shihab Nye, drawing attention to the ways their voices reveal more of the story hidden in the poem. And, encourage students to perform their own poetry through poetry cafes and slams, which have the power to become community events. With my fourth graders, I held an annual Hot Chocolate House designed to mirror the coffee house experience of an open mic night where students shared poems, stories, and songs. With middle- and high-school students, listen to performances from New York's famed Nuyorican Poets' Café and the annual New York Knicks/Urban Word poetry slam. Watch the documentary from Chicago's poetry teams titled "Louder than a Bomb."

Find ways to bridge poetry and art by providing visual images for students to write about. I have a box of postcards from museums that I use for this purpose, but images can easily be found online to spark student poetry writing. The example in Figure 3.1 is by a fifth-grade student who chose a postcard of Van Gogh's (1887) *Bridge in the Rain* to draw inspiration from.

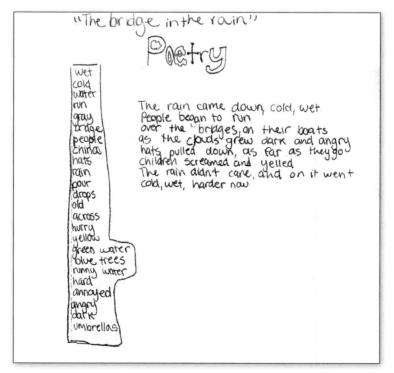

Figure 3.1 Student poetry in response to Van Gogh's painting *Bridge in the Rain*

I encourage students to start by listing what they see and move from their lists into lines of poetry. I also encourage students to start with their own art as the basis for poetry. Drawing from their newfound favorite poets and from their own lives and dreams, students can begin to see themselves as poets, full of stories to tell in a myriad of ways.

In Music

As a young girl, I was subjected (sorry, Mom and Dad) to piano lessons and then violin lessons and then orchestra rehearsals and dreaded performances on stage—with me in the fifth or sixth violin chair. Music has always been something I've loved but never understood. It is a language I struggled to participate in despite a host of models, small-group experiences, and one-on-one lessons. As a fourth-grade teacher, I recognized that several of my students had an affinity for music, and in some cases extraordinary musical talents. My students were allowed to bring in music and play their favorite songs on the class computers during free time, sharing their favorites with one another ranging from Led Zeppelin to Green Day to Mariah Carey. Several students brought their own instruments to school and would strum chords together, learning new techniques from one another during snack time. I was amazed at their collaboration, skills, and ability to talk about music. They had a connection to music as a vehicle for story that I had never known as a young person.

As a literacy consultant at PS 49 in Queens, New York, I finally learned about where stories live in music. This forever changed the ways I listen to music and teach through music—by centering its power to convey stories. A kindergarten through eighth-grade public school, PS 49 is dedicated to a balanced literacy curriculum that emphasizes deep understanding of the arts as an integral part of being a literacy learner. In every classroom every week there is a shared poem, a shared work of art, and a shared song as part of the classroom routine for reading, discussing, and interpreting a variety of texts that we make meaning from and often don't have the tools for understanding more deeply. I owe a debt of gratitude for any understanding I have of music to the leaders and teachers of this great school.

The first thing I noticed about how music is integrated across the school is in the use of terms for talking about how songwriters and musicians play with elements, much as storywriters do to convey meaning. Terms that express how musicians use sound to affect meaning include but are not limited to:

Adagio - *slow*

Allegro - *to play music brisk and happily, sometimes fast*

Alto - *high pitched, an alto voice is lower than a soprano, but higher than a tenor*

Bass - *low, the lowest of the voices and the lowest part of the harmony*

Bravura - *to play music boldly*

Crescendo - *growing steadily louder*

Harmony - *when several notes or chords come together to create a certain sound*

Meter - *a pattern of strong and soft beats throughout the music*

Staccato - *when each note is played sharply and by itself*

Tempo – *the timing or speed of the music*

Terms that express how musicians use structure to affect meaning include but are not limited to:

Bridge - *the part of a song that connects two main parts*

Measure – *a short group of notes within a piece of music*

Stanza - *a verse of a song*

Anchor charts with these terms hang in all the P.S. 49 classrooms, encouraging students to use the language of music to talk about how musicians and songwriters make choices that affect how we listen to and interpret music. At P.S. 49, the song of the week is played on Monday morning to support students with a general understanding or first impression of what a song is mostly about. They draw on their personal connections to the content and share initial questions about its meanings. In subsequent lessons throughout the week, they study particular lines of the song as they would a sentence in a novel or a line of poetry. They read with a linguistic lens, noting word choice, repetition of words, rhyme, and alliteration. As the days progress, they incorporate the academic language of music to deepen their interpretations, and they listen to the songs with a rhythm lens or a syntactic lens, noticing how the sounds of voices and instruments contribute to the overall meaning and emotion of a piece. They have tools for talking about why the story portrayed through the song is effective by looking specifically at the language, sounds, and structures of songs.

In the Language

I have often thought that the language choices songwriters make are very similar to the choices poets make, but in many ways songwriters rely on simpler language to tell their stories. I learned more about this from some experts—notably the great Phil Collins—during an episode of *This American Life* (Glass 2007) titled "339: Break-Up" on National Public Radio. These days NPR is my most trusted source of news and my driving companion. Such was the case on my drive to work one day when I came upon an episode about break-ups. Writer Starlee Kine kicked off the episode with questions many of us may share—what makes the perfect breakup song, and can really sad music actually make you feel better? Kine went on to interview the king of ballads, Phil Collins, who has united many of us under the golden lyrics of the song "Against All Odds" (1984):

> *How can I just let you walk away,*
> *just let you leave without a trace,*
> *when I stand here taking every breath with you?*
> *Ooh, ooh.*
> *You're the only one*
> *who really knew me at all.*

The words are simple. So simple. Yet they convey something that anyone who has been in a relationship can understand. When something is over, it's like the person has left without a trace. They are just gone. In the interview with Kine, Collins talks about lyrics and the language he chose to make the song effective:

> *Most of the time, it's the direct—I mean, if it's a good song, that's what makes it good is the fact that it's—so many people try to fluff things up or disguise them or make them a little bit too clever. But sometimes, it's the simplest thing that actually reaches people.*
> (Glass 2007)

Kine went on to walk us through her own songwriting experience, where the most powerful lyric she wrote for her own breakup song was from what she referred to as the "junk pile." The lyric, "It doesn't do me any good. In fact, it does me bad," was applauded by her songwriting friends and even Phil Collins himself. It was so simple. And then I thought—yes—we can teach students to notice the simple language that moves us the most and to learn from the combination of words and phrases songwriters use to convey meaning.

My fourth graders were actually masters at this, and I had never realized it. The lyrics to their snack-time strumming sessions were simple but powerful. I now encourage students, through the close reading of songs, to better understand how the combination of words on the page—the choices the songwriter made—help us understand ourselves and others. We read and listen to Sara Bareilles's (2013) "Brave" to define bravery for ourselves. In what ways is being an outcast brave? How can a phrase be as powerful as a weapon or a drug?

> *You can be amazing*
> *You can turn a phrase into a weapon or a drug*
> *You can be the outcast*
> *Or be the backlash of somebody's lack of love*
> *Or you can start speaking up*

We listen to and read Cat Stevens's (1970) "Trouble" to consider whose story is being told. What represents trouble for different people? What do students want to be set free of in their own lives?

> *Trouble*
> *Oh trouble set me free*
> *I have seen your face*
> *And it's too much too much for me*
> *Trouble*
> *Oh trouble can't you see*
> *You're eating my heart away*
> *And there's nothing much left of me*

I now listen to lyrics with greater interest. I encourage teachers to immerse students in music throughout the year, and especially at the beginning of a unit, to help them analyze simple forms of language that are chosen to convey larger meanings.

In the Sounds

Fritz et al. (2009) reported that people from other parts of the world who have never listened to the radio before can pick up on happiness, sadness, and fear emotions in Western music. What does this show us? It shows that basic emotions in music can be universally recognized. The ways we read emotions on other people's faces can be applied to our understanding of what makes music effective. Emotion is a fundamental part of why we turn to music both in times of joy and celebration and in times of great pain. When we explicitly teach students how to listen for the sounds of music in combination with the words, we are teaching them to notice what kinds of sounds evoke which emotions.

Even before our students have mastered the musical terminology for what musicians do with sound, we can talk about pauses for effect, volume, and the rate of sounds we hear to help them understand the stories that music conveys. Take the time to re-listen to your own favorite songs: those that you turn to again and again on your playlists, in your iTunes files, or from your record or CD collections. These days I use Songza to select music. I find myself returning over and over to the same playlists—*Wintertime Warmth* when I'm sitting by the fire on yet another snow day or *Girls: Marnie* when I'm gearing up to cook a new recipe or when I'm prepping for demos. What are the songs you return to? What are the sounds you hear, and how do they convey happiness, sadness, or fear? Our students have many of the same songs in their own collections, and we can help them to read and listen to songs to better understand how words work, how authors put sounds together, and what that has to do with us as writers.

The auditory choices musicians make can help students as readers across texts but also as listeners and speakers. What should their voices do when reading aloud a poem, persuasive essay, or speech? Where should they pause for effect? Where should they raise their voices? When should they speak quickly or draw their words out? How do our choices as speakers affect our listeners?

In the Structure

Like all writers, songwriters make choices about the structures of their pieces. They choose to repeat words and lines for effect, and they organize their thinking into groups of ideas. Take "Blackbird" by the Beatles (1968) as an example:

> *Blackbird singing in the dead of night*
> *Take these broken wings and learn to fly*
> *All your life*
>
> *You were only waiting for this moment to arise.*
>
> *Blackbird singing in the dead of night*
> *Take these sunken eyes and learn to see*
> *All your life*
> *You were only waiting for this moment to be free.*
>
> *Blackbird fly Blackbird fly*
> *Into the light of the dark black night.*
>
> *Blackbird fly Blackbird fly*
> *Into the light of the dark black night.*

We can encourage students to notice the common threads across the first two verses and to notice the initial repetition but also critical differences in the use of "Take these broken wings and learn to fly" and "Take these sunken eyes and learn to see." We can encourage them to notice that the phrase "Blackbird fly" is repeated in several places. Finally, we can encourage students to find other examples from songs they love, to better understand how writers organize their thinking and use repetition for effect. Imagine if we started with the text structures within songs before we launched our readers and writers into the text structures of literary essays or informational texts. When we lead with the structural choices poets and songwriters make, we create a bridge for understanding text structure in other genres. The underpinnings remain the same, but we provide a foundation for students to build on when we start with texts they know and can gain confidence from.

In the Visual Arts and Illustration

As I shared in Chapter 2, before I was a teacher I studied architecture, and before I studied architecture, I fell in love with art history. A big thank you must be given to Mr. McClellan, my high school art history teacher, for opening this world to me. With the lights turned off and the slide reel turning, characters on canvas and formed from clay came alive for me. Mr. McClellan made his love of art a newfound love in his students, as evidenced by the Vermeer print that has hung in my kitchen for nearly twenty years. I would have never known the beauty and value of *Girl with a Pearl Earring* (Vermeer 1665), Rodin's *The Thinker* (1902), or Van Gogh's self-portraits if he hadn't shared them with me.

Many of our students are not wordsmiths at first. Many of them make their way through the world with an eye towards color, shape, and lines, and use those codes to better understand and make meaning. They are the students who pay particular attention to the changing of the seasons. They notice shades of eye color. They appreciate book covers and linger over illustrations. They love trips to museums when they are possible, and they would rather hold a paintbrush or piece of chalk than a pencil (see Figure 3.2).

Figure 3.2 My son Jack's version of Van Gogh's *Sunflowers*

The world is an increasingly visual place. Since the first billboard was displayed at the Paris Exposition in 1889, billboards have been changing the way we experience advertising. Today, Apple and Nike have perfected the wordless billboard. The advertising teams for these commercial giants know the codes and conventions of visual literacy and are rooted in the work of artists that came before them.

The codes that visual artists use to convey their stories include color, texture, line, shape, and form. When we interpret the stories that visual artists have shared with us, we can use these codes to more aptly and specifically discuss the techniques the artists have used and how those techniques convey the artists' messages. The codes apply to the Vermeer print that hangs in my kitchen as well as the Apple ad for the latest iPad. They also apply to the choices illustrators make in beloved picture books.

Today, we can turn to our favorite picture book illustrations, but we can also use Google image search to find works of art and advertisements to support students as they read and discuss visual images, using the codes that visual artists apply to their work. Some of my favorites are Matisse, Mondrian, and Georgia O'Keefe. Do an image search and interpret their work and the choices the artists made to convey a story. Are the colors bold and bright or subdued? Is there an absence of color in places, or does the image make targeted use of a specific color (as in Apple advertising)? What is the texture of the image? Is there thick paint or is there a glossy shine? In what direction are the lines moving? Are our eyes drawn up and down or side to side, or to a particular corner or to the center of the image? What shapes are used? Are they rounded or sharp? Is there a dominant shape? What is the overall form or composition of the work? What are the layout choices? What do these choices reveal about the story the image is trying to tell? What mood is created? Is there a central character, and how do you feel about him or her? Why?

When we use the language of visual codes to interpret an image, and when we encourage our students to do the same, we are helping them provide text evidence for their thinking. We are bringing them back to the image itself as they form interpretations. When we engage students as thinkers using text evidence with images, we can transfer the same thought process to print texts, which have more comprehension barriers for some students who are still developing their decoding and fluency skills.

In Multimedia

Many of us may remember when YouTube first came out. I thought at first that it was mostly dedicated to stunt videos that featured the antics of anyone with a portable video camera. I admit it took me a while to notice the power of YouTube and Vimeo to support everyone in creating and sharing stories. I now routinely turn to multimedia platforms to help me support preservice and inservice teachers. I don't know where I would be without the Teaching Channel. I have also watched as my own children have made meaning from the audio and video stories that have captivated their imaginations and turned them on to new topics, new ways of thinking, and new aspirations for ways to participate in the world (I say more on this in Chapter 5, "How Do We Build Stories?"). I don't think any book I could have read aloud would have come close to affecting my oldest son's three-year-old self as much as the movie *Cars*. Both of my boys love "silent" videos like the *Road Runner* cartoons and *Zig and Sharko*. We watch, interpret, and make meaning. In my own life, I am moved and changed by the films I love that tap into different parts of myself—*Mona Lisa Smile* fuels my teacher self; *Love, Actually* my romantic self; and *Bully* my parent self. Our students are no different.

The world of multimedia is rich with possibility, offering us countless platforms for supporting students as interpreters of stories and as storytellers themselves. This section will detail the ways that multimedia supports our understanding of stories through the power of voice, the power of video, the power of mash-ups, and the power of curation.

The Power of Voice

As a family we often take long car trips to visit relatives, and we listen to audiobooks to pass the time with stories. We have all fallen in love over and over again with Peter, Susan, Lucy, and Edmund (okay, not so much Edmund) from *The Lion, the Witch and the Wardrobe* (Lewis 1950), Jack and Annie from the Magic Tree House series, and classic characters from Aesop's fables, including the Tortoise and the Hare, and even the Tortoise and the Hedgehog (who knew?). When I am waiting for my oldest son to get off the bus, I often listen to National Public Radio's *StoryCorps* podcast, hearing concise but affecting stories of people's lives. The first gay man to adopt a child in California reflects on the life of his son. A mother asks her son's friend what it was like the day her son died in combat. These stories make me notice things a little more sharply and feel things a little more completely.

As a second-grade teacher, I was in a school that routinely turned to stories during transitional times in the day. It led to such rich days. When my voice wasn't sharing a story and students were engaged in something that could support background noise, we listened attentively to audiobooks of *Harry Potter and the Sorcerer's Stone* (Rowling 2001) and *The Bad Beginning* (Snicket 1999), the first book in A Series of Unfortunate Events. They were an instant classroom management tool. The voices conveyed the stories and sometimes did a much better job than I could.

As with poetry, when we listen to stories through podcasts and audiobooks, we are affected by the power of the voices telling the stories. We can encourage students to listen closely and notice features that make the voices even more powerful in conveying their stories with feeling. This, in turn, can help students read with greater expression and speak with greater awareness of the power of their own voices. We can specifically encourage students to notice the following:

- How voices rise with a question or with enthusiasm
- How the volume of voices demonstrates meaning
- How pauses are used for effect
- How multiple voices reveal more about the speaker's position and character
- Moments when the narrator steps forward

I will always remember the anticipation of hearing a new chapter of *Harry Potter*, my students anticipating the voices as they hushed one another to better hear the story and consider its meaning. I continue to laugh out loud or cry at the steering wheel as the brave voices of programs like *The Moth* share their personal successes and tragedies. And, as a listener, I am now more conscious of the impact their voices have on the story.

The Power of Video

With video, stories naturally come to life. Whether we are watching vines, gifs, YouTube videos, animated classics, sitcoms, or films, there is power in video, and it has never been easier to create videos in an instant. That does not mean that every video made on a camera phone is an Oscar-winning production, but it does mean that, increasingly, anyone has the tools to create videos that others can view, interpret, and benefit from. As a consultant, I often use videos to set the stage for a unit, such as supporting second graders with a viewing of Scholastic's video version of *Lon Po Po* (1996) before or after reading the story by Ed Young. I want them to notice choices that the moviemakers made to move the book from printed images to a series of rolling images and to compare the two texts. What is left out? What is centered by each medium? How do the choices made by the author and illustrator, and the moviemakers, impact our interpretations of the story? With fifth graders, I often turn to the short film *Belonging* (Filimon 2012) to support conversations about ways that characters in the books they are reading belong to different groups or the ways they feel like they belong and when they do not. I pair this with the short film about the Panyee Football Club (Grant 2011), which tells the story of a group of young boys who transformed themselves into a masterful soccer club, hammering nails and collecting wood to build a barge to practice on, playing barefoot, and responding to the doubts members of their community had about them. With eighth graders, I show commercials such as the Apple iPad Air's "Your Verse" commercials to have them consider the power of when images, text, and sound come together. I want them to notice how the producers made choices about which moving images to include to convey wonder and possibility.

Moving images have their own set of guiding codes to make their stories clearer and more effective. The Jacob Burns Film Center, a leader in film education and storytelling, has curated a collection of film clips that explore and explain the language of film on their website (https://education.burnsfilmcenter.org/education). I strongly recommend turning to their site both as a source for your own learning and to support your students as interpreters of film. Some of my favorite clips show the impact of close-ups on a single character and the power of extreme close-ups, such as zooming in on a tear rolling down a cheek. I also love noticing panoramic shots and how they often begin movies, serving as a hook for the viewer much the way authors use dialogue or dense description to bring us into a story. Encourage students to use the language of film to interpret movies with greater attention to the choices made by moviemakers to convey their stories.

When selecting videos for use in your own classroom, consider your reasons for sharing the videos. Do you want to help students connect to other texts such as books, poems, images, and songs? Do you want them to notice the craft techniques that moviemakers use so they can create their own movies? Do you want them to notice the central message in a short clip before moving to print texts? Make your purposes explicit for students, but also leave room for their own purposes, as they will see things we may never have considered.

The Power of Mash-ups

In an increasingly digital world, we have an array of artists and storytellers who know how to select existing material, combine selections, and make something completely new and original. One term for these new creations is *mash-ups*. The genius of DJ Danger Mouse gives us one example of this phenomenon. By taking The Beatles' *White Album* and JZ's *Black Album* and "mashing" them together, DJ Danger Mouse created *The Grey Album* (2004). While the term *mash-up* often refers to sound, the same theory can apply to other media. Consider picture book illustrators like Mo Willems, who use photographs with drawings laid on top of them. Consider poets who create found poems from lines of text they find in newspapers or magazines or from other poets. One could apply the term *mash-up* to better understand how these pieces were created.

Our students are primed for creating mash-ups to tell their own stories. By encouraging students to select works that already exist and put them together to convey a new story, we are providing a framework that frees up creativity. Consider collaborating with the music teacher in your building to support students in creating sound mash-ups of existing songs. Partner with art teachers to consider paintings and photographs that can serve as a background for students to overlay their own drawings on. The picture book author and illustrator Oliver Jeffers uses this technique in his book *This Moose Belongs to Me* (2012). He shared in a book talk I attended that he had found discarded paintings on the street of his neighborhood in Brooklyn. He gathered these treasures destined for the garbage, scanned them, and drew his characters right on top.

When we embrace the possibility of mash-ups as a process and product in our classrooms, we are building from the foundation of mentor texts but with a twenty-first-century recognition that sometimes the stories we want to tell are best told by standing on the foundation of texts that came before us.

The Power of Curation

The site Cowbird is rooted in the power of curation—the idea that we can build an array of stories that we love and want to return to, thanks to the global network of story sharing we live in today. The same principle applies to Pinterest. Our pinboards reveal different parts of ourselves and collectively tell part of our story. Our bookshelves are our old-fashioned curation systems. When I look at my home bookshelf, I have architecture books, art history collections, novels I cherished in middle school, the books that have nourished my adulthood, and books I read with my children. My classroom library always had an array of various genres, authors, series, and nonfiction topics represented. As teachers, we curate the reading lives of our classrooms by making choices about the texts that build our collections. We want our students to see that their book baggies, reading lists, and online reading and writing spaces are part of their own stories—that they have the power to curate their own reading lives.

I work in an afterschool setting with third-, fourth-, and fifth-graders who often do not see themselves as readers or writers. They cannot tell you an author or book they love. Yet, they yearn to be part of the reading and writing world. They see reading and writing as a kind of club and they want in. It takes several weeks to support students as they curate their own reading lives and come to see the myriad of texts that I share and our time in the library stacks as worthwhile. By the fourth or fifth week, they want to share pages from the books they are reading with one another. They want to read aloud in front of the group, despite their own recognition that it will be hard and they may not get it right.

In our own classrooms, we can emphasize the importance of building or curating our own reading lives by valuing the multiple genres and text types our students are drawn to. What do their choices say about them? What kinds of texts are they finding that they like? What do they notice about how authors write when they write across a series? Are there bloggers or podcasters whose voices resonate with their own? Encourage students to build digital pinboards of their reading lives or to create Shelfies on Instagram displaying the types of reading they like to do. Value responses that include reading texts such as the sports page alongside award-winning novels.

In Play

Anyone who has spent time with young children knows that they are creatures of story. As I write this book, my own sons, ages three and six, immerse themselves completely in stories. Matthew is jumping on the couch pretending to be Captain Hook, trying to escape the tick-tocking crocodile below. Jack is walking around making video game sounds, narrating a Skylanders adventure. He's Pop Fizz and Kaos is on the loose. Their story world, the world of make-believe, is psychologically and physically compulsory. They don't need explicit lessons or afterschool tutoring in make-believe. They play alone and in groups instinctually. Often character- and situation-driven, children's play is usually about caretaking, superheroes, dragons, knights, and princesses, but it is nearly always rooted in a character getting into trouble and having to get out.

Yet, the kind of trouble that drives the imaginative play of many children is uncomfortable for some teachers, especially the imaginative play of boys. Pirates, robbers, blasters, starships, wrestlers, and X-men can struggle to find a home in some classrooms or can even be made into villains, especially in kindergarten, where time for active imaginative play is often limited and where reading and writing are frequently restricted to "safe" topics, small moments, and stories from your own life. Ali Carr-Chellman (2010) in her influential TED Talk describes the ways the culture and play of boys is not in sync with the culture of school. Even the defender of play, Vivian Paley (2014), the author of *Boys and Girls: Superheroes in the Doll Corner*, writes about how it was easier to let "girls be girls" and much harder to let "boys be boys." The boys pretending to be pirates and superheroes today are playing video games tomorrow—securing spaces for play that activate their imaginative, story-driven selves.

The pieces of student writing in Figures 3.3 and 3.4 exemplify some of the best ways we can honor the imaginative, playful spirits of students throughout the grades. In their fourth-grade unit on mythological narratives, Eian and Jay took on the identities of Hercules and Perseus and placed themselves at the helm of battle and adventure. Full of literary craft techniques, they achieve a great deal as writers in these pieces, playing with gore in ways that propelled them as writers.

Hercules And The Battle With Cerberus
By Eian

I could taste the blood and see the flesh of Cerberus. I punch Cerberus in the stomach. I can hear him howl as I am being thrown around and could feel the flesh of Cerberus. Finally Cerberus was holding me in front of his eyes and I could see his eyes that were black before but were now red. I bit his hand and he dropped me. I climbed on him and got kicked in the face and tasted my blood again then I smelt his breath and I could hear him panting. After the fight Cerberus got tired and I put him in a metal collar and went back to my cousins palace and gave him the dog. Then we started talking he said that I needed to keep the dog but I said that was not part of the deal so I let go of the collar and left the dog. I went back to my hometown and was congratulated by the people. Even the gods were talking about me on Mount Olympus. Since I had nothing to do I continued doing good deeds for no reason. Hera and my cousin were both mad because I lived.

Figure 3.3 Mythological Narratives: Playing with Genre

Perseus
By Jay

I have been sent on an intrepid adventure by the king of Argos to slay the creature, Medusa, and bring him her head. I have received a shield from Athena, a sword from Hermes, winged sandals, and a magical bag. To find the gorgons cave, I must search for the Gray Sisters, since only they know the way to the island the cave is set upon, for they are the gorgons sisters. The trek is tiring. Soon after, I come across the Gray Sisters, which only have one eye between them. I snatch the eye as it is in the motion of being passed to one sister. Any other mortal who came across them by chance would leave at once of disgustment. I demand, "I will not give your eye back, unless you tell me the location to the gorgons cave!" The eye felt gelatinous and gooey in my hand, and almost slipped away. They tell me the way, and I give them their eye back. I was actually looking forward to giving back the eye. It was engrossing.

Once I find the cave, I see the gorgons sleeping. Their view is sickening. I do not gaze directly at Medusa, for her look can turn whoever glimpses at her to stone. Instead, I look into the shield's mirror reflection. I fly over Medusa with the winged sandals I was provided by Hermes, and with one single swipe, I slice the beast's head off. The snakes on Medusa's head wriggle in my hand, looking for a space of which to flee. Abruptly, a winged horse, Pegasus, sprouts out from where Medusa's head

Figure 3.4 Mythological Narratives: Playing with Genre

had once been. He neighs loudly, disturbing the sleeping gorgon sisters from rest. They chase me relentlessly, but I am too fast for them, and they are quickly out of sight and reach. I am astonished. I, Perseus, have defeated the horrifying Medusa. What an accomplishment! This quest was long, but the journey was worth the travel.

Along the path home to Argos, I spot a maiden chained to a rock above the sea. I swoop down to free the maiden. She beckons, "Leave! Before it's too late!" Fortunately, I resisted. "No, not until you are free from your chains!" Finally, she tells her sad story. "My name is Andromeda, daughter of King Cepheus and Queen Cassiopeia. My mother had boasted that she was lovelier than the Nereids. Poseidon was quite enraged, for no mortal was lovelier than the goddesses of the seas, so he sent a giant sea monster to punish Ethiopia. As sacrifice, King Cepheus chained me to this stone in the sea, to be devoured by the sea monster. I called to the prince whom I was engaged to, yet he had fled in terror. Surely, there is no hope left, and you can't be of assistance!" I told her, "I will free you of your terrible fate!", and told her I would marry her after the ordeal. As I had spoken, the monster arose from the seas. I flew toward it, and with a few swipes of the sword I was given, the sea monster was dead. I cut Andromeda free from her binds, and the prince she had spoken of returned to reclaim her as his bride. I shouted, "Andromeda, shield your eyes!" as I faced the Medusa's head in his direction. He had instantly turned to stone. Unfortunately, the king and queen were also in the direction of the prince, and they too turned to stone. The gods were upset,

Figure 3.4 (continued)

but me, a child of the almighty Zeus, who was to marry a daughter of the king and queen of Ethiopia, placed them willingly into the heavens. Andromeda and I flew off to Argos, to live together for as long as we live.

Figure 3.4 (*continued*)

In the book *The Storytelling Animal: How Stories Make Us Human*, Jonathan Gottschall (2013) argues that as humans we are addicted to stories and that throughout our lives we live in an imaginative realm. We saturate our lives with stories, from television commercials to daydreams. Imaginative play in childhood becomes our adolescent and adult love of novels, plays, films, and even video games. He writes, "Story is for a human as water is for a fish—all encompassing and not quite palpable" (2013, xiv). While our bodies are fixed in time and space, our minds are free to wander and frequently do. Even our dreams are saturating our minds with story all through the night. While play is where story may live most cogently in our young children, we never lose a love of story, or of play for that matter. We play with language, thinking of new lyrics for songs we love. We play with food, trying new recipes. We play when we pick up a paintbrush, go for a walk in the woods, and dance in our living rooms. As the field of teaching maintains a gender bias towards women, we have to work even harder to recognize the play of all of our students and find new ways of making the curriculum playful, joyful, and story-driven.

Final Thoughts

So, what does all this mean for our teaching and our students' learning? That stories lie everywhere. That we want to recognize the humanity behind each of the places where stories live. That the spaces where stories live should always help us continue to explore our place in a complex world system—whether we are moved by characters in a book, an image on a screen, or the experience of hearing someone's words. What stories should always give us is an opportunity to wonder. And wonder, as Plato's Socrates suggests, is the beginning of wisdom.

TOOLKIT Where to Find Stories

Our students need to know that we value the many places where stories live. Consider creating a classroom bulletin board in your classroom space or online that reads "Stories Live Here." This interactive board can encourage students to share books, excerpts, poems, images, and screenshots that have impacted them in some way. You may want to guide students to write short responses based in a genre study, or you may want the board to serve as an invitation for ongoing participation driven by choice.

We can ask ourselves whether we value and balance the different places where stories live across our curriculum, using the following toolkit as a guide. Ask yourself the question "Where Do Stories Live in My Classroom?"

In literature	What are the stories you read aloud that best exemplify authentic characters, compelling events, and small scenes that reveal big themes?
In poetry	What are the poets and poems you share with students? How often are they shared? Where in the curriculum could a study of poetry contribute to student understanding of themes and language? In what ways do you help students to notice the sounds, structures, and language of poems?
In music	What songs do you share with students? How often are they shared? Where in the curriculum could a study of music contribute to student understanding of themes and language? How can analysis of the sounds, structures, and language of songs support students as meaning makers?
In the visual arts and illustration	What kinds of visual images do you share with students? How often are they shared? Where in the curriculum could attention to visuals add to meaning-making possibilities for students? In what ways can an understanding of the codes of visual images strengthen student under-standing and speech?
In multimedia	What multimedia selections do you share with students? When do you share them? How often? In what ways can an understanding of the language of film strengthen student understanding both of film itself and of other text types?
In play	What are the ways you encourage your students to create through play? Imaginative play? Word play? By playing with genre and format?

Chapter 4

How Can Stories Come to Life?

Everything you can imagine is real.

–Pablo Picasso

In Akira Kurosawa's (1990) film *Dreams*, we witness eight vignettes that explore how we think about dreams coming to life. My favorite tells the story of an art student inside a museum hall looking at Van Gogh's (1890) *Wheat Field with Crows*. All of a sudden, the art student finds himself inside the painting, roaming among the wheat fields talking to Van Gogh himself. The student asks Van Gogh (played by the brilliant Martin Scorsese), "Why are you painting?" and Van Gogh replies,

> *To me, this scene is beyond belief. A scene that looks like a painting does not make a painting. If you take the time and look closely, all of nature has its own beauty. And when that natural beauty is there, I just lose myself in it. And then, as if it's in a dream, the scene just paints itself for me. Yes! I consume this natural setting. I devour it completely and whole. And then when I'm through, the picture appears before me complete. But it's so difficult to hold it inside.* (Kurosawa 1990)

Kurosawa uses film to imagine an art student's realized dream of wandering around a work of art and speaking to its maker.

This is the same premise as in Leo Lionni's wondrous picture book *Matthew's Dream*, where a young mouse decides he wants to become a painter as a means of seeing the world. Following his first trip to an art museum with his class, he has a dream much like the art student in Kurosawa's film. Matthew imagines himself roaming inside the world of shapes and colors on the canvas. The story within the painting comes to life for Matthew both while standing inside the museum and then again in his dream. In these moments, his life is changed. Painting becomes his story.

As teachers, we have the incredible power of bringing stories to life. When we select thought-pro-voking and powerful books, images, and multimedia, our students want to hold these stories inside themselves. They want to linger in the story, enter its world, and roam around for a while. And many times, these stories have the power to change our students' lives, much like the art student and the mouse Matthew are forever changed.

Knowing my passion for thinking about how stories can come to life, my husband recently asked me on a rare date night, "If you could invite anyone to dinner who would it be?" I was now the art student, thinking about the world I would enter, if I could, and with whom I would like to speak. I was full of more questions than answers. Is the person living or dead? Fictional or real? Oh, to speak with Ruby Bridges as a young girl and hear her tell the story of her bravery as she stepped into an all-white school. To ask Anne Boleyn about the terror she felt. To ask Fitzgerald to retell his days in Paris. The possibilities came pouring out. I then wondered about what characters I would have to dinner, if I could will them to be real. What would I say to Jo from *Little Women* (Alcott 1880)? What would my sons say to Max from *Where the Wild Things Are* (Sendak 1963) or to the wild things themselves? What if we asked our students the same kinds of questions as a way of bringing stories to life:

- If you could have any character join our class who would it be? Why?
- If you could have a real figure from history, living or past, as a guest visitor who would it be? Why?
- Which story would you step into if you could? How do you think you would contribute to or change the story?

We can encourage students to imagine written correspondence with figures and characters in the same way. When we do so, we expand the ways our students respond to their reading and we help them to engage in critical and creative thinking. Figure 4.1 shows a letter written by a second grader to Stuart after reading E. B. White's *Stuart Little* (1945), and Figure 4.2 shows a letter by a fourth grader written to William Shakespeare following a study of his work using the Shakespeare Can Be Fun! series.

As a reader, listener, or viewer, the characters and figures we come to love (or despise) through stories become part of our imagination and sustain us in childhood and well beyond. Some stories stay with us for years, even decades. As a girl I imagined myself as Claudia and Jamie, the children from E. L. Konigsburg's *From the Mixed-Up Files of Mrs. Basil E. Frankweiler* (1967) who ran away to the Metropolitan Museum of Art. What a night they must have had! I turned to books and the characters I loved to figure out the girl I wanted to be.

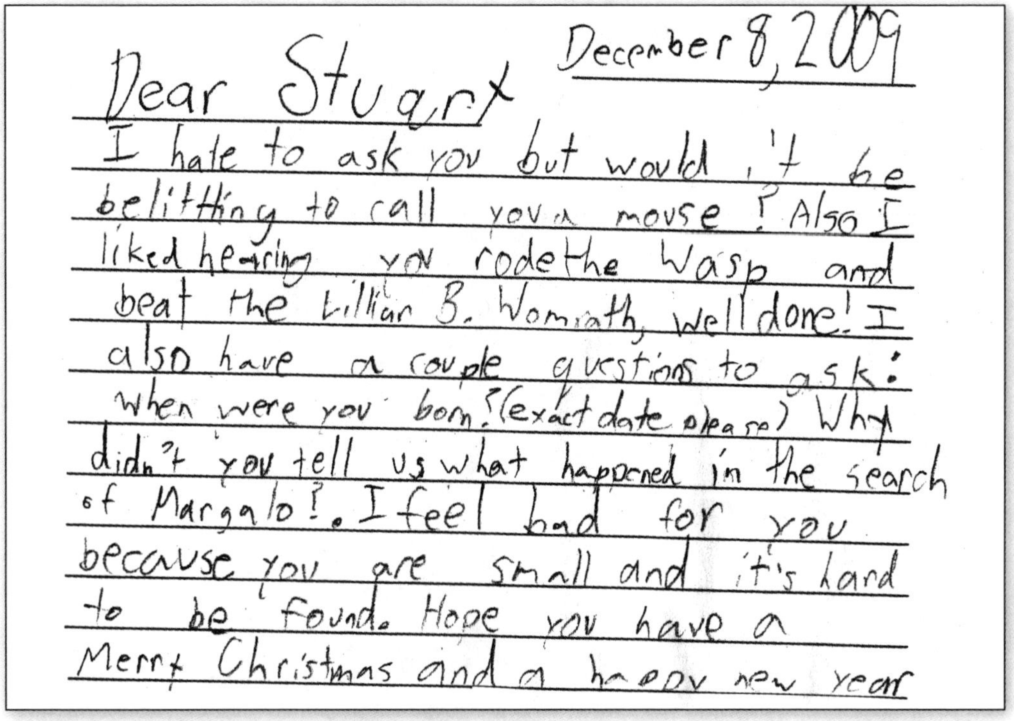
December 8, 2009

Dear Stuart

I hate to ask you but would it be belitting to call you a mouse? Also I liked hearing you rode the Wasp and beat the Lillian B. Womrath, well done! I also have a couple questions to ask: when were you born? (exact date please) Why didn't you tell us what happened in the search of Margalo?. I feel bad for you because you are small and it's hard to be found. Hope you have a Merry Christmas and a happy new year

Figure 4.1 Student letter to Stuart Little

As a viewer, you might find yourself, like me, binge-viewing episodes of *Breaking Bad*, *House of Cards*, or *Downton Abbey*. These are stories where the characters and the storylines are so enthralling we have to see more. We don't want the stories to end, and we experience loss when the season or the show reaches its finale. Our students have the same passion for the stories they love to watch, be it *Power Rangers*, *Dinosaur King*, *Hannah Montana*, or *Wizards of Waverly Place*. Our students imagine themselves entering the worlds of these stories, bringing them to life often on repeat.

Story and Technique

As a teacher, my favorite times of the day have always been read-alouds, especially ritual read-alouds, when the room stood still and silent before lunchtime, or before we packed up for the day, as I read from *Charlotte's Web* (White 1952), *My Brother Sam Is Dead* (Collier and Collier 1974), *Seedfolks*

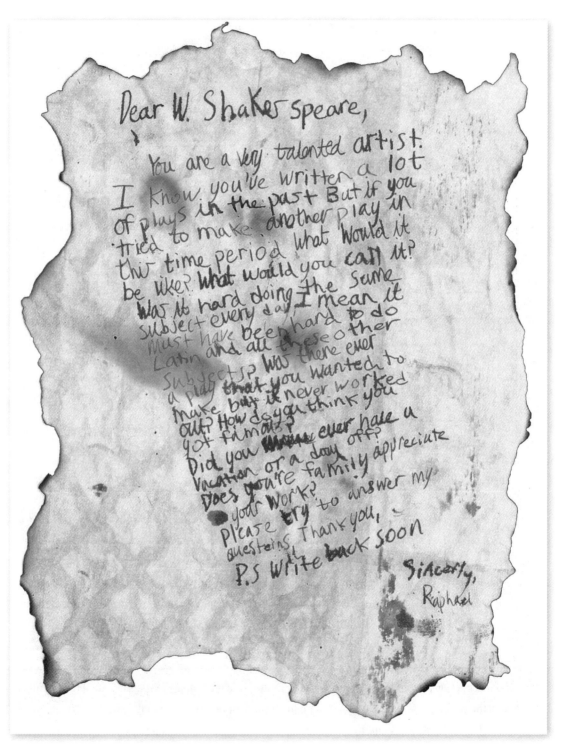

Figure 4.2 Student letter to William Shakespeare

(Fleischman 1997), and these days from *Wonder* (Palacio 2012). When I first started teaching, I was not as metacognitive about my techniques. I turned to timeless and timely stories, and I let the authors' language choices and sentence structure drive my performance. Today, I can name the things I do as I bring stories to life for students, and I encourage my graduate and undergraduate students to think, plan, and practice their techniques with greater purpose. I ask them to use techniques to bring stories to life—stories that are worth sharing. Whether you are a teacher early in your career or a veteran teacher with decades of experience, or if you are a supervisor or coach of teachers, there are techniques you can use to help you think about the choices you make to help all students lean in to great stories. After all, as educators, we are the best readers in the room.

Think about how you make stories come to life in your own teaching. Picture a recent text you shared and the choices you made to reflect the message of the story, or to emphasize word choices or significant moments. It is through our voices, gestures, intonation, and expression that stories become part of the fabric of our classrooms. It is through our think-alouds that we bring students into our experienced readers' minds. It is also through the ways we support our students as they share their thinking through interactive engagements, such as turning and talking, stopping and jotting, or stopping and acting. What we choose to read is critical, but so are our choices about how we read, how we engage students, and how we build a world of story in our classrooms. This chapter explores various teaching techniques to support you in your journey as stories come to life in your classroom. Whether you are in a school that uses a workshop-based approach to teaching or a school that embraces other frameworks, this chapter can support you with methods that will make a difference to your teaching and your students' learning.

Read-Alouds: Our Voices and Choices Matter

One of the many reasons I fell in love with my husband was that he read aloud to me. He read aloud Neil Gaiman's (1996) *Neverwhere*. He read aloud haikus. He read aloud articles he found interesting. He read aloud his own writing. I was hooked. These days we have different read-aloud rituals that involve books with our sons, but I still love hearing the sound of his voice.

In the research-based pamphlet "Why Read Aloud to Children" (2009), Jim Trelease, the author of *The Read-Aloud Handbook* (2013), gives reasons we read aloud that parallel the reasons we engage children in conversation: to "reassure; entertain; bond; inform; arouse curiosity; and inspire." He also suggests that when we read aloud, we do specific things that conversation alone cannot do. We teach children to associate reading with pleasure. We build background knowledge into new topics and build new areas of interest. We provide a reading role model. And we use words we wouldn't otherwise. In fact, as Trelease states, "A good children's book is three times richer in vocabulary than conversation." Great stories bring us into a world of words, make new words interesting, and invite us to wonder what they mean. Trelease argues that the time when we begin to lose students as readers, in the middle school years, is often the time when read-alouds are dropped as a classroom structure and predictable routine. The shared comfort of hearing a story well told is gone, and with it the motivation for our developing readers to engage with stories themselves.

One of the techniques my mother-in-law used to inspire her sons as readers, which I co-opted as my own technique at home and in my classrooms, is the old "we're going to have to pick up here tomorrow." This is used best when you are right at the most exciting part. The moans and groans for more of the story let us know that we're inspiring readers and that we are encouraging our students to associate reading with pleasure. They want to hold on to the story, and so do we.

There are other techniques we can employ to make read-alouds interactive. Balance is key here. Too much interaction and our students struggle to hold onto the story line. Words and concepts are lost. Yet, some level of interaction brings students deeper into the story. This is where planning and purpose are essential. When I plan for an interactive read-aloud I plan for three kinds of interactions: my own modeling of thinking, opportunities for students to rehearse and share their thinking, and opportunities to get closer to what's happening on the page. The following sections explore think-alouds and increasing student interactions with greater detail as part of the read-aloud.

Think-Alouds: Making Thinking Visible

As Dorothy Barnhouse (2014) describes in *Readers Front and Center: Helping All Students Engage with Complex Texts*, the thinking work we do as readers is often invisible. That goes for our students, but also for us. We can help students understand the strategies readers use to make meaning by modeling our thinking through what we call *think-alouds*. Specifically, we can draw on research about proficient readers to model moments in the text where we naturally

- recognize a connection to our own lives, other texts, or the world, known as text-to-self, text-to-text, and text-to-world connections;
- picture something vividly in our minds using sensory details;
- ask a question;
- pause to summarize what has happened so far;
- use context clues to understand an unknown word;
- make an inference based on our own background knowledge and clues from the text;
- determine what's important so far and how we know;
- pause to monitor our own comprehension; and
- reread to clarify our thinking and repair confusion.

My general rule of thumb is to plan for two to three think-alouds throughout the course of a single read-aloud experience, but this depends on the complexity of the text. Remember, if there are too many think-alouds in a read-aloud sitting, students may lose valuable momentum with the story, and we may privilege our own interpretations of a text at the expense of our students' emerging ideas. I tend to think aloud about the meanings of difficult and unfamiliar vocabulary words and then choose one or two strategies to model that feel natural to my own reading process. This is where I find scripted curriculum becomes difficult for teachers to enact—if a think-aloud is not your own, it can feel inauthentic, and students will know this. Students love to hear about our genuine connections and questions, and we serve our students best when we plan in advance for these moments. Our think-alouds bring our students into our thought processes. They, in turn, remember the details of our thinking, which strengthens their experience with the story. This builds stronger memories for drawing upon and taking note of their use of thinking strategies in their own reading.

Interactions That Deepen Meaning

I was fortunate to teach in a school that believed that structure and nurture were the cornerstones of elementary school teaching. I still believe this to be true. Interactive read-alouds give us the best opportunity to build a predictable structure and to nurture students in their developing literacy practices. As readers, when we have a chance to pause, ponder over meanings we are making, and share our thinking with others, we have an opportunity to deepen our understanding and learn from others. Not every read-aloud needs to be interactive, but when we incorporate an interactive read-aloud into our daily routine, we build expectations and a consistent routine for students to participate and share their thinking. This helps us break down the invisibility of reading. So, what are some of the most effective techniques we can use to make read-alouds interactive?

One of the most interactive structures to build into your routine is the turn and talk. This is an opportunity for students to turn to each other (in elementary classrooms, knee to knee and eye to eye) and share their thinking with a partner. Our youngest students, who may not yet be ready for turning and sharing their thinking with a partner, can talk into their own hands as a rehearsal of their ideas or can even talk to stickers placed in their palms to give them a sense of audience. The same research on proficient readers that guides our planning about think-alouds becomes our anchor when planning for our students to turn and talk. What are the connections—or disconnections—students have to characters, setting, or events? What are the questions they have so far? What do they think is important? What do they think a word means? How do they know? What inferences are they making about how a character feels or what she is thinking? What are they confused about? What predictions do they have about what will happen next? What is guiding their thinking?

As my yogi friend tells me, "progress not perfection." We cannot expect students to have the "right answer" every time they share their thinking with a partner. We can expect, though, that they participate—that they take a risk, share an idea, and vocalize their thought process even if they're not sure it's right.

The same is true when asking students to stop and jot down their ideas. For our youngest learners this can be in the form of a quick sketch on paper or by skywriting in the air. When we ask students to stop and jot down an idea, we are activating their thinking. In my own teaching practice, I often ask students to stop and jot down an idea, about a word, phrase, character, or event, and then I have them turn and talk to a partner. I choose the technique of stop and jot when the content is complex enough that I want everyone to first form their own ideas, using the space of the paper or the air as a rehearsal for their ideas. I also use this technique when I want a quick written assessment from students. I want to see everyone's thinking, and I'm not sure I will capture that if I try to listen in to each turn and talk.

Finally, one of the most interactive engagements we can use in our teaching is to have students stop and act out a part. Not everyone is comfortable on a stage, least of all me. Yet, there are small ways we can ask students (and ourselves) to use their voices and their bodies to bring stories to life. We can share lines from the text with students and ask them to read in a character's voice. My three-year-old son, Matthew, is actually the best person I know at this, so age need not be an obstacle. Unprompted he will often leap up from my arms during a read-aloud at home to pantomime the way a character might move or to repeat a line of dialogue in a character's voice. He loves to become a part of, or embody, the story. We can first model and then help students to pantomime (acting without words), to use their bodies and gestures to indicate feeling and action. We can have students share the things they think the characters must have thought at the time, or dialogue that may have taken place behind the scenes. What would that look like? What would that sound like? In this way, students are embodying the story, bringing it to life through their voices and bodies, imprinting story in memory in a physical way.

As a fourth-grade teacher, I read with students selections from the series Shakespeare Can Be Fun! We read *The Tempest for Kids* (Burdett 1999) when studying weather as an interdisciplinary unit and *Macbeth for Kids* (Burdett 1996) in the days before Halloween. Prior to reading and acting out the scenes, I would extract lines of dialogue from the play, type them up, and cut the paper into strips, and each student would draw a line from a paper bag. I had students say their lines all at once. I had students walk around the room and share their lines. I had students line up according to the numbers on the back of the paper, reading their lines in the sequence in which they appear in the play. Through these interactions, the students were activating their thinking about what they thought the story was about. They were all speaking and all listening. We didn't need a stage or an outside audience. The interactions and opportunities to move, think, and participate were building meaning, memory, and potentially confidence.

Like our think-alouds, supporting our students through their brief but meaningful interactions around texts requires purposefulness and planning. I plan for two to three opportunities for interactions in a single read-aloud. I draw most heavily on turn and talks, since they are often the quickest and most immediately collaborative way to create engagement for all students. The toolkit at the end of this chapter has a detailed read-aloud planning guide that can be used to encourage students to deepen their understanding and to increase their interactions. In addition, there is a sample created by a teacher I have been fortunate to work with that provides planning details for a powerful read-aloud text, *Let's Talk About Race* by Julius Lester (2005). The toolkit is designed to support you in your planning, and to help you make decisions about which texts will best support you and your readers as you bring read-aloud texts to life.

Shared Reading: Fostering Close Reading

When I first started teaching, I have to admit I was hesitant about shared reading. I knew its roots in Australian classrooms and the work of Don Holdaway (1979). I knew shared reading was a practice using Big Books or enlarged texts. I knew it was an instructional approach where I explicitly modeled the strategies and skills of proficient readers, where students had access to the print and could participate or share in the reading of a text. But, I struggled with how to bring these texts to life. I believed in the structure and knew that the method was designed to support our emerging readers with access to print, but I wanted the text to come to life more.

Shared reading often uses the same enlarged text for a series of lessons and usually follows a predictable structure that supports emerging readers with important reading strategies and skills such as those in Figure 4.3.

This is a structure that works best for our early and emerging readers to grab hold of print as they learn to apply primarily print strategies themselves. The thinking strategy work modeled and practiced with shared reading texts is often limited, because the texts are often simplistic. As students get older, they too benefit from shared reading experiences, but the focus needs to shift from primarily print strategies to primarily thinking strategies, including close reading strategies across text types.

Shared reading started to have greater meaning for me when I saw teachers incorporate other media into the shared reading routine across grade levels. A lightbulb came on—aha!—this is a method that helps bring stories across media to life for all students. As described in Chapter 3, PS 49 in Queens, New York, has a shared reading structure that incorporates song, poetry, and art each week *in addition to* shared Big Books in the early grades. In this way, thinking within and across media becomes visible, and students learn how to read print, visual, and audio texts with greater purpose and flexibility.

Monday	Tuesday	Wednesday	Thursday	Friday
Reread a previously shared text; introduce a new text; encourage students to make predictions; read for the story line and enjoyment.	Read the same text with a focus on conventions of print, including noticing front and back covers, reading left to right, word spacing, and identification of letters and words. Students participate more in the reading through echo reading.	Read the same text with a focus on print by covering up certain words and having students think of words that make sense. Students participate more in the reading through increased choral reading	Read the same text with a focus on story sequence and retelling.	Students write, draw, or dictate responses to the text.

Figure 4.3 Typical Shared Reading Schedule

When you incorporate a variety of genres and media into the routine, the structure changes. It can look something like Figure 4.4.

In this way, the shared reading routine becomes a close reading routine across the grade levels in a way that supports students not only with strategies and skills, but also with habits of zooming in more closely over time. When we reconsider shared reading from a multimodal and multimedia perspective, we encourage students to become close readers—to slow down and analyze complex texts with greater purpose.

Close Reading as Shared Reading

"Close reading" has been at the center of the field's discourse since the Common Core began to take a greater foothold in classrooms in 2010. *Notice and Note: Strategies for Close Reading* by Kylene Beers and Robert Probst (2012), *Falling in Love with Close Reading: Lessons for Analyzing Texts—and Life* by Chris Lehman and Kathleen Roberts (2013), and *Text Complexity: Raising Rigor in Reading* by Nancy Frey and Douglas Fisher (2012) are among the texts that many teachers have been reading closely themselves to better understand close reading strategies. While there are different approaches to and interpretations of what we mean by close reading, in practice close reading is about paying attention to a complex text in front of you, engaging in some analysis, and forming an interpretation of the text. Close reading is about rereading with purpose, including what is important in the text, what is confusing about the text, the multiple meanings of words and passages, and reading like a writer. It is human nature to draw upon what you know and what you have experienced to better understand the text. Close reading theorists argue that despite a potential lack of connection with a text's topic or language, we can develop the literacy tools to analyze and interpret an unfamiliar and complex text. I happen to agree, but I also argue that we need to rethink how we valorize the close reading of print and often dismiss the close reading of visual art and multimedia.

Medium	Monday	Tuesday	Wednesday	Thursday	Friday
Song	Listen and read for overall meaning: What is the song about? How do you know?	Listen for melody and sound: What instruments are used? What are the voices doing? Why is that important to the message?	Listen and read for structural choices, such as repetition of lines, that indicate importance.	Listen and read for word patterns such as rhyming and alliteration and for word choice.	Listen and read for craft or to form an opinion with text evidence. What can you apply as a songwriter? What do you think and know now about the song?
Poem	Listen and read for overall meaning: What is the poem mostly about? How do you know?	Listen and read for significance demonstrated by things such as repetition of lines. What repeats itself? How does the poet let you know these words or ideas are important?	Listen and read for other structural choices such as line breaks, stanza breaks, and use of white space. Why did the poet make these choices?	Listen and read for word patterns such as rhyming and alliteration and word choice. What sounds do you hear? How do they better help you understand the mood generated by the poem?	Listen and read for craft or to form an opinion with text evidence. What can you apply as a poet? What do you think and know now about the poem?
Art	View for general understanding: who is pictured? What is happening? (characters and action)	View with attention to where your eyes are drawn. How do you know what's important?	View with attention to color and light. What mood is created?	View with attention to perspective. Where are you in relation to this image? Why is that important?	View with consideration of craft and to form an opinion with text evidence. What can you apply as an image maker? What do you think and know now about the work of art?

Figure 4.4 Shared Reading as Shared Media Schedule

At PS 49, we engaged in a year-long study of close reading. Many of the teachers incorporated close reading into their shared reading routines. Others incorporated close reading into their small-group instruction. The goal was to encourage students to repeatedly practice close reading through a structure that they could apply themselves. In my experience as a classroom teacher and literacy specialist, students are naturally close readers, especially when we support them as they closely read visuals and multimedia first and then carry that thinking into increasingly complex print texts.

At PS 49, we wanted to arm students with passion and purpose and to instill in them the habits of mind needed to be close readers across a variety of text types. When we think about how and when we read closely, it's when we are invested in remembering the text. At PS 49, we wanted to establish a framework for helping students to both *want* to and know *how* to form stronger interpretations of new texts.

When we read closely, it is often because we want to remember what we are reading or we recognize that the content is challenging, and we slow ourselves down, rereading with purpose to better understand. This past year, I found myself closely reading *The Goldfinch* by Donna Tartt (2013). For me, that book was literature with a capital L. It took me weeks to read, but I thoroughly enjoyed all the scenes of New York City, references to restaurants I frequented, and the drama of the art world. My own background in the art world and my passion for New York City partly drove my close reading. I also found myself this year closely reading the narrative nonfiction text *Bringing Up Bebe* (Druckerman 2014) about an expat mother raising her children in France. As a parent of young children, I read and reread, pausing to think about how her methods of parenting overlapped with my own, where they differed, and what I potentially could be doing better. Think about the texts you read closely and why you are driven to read them closely.

When I think of close reading, I think of a photographer who wants to capture a shot to remember the moment. As readers, we are a lot like photographers. We have different lenses we can apply to better make meaning. When we first encounter a text, we often start with a panoramic shot. We start big. With narrative texts, we look for who is there, what is happening, and where the story is taking place. These are primary understandings that support more nuanced understanding. As we zoom in closer, we notice what's important, often revealed to us through patterns and compelling events. As we zoom in even closer, we begin to notice specific word choices in print text, and we work to understand their meaning in context. When we zoom in more closely on images, we move from what's important to noticing details revealed through shapes, the use of light, and the use or absence of color. When looking at film, we zoom in to notice things like camera angles, changes in the speed of the frames, or the absence of sound. We begin to form interpretations of our own, using the text to guide our thinking. When our students closely read in this way, starting with panoramic shots and slowly and repeatedly zooming in, their interpretations are stronger, more nuanced, and more text-based. What did we find at PS 49? That more voices were contributing to conversations about complex texts. That students were able to apply close reading techniques to print, image, and multimedia texts. That student interpretations were more specific and text-based. That teachers began to see themselves as lens makers, or guides who helped students read more closely and more meaningfully, and ultimately, to commit what they read to memory.

Small-Group Instruction: More Than Strategy and Skills

One of the greatest opportunities we have as teachers to nurture readers and writers is to gather small groups of students who need support with particular strategies and skills. This is another area where, in my observations across schools, I see more targeted, more purposeful, and more data-driven instruction. All of that is good. Teachers are thinking about why they are pulling small groups together, what skills and strategies they can reinforce, and what their methods will be. Yet, whether you form leveled groups and use a guided reading structure, or you gather students in other formations such as strategy groups, the shared experience of coming together in a small group can impact learners when we do *more* than simply teach strategy and skills. When we plan carefully for bridging story with strategy and skills, we invite students to remember more of the learning experience. I'm often asked by teachers which materials they should use for small-group instruction especially when students are past the emergent stage as readers. Finding compelling materials that students want to read and will remember reading is hard at the early and emergent stages. The books are purposefully repetitive, and the skills our earliest readers are developing are focused more on one-to-one matching, reading across CVC words, more consistently and automatically recognizing sight words, and increasing fluency through strategies such as rereading. Even at the earliest levels, however, if we draw students into reading by making them want to find out what happens, we have an opportunity to hook more readers.

As students apply more print and thinking strategies to their reading, we want to be selective about what materials we use. Proficient reader research has guided us to focus on strategies raised earlier in the chapter. However, we know that developing schema requires forming connections to characters, events, and topics within and across texts. We know that asking questions is critical to making meaning. We know that visualization helps readers bring stories to life in their minds. We teach these and other strategies to strengthen our readers, but we often gather small groups of readers hurriedly, hyper-focused on our teaching points and the strategies we want students to try. Have you ever wondered whether these strategies are sticking? Or how you know? When we select materials driven by compelling stories, we encourage students to make more natural and meaningful connections, to raise authentic questions worth asking, to picture more vividly in their minds, and to synthesize across pages. When we don't select compelling stories, we miss opportunities by over-teaching strategies devoid of memorable and impacting text.

In my work with schools, particularly in third grade and above, I have advocated for teachers to engage students in small groups through at least one compelling extended text in each small group during the year. That means balancing short and long texts, and the extended texts you (and your students) choose may require multiple small-group sessions to complete. We can expect our students to hold on to stories and to yearn to read more when the stories grab their interest. We can trust them to hold on to their small-group story, their independent reading books, and a book we may be reading aloud. Think of your own nightstand or e-reader. You likely have several different texts you are reading at different times, depending on your interests and mood that day.

To plan your small-group instruction to bridge strategy and skills instruction with powerful and memorable stories, consider your daily, weekly, and monthly small-group instruction schedule. If you meet with each small group of students once or twice a week, you have the capacity to consider building text sets that can support your students with the skills and strategies they need, while also tapping into their interests and identities through compelling stories. One resource to turn to for leveled books that represent diverse society at the early reading levels is the imprint BeBop Books, published by Lee and Low Books. These stories are written to support early readers through interesting, engaging story lines and illustrations. You might also turn to series books that will help your students to read and apply strategies in their small groups but also keep them engaged in their independent reading as they fall in love with characters and form more accurate predictions and meaningful connections. As students are ready for increasingly complex texts, we can help them to apply purposeful strategies within texts such as the American Library Association award winners. Yes, we can use these great books as read-alouds, we can pull excerpts for shared reading, and we can help students to find the great books that anchor them to their truest selves as independent readers, but we should not shy away from compelling stories to support our small-group instruction.

I increasingly meet teachers who are fearful that they will be focusing too much on the story and not enough on strategy, so they avoid compelling stories altogether for their small-group instruction. What a loss for our readers! When we plan with strategy in mind, using great stories, we deepen our students' connections with reading and encourage them to read in community. I firmly believe that literacy is a social practice. I far prefer to talk about books with others than to read in isolation, and having a great story to apply strategic thinking to and discuss over time with others is something that can benefit all students, at every level.

Independent Reading: An Invitation to Make Meaning

It has been one of my greatest joys to watch my sons become readers. Seeing them grab hold of print, read across letters and words, and celebrate their access to words is absolutely thrilling. I look forward to my kindergartner's book baggie coming home each day. I say a little thank you in my mind to his teacher when he talks about how much he loves reading and writing workshop. He already knows that words have power and that while literacy is a social practice, the act of reading can feel rather independent. He doesn't want me to read or write for him. He wants to do it himself, and he knows how to apply strategies, or reading powers, to feel successful. He's working on his pointer power, prediction power, picture power, and punctuation power as ways to attend to print, think about stories, and read with enthusiasm. When we read from a place of power, we believe we can master any text. I saw this as my six-year-old super-reader picked up a well-worn paperback copy of Dostoyevsky's (1956) *Crime and Punishment* that was sitting on the kitchen table. (My husband often leaves a trail of books behind him, much like the crumbs left by Hansel and Gretel to find their way home.) He said, "Mom, I know some of these words," as he started to read from a random page, "he, is, not, was, the." He was unafraid. He was empowered and knew that today he read from a book that held some big-time meaning in the world. I want this for all of the students I work with, at all of the schools I work in. They all deserve to feel like they can tackle *Crime and Punishment*.

Much of my work in schools is designed to encourage teachers to make independent reading the heart of their workshops. Students know what counts. They know whether we value their reading and meaning-making processes. They know this when we carve out time in the school day to encourage them to dive into stories. We invite them to make meaning and to bring stories to life in their own minds. To visualize. To challenge. To wonder. To celebrate. Nancie Atwell refers to the flow that we get into as readers as the "reading zone." While often invisible, our minds are a valuable place where stories come to life. It's time to start thinking of this time as a place to fine-tune one's reading powers at any age.

Choral Reading: Joyful Noise

One of my favorite poems is Allan Ahlberg's (1991) "Heard It in the Playground." I first read it when I had the opportunity to spend a summer in Oxford, England. I was so fortunate to walk along the roads that inspired Lewis Carroll (1865) to write *Alice in Wonderland*, and Philip Pullman (1995) to write *Northern Lights*. Doorways looked like hobbit holes and rabbit holes, like places where you could step inside a dream and make it come alive. It was here with the spirits of children's book characters all around me that I first read "Heard It in the Playground" and was asked to perform the poem as a choral reading with fellow graduate students. The repetitive and incremental nature of the text allows for the blending of voices: "Heard/Heard it/Heard it in/Heard it in the/Heard it in the play/Heard it in the playground/The playground/The playground/The play/The play." As I type the lines of text I can't help but hear the chorus of voices in my head. To see the poem at its best, watch one teacher's blending of student voices performing the lines of the poem on Vimeo at https://vimeo.com/13766287.

"Heard It in the Playground" is a great text to engage students through choral reading. It also serves as a wonderful mentor text for students as poets. Other poems that yearn to come alive include the ones in Paul Fleischman's (1988) collection *Joyful Noise: Poems for Two Voices*. They invite readers to bring the stories on the pages to life.

Some of the techniques we can use to support students as they bring poems and other choral readings to life include the following:

- Make your voice get louder and softer at important moments
- Pause for effect
- Use your body to say more
- Listen for the rhythm of the reading

When we support students through choral reading, we encourage them to celebrate in the joyful, purposeful noise that is poetry, song, and chant; we also let them know that they are valued in a community of readers. Their voices are heard. They are not alone.

Wordless Picture Books: What Just Happened and What's Next

One of the most powerful resources we have for supporting students as they bring stories to life is wordless picture books. Absent any words or with sparsely written text, it is our voices, our students' voices, and the images that create the story.

When we use wordless picture books with our youngest learners, we are letting them know that they are readers—that reading images matters and counts and is an important form of reading. After all, our youngest learners read the natural world closely as part of their everyday experiences. Without print to make meaning from, they read the visuals in front of them, from the changing of the seasons to their friends' facial expressions. When we engage our youngest learners with wordless picture books, we are valuing the visual and capitalizing on their access to the world. Some of the books I use again and again in my work with young children are *Good Night, Gorilla* by Peggy Rathmann (1996), *Hug* by Jez Alborough (2009), *Pancakes for Breakfast* by Tomie dePaola (1978), and *Flora and the Flamingo* by Molly Idle (2013). These are all stories with simple plotlines, but the more closely you read each page, the more you find to see and interpret. With each telling of these stories I find myself noticing a detail I hadn't noticed before—the mouse who holds the banana on each page in *Goodnight, Gorilla* and the facial expressions of the dog and cat in *Pancakes for Breakfast*.

Not to be dismissed as a format strictly for young students, wordless picture books offer readers a world of complex texts that require post-modern ways of thinking about the nature of text itself. Goldstone (2004) defines post-modern picture books as a subgenre of picture books where authors and illustrators play with multiple story lines, narrators, and perspectives. Goldstone further describes how these books are characterized by fragmentation, chance, contradiction, irony, and repositioning of the reader as a coauthor making choices about how the text is read. As students move into more sophisticated ways of thinking about stories, they can linger over David Wiesner's *Tuesday* (2011) and *Flotsam* (2006), visual masterpieces that leave readers wondering who's telling the story, where does it begin, and where does it end. Likewise, *The Red Book* by Barbara Lehman (2004) inspires wonder each time I read it and has opened up conversations with students with a range of life experiences and at various stages of English language acquisition. In this story, a young girl picks up a red book from the sidewalk on her way to school. She opens it to see a boy on a desert island reading a red book, viewing her in her classroom reading a red book. The illustrations captivate readers, begging you to turn back to revisit what just happened but eager to find out what is going to happen next. And then there is the brilliant work of Shaun Tan, whose books include *The Arrival* (2007) and *Rules of Summer* (2014), postmodern blends of fantasy and reality that tackle complex social issues of immigration, identity, belonging, and family.

When using wordless picture books with any age group, we can return to thought-provoking questions that encourage students to read more closely and say more:

- What happened?
- What's next?
- Who's telling the story?
- How do you know?
- Why do you think so?
- What questions do you still have?

When we use wordless picture books, we bridge our students' visual literacy skills and challenge them to rethink how stories work. Each time you share a wordless picture book, you invite students' voices into the telling and the story comes to life in a new way.

Storytelling

If wordless picture books provide us with a series of images to anchor our thoughts around stories, oral storytelling challenges us as teachers to be, perhaps, our most imaginative selves when bringing stories to life. We have the stories we want to tell, our voices, our bodies, and above all, our students' participation. Masters of storytelling have a host of techniques that guide their work. I have to admit I am a novice storyteller. I am far more comfortable with a book or an image in my hand to guide my performance in bringing a story to life. Yet, I revel in the challenge that storytelling brings, and I am always amazed at the results of encouraging students to hold on to stories with greater memory and purpose, especially when they are asked to join in the storytelling performance.

In my study of read-alouds across four New York City schools, I had the privilege of watching a teacher engage her students with oral storytelling as a springboard for understanding a new story. Prior to her read-aloud of *September Roses* by Jeanette Winter (2004), Melissa engaged her students in three different rounds of storytelling, leading up to remembrance of September 11th. Taking Fred Rogers's advice for addressing tragedy, this teacher focused on the helpers in the story. In her first oral storytelling round, she told the story of two women who were flower artists and their big trip to New York. She told the story of how their arrival was marked by tragedy, but how they were invited to stay with someone they met at the airport. She told the story of how the women displayed their flowers in Union Square to bring hope to the people of New York. In her second round of storytelling she moved beyond who and what. She included dialogue as it was expressed in the picture book and added some from her own imagination of what the women might have said. In this round, the students were able to join in telling the basic plot, as she repeated words and phrases to bring them into the role of storyteller. In her third round of storytelling, she repeated the plot points and dialogue and added in the characters' thoughts as she imagined them. Each day her students' voices were more and more of the shared experience. Then, on the fourth day she read the story aloud without showing the illustrations, inviting students to illustrate each page in typed books she made for them. Not until the fifth day of sharing did she read both the words and pictures as Jeannette Winters intended.

As a participant-observer, I have always remembered this powerful week of storytelling. The process is replicable with any story that you want students to more deeply and purposefully connect with, using their imaginations before seeing the print or the illustrations.

> **Day One:** *Tell the basic plot points: who the main characters are and what happened (focus on the good where possible).*
> **Day Two:** *Add dialogue.*
> **Day Three:** *Add the characters' thoughts.*
> **Day Four:** *Invite students to illustrate a printed version of the story.*

Day Five: *If the story is in book form, share the words and illustrations through a read-aloud.*

Other techniques for storytelling include adding your own gestures or inviting students to engage in physical actions such as clapping, stomping, or jumping, adding facial expressions, and pantomiming stories without words. All these techniques help bring stories to life. They often fill classrooms with the kind of laughter that fosters community building and engaged learning. To be a storyteller is to let go—of worry, of judgment, of fear of missing something or looking a bit silly.

Reader's Theater and Story Scripting

As a fourth-grade teacher, I had the opportunity to support a group of girls as they wrote, staged, and performed their own portrayal of women's protests for the right to vote. They researched Susan B. Anthony and watched select clips from HBO's *Iron Jawed Angels* (2004). They designed their own costumes and delivered their scenes as part of our class study of democracy. Becoming the women on the picket lines was far more powerful than simply reading or writing about these historical events. When students engage in dramatic performances, they take on a character or figure's persona and use their voices and bodies to make the character believable. They embody and they remember.

Dramatic interpretations can range from simple reader's theater productions to multifaceted productions of plays. Reader's theater is an instructional technique used to support students as readers and performers. The goal is often to have students practice oral reading fluency by reading from a script. Reader's theater gives them a new purpose for reading and supports rereading. Students often stand or sit in a semicircle, starting with short, simple scripts with repetitive text. As students become more comfortable with the process, you can start to play with script writing and movement. By living the story, students linger over lines longer, playing with the various ways they can portray a character, an event, or a feeling. Some of my favorite stories to bring to life are fables—Aesop's, Arnold Lobel's, and Leo Lionni's. Lifting lines from the text of these stories, we can help students to become the tortoise or the hare, the lion or the mouse. In these stories we admire characters for trying to overcome a challenge despite various obstacles. In these stories the underdog often succeeds, thanks to great efforts. In these stories the plot lines are fairly simple, making it easier for young students to remember the sequence of events (Once there was _____. One day, _____. Because of that, _____. Until finally, _____.). And, of course, we learn something from these stories that applies to our own lives: slow and steady wins the race (well, sometimes), help those in need, unlikely friendships can happen when you least expect it, things are not always what they seem.

As students progress from early childhood to the elementary and middle school years, we can support them to reenact more complex story lines and to craft story lines of their own from the foundation of existing texts. We want them to imagine how they would feel if they were a character and how they can show that emotion to their audience using facial expressions, tone, rate of speech, and body language. What reasons does the audience have for rooting for their character? What do they want their audience to remember?

Readers' theater and story scripting give students an opportunity to share what they know about how stories work and how to make them come alive. As a classroom teacher, I often had students use reader's theater and story scripting as a performance-based assessment following book clubs. I wanted to know more than their overall comprehension of the books. I wanted to know how they interpreted the texts, what they found important about the characters and events, and what compelling message the books left them with. Rather than a traditional writing exercise at the end of the books, role-playing and acting allow students to use what they know and become the characters they have grown to love, question, and form connections with. Rather than write about the hero or villain, they get to become these characters. As professional actors attest, you need to be yourself in order to be the character. In this way, students further understand themselves and think about their best qualities, as they transform their own personalities into those of a character.

Finally, reader's theater and story scripting allow us to break down social barriers and reimagine stories as our own with characters of all social backgrounds. Lee and Low Books has conducted a series of diversity gap studies, including not only the plateauing of multicultural content in children's books (as described in Chapter 1), but also the lack of diversity in the Emmy and Tony awards. The researchers found that while television shows are becoming more diverse, those shows are not winning media awards. According to Lee and Low Books, in the 2014 Emmys, "not one person of color won in any of the lead or supporting actor/actress categories, with only six total African Americans amongst the 54 white nominees" (Schneider 2014). On stage, the figures are even more alarming. The Asian American Performers Action Coalition (2012) found that "on New York City stages during the 2011–2012 season, African American actors were cast in 16% of all roles, Latino actors in 3%, Asian American actors in 3%, and other minorities comprised 1%. Caucasian actors filled 77% of all roles. Caucasians continue to be the only ethnicity to over-represent compared to their respective population size in New York City or the Tri-State area." In an interview Christine Toy Johnson, an award-winning writer, actor, filmmaker, and advocate for inclusion, said that, "No Asian American female playwright has ever been produced on Broadway. Ever" (Low 2013). These are alarming statistics about the state of diversity in the world's best-known theater hub, New York City. In our classrooms we can counter these cultural trends and help students to see themselves as playwrights, actors, producers, and set and prop designers. In this way, reader's theater and story scripting are methods that not only support students as readers, writers, speakers, and listeners but also serve as opportunities to create diverse representations of characters.

Quite often, there is nothing in a story to indicate the race or ethnicity of the characters, yet media portrayals and book covers often position characters as white and middle class. As a result, we may often see white as the default for characters. There is a growing trend on spaces like Tumblr to create "racebent" characters, that is, characters that reset the default, including versions of characters from *Harry Potter*, *The Avengers*, and *Star Wars*. As we encourage students to become their favorite characters, we can turn to portrayals of "racebent" characters to help all students to see themselves as having every right to be Hermione Granger, Bilbo Baggins, or Katniss Everdeen.

Final Thoughts

Stories matter. So do our methods. We have come a long way as a field in recognizing the impact of our methods on student learning. In my work in schools, I am overwhelmingly impressed by the ways teachers use techniques to build purposeful interaction into their read-alouds. I am constantly learning from the ways shared reading is being repositioned to consider other media including images, songs, and multimedia. I am amazed at the wordless picture books that come out each year, and I linger over the pages with students, seeing new details with each reading. I am hopeful about the small and big ways students are asking to become the characters they've read about, to bring history to life, and to interpret stories with their bodies, hearts, and minds.

Think about your own classroom. What techniques from this chapter do you use to bring stories to life? In what ways do you position your students as close readers? Interpreters? Storytellers? Actors? Scriptwriters? All of the methods I have described are invitations to independence for your students. They are the ones who will ultimately bring stories to life beyond the walls of your classroom. Now is the time for you to model and then invite students to participate, making stories their own.

 TOOLKIT Read-Aloud Planning Guide to Increase Understanding and Interaction

This tool is designed as a scaffold to strengthen the ways you plan for read-alouds by first closely attending to the text and then building opportunities for increasing your students' interactions with the story. There are many more possible ways to plan for effective, joyful, and purposeful read-alouds. This tool is simply one way to start thinking about stories. Over time, some of these components will become second nature when you pick up and read any new book you're considering for a read-aloud. Play with the components, and plan for the things you think will be most effective in your classroom.

Text Features

Supportive

Text

Content

Challenging

Text

Content

Vocabulary: Think-Alouds and/or Extended Instruction

Developing Phonics and Word Study Strategies

Developing Fluency

Turn and Talk and/or Shared Conversation

Before Reading

During Reading

After Reading

Developing Understanding

Within the Text

Beyond the Text

About the Text

Visual Literacy

Curricular Extensions

Reading

Writing

Other

Sample for *Let's Talk About Race* by Julius Lester
by Francesca DeLio

Text Features

Supportive

Text

- It is clear that the author Julius Lester is telling the reader about his "story" (his life story).
- The text invites the readers to explore who they are and their personal stories as they read along.
- The illustrations are very vibrant, colorful, and dramatic. Each is a painting filled with detail.

Content

- There is a clear beginning, middle, and end. This book invites the readers to explore their own stories, and in the end decide if they will share who they are under their skin.
- The theme of this story is easily understood, since the author tells his story as he introduces the idea of race and who we are. The readers are then able to explore their life stories and their race alongside the author.
- The book deals with learning about race and what makes us special. In the younger grades students often share about their personal lives, and who they are.

Challenging

Text

- At times the text stretches across pages and does not follow the systematic reading format. Students may get confused about what order to read the text in.
- Some of the text is put in parentheses, and blanks sometimes are left to fill in an answer. Students may be unfamiliar with this. For example it is stated, "I'm better than you because I live in _____." "I'm better than you because my dad (mom) makes more money than your dad (mom)."
- There are a few challenging vocabulary words.

Content

- Students who may attend less-diverse schools may not have experienced being around many different races.

- It would be helpful for the teacher to discuss what race is before reading the book.
- Allowing students to share and interact while reading the book would provide them with a better understanding of race and what our "stories" consist of.

Vocabulary: Think-Alouds and Extended Instruction

There are several words that may need to be explained to students to provide them with a better understanding, or to make sure they know what they mean.

- *Race* (in the title and stated throughout the book): A group of people who share the same culture, history, or language. Has to do with skin color and physical characteristics.

  o   Page 10: "Whether you're black like me or Asian, Hispanic, or White, each race has a story about itself."

- *Elements*: a part or features of something.

  o   Page 5: "My story and yours have many elements. Such as..."

- *Nationality*: Where you are from or were born.

  o   Page 5: "Nationality: I'm from the United States."

- *Texture*: The way something feels when you touch it.

  o   Page 21: "The texture of your hair?"

Developing Phonics and Word Study Strategies

- Point out words ending in *–ing* (*happening*, *telling*).
- Point out which words are upper case and why. (St. Louis, Missouri, is a place. Asian and Hispanic are names of races.)
- Students can sort the words that make up the different elements of a person's story found throughout the book.

Developing Fluency

- Model fluent reading during the interactive read-aloud.
- Read with expression throughout the book.
- Change tone of voice when reading the questions in the book.

- Put the story on the Smart Board overhead projector to have students read along, or pick students to read certain pages. Students can practice reading fluently and with expression.

Turn and Talk and/or Shared Conversation

Before Reading

- Look at the title and cover of the book. What does race mean? (Allow the students to discuss what race is.) What do you think this story is going to be about?

During Reading

- "How does your story begin?" (on page 3) "Where were you born?" This question is asked in the story. I would allow students to share out.
- Would anyone like to share any elements of their story?
- Has anyone ever heard a statement similar to that one, "My race is better than your race"? How did it make you feel?
- Do you think these stories are true? Are we better than others because of our gender or the money our families have?
- The book directs the students to "take your fingers and press them softly against your skin right below your eye..." They are asked to do the same with a partner. I would have the students do as the book asks. Then I would ask, Do you all feel the bone beneath your skin?
- What do you wonder when you see people you don't know?

After Reading

- What does the author mean by "I'll take off my skin. Will you take off yours?" at the end of the book?
- Now I want you all to take off your skin, turn, and tell a partner something about yourselves.
- Then have a few students share something about themselves (where they are from, something about their family, their hobbies, favorite food, something interesting we don't know, etc.).

Developing Understanding

Within the Text

The main thing I want students to understand while reading the text is, we all have a story that makes us special. I want students to understand what race is and that it is just a small part of who we are.

Beyond the Text

I want students to think about what makes up their story, as well as other people's stories. How do they perceive people when they see strangers or meet someone for the first time? From now on will they judge them based on their race and how they look, or will they look past the physical characteristics and learn about who the person is underneath his or her skin?

About the Text

I want to direct students' attention to how the author is the one who is speaking in the story. He is the one telling us about his story. The author also uses personal examples of his life and his story to get the readers thinking about their own stories. I want to show students how the author uses questions in his writing and asks readers to do certain things. This engages readers and allows them to interact with the book..

Visual Literacy

Each of these pictures invokes much feeling and meaning. They tell a story all on their own. Allowing the students to take the time to interpret the pictures and see how they relate to the words can get them thinking deeply about the text.

Curricular Extensions

Reading

Have students read other books about race, heritage, and culture. Students can also read about other people's lives and stories. They can then compare and contrast the books, or find more elements that make up a person's story.

Writing

Have students create their own books about their "stories." Where do their stories begin? What are the different elements of their stories? (Family, favorite food, religion, nationality, favorite color, race, etc.). Students will be able to construct books about their stories, just as Julius Lester did. In the end they can present their stories. They will then be able to see the similarities and differences they have with one another. They will see that we are far more than just our skin colors. We all have a story, and this story will now be told.

Other

This book could be used to introduce students to different races and to the idea of not judging or stereotyping others. Students could interview a student from another class or someone they do not know very well. The student will then find out the person's story. Did the student find out something about the other person that surprised him or her? Do they have any similarities? Do they like or dislike the same things? This activity will help students see how important it is to take the time to get to know one another and look beneath the skin. Students can then share what they learned about the person they interviewed.

Chapter 5

How Do We Build Stories?

Stories, like people and butterflies and songbirds' eggs and human hearts and dreams, are also fragile things, made up of nothing stronger or more lasting than twenty-six letters and a handful of punctuation marks...But some stories, small, simple ones about setting out on adventures or people doing wonders, tales of miracles and monsters, have outlasted all the people who told them, and some of them have outlasted the lands in which they were created.

—Neil Gaiman, *Fragile Things: Short Fictions and Wonders*

*T*he Incredibles. Ratatouille. Toy Story. Monsters, Inc. Cars. Big Hero 6. When we are supporting students as writers, we should turn to the pros. That's right, Pixar. They are undeniably masters at creating stories that so many of our students (not to mention us) return to again and again. They are mentor texts for growing stories in our classrooms. Above all, they encourage our students to start with a source many of them know, value, and love.

Emma Coats (2013), Pixar's story artist, tweeted Pixar's 22 rules for phenomenal storytelling, and the list has been widely circulated and designed by graphic artists all over the web. You can find them through a simple Google search and can even find downloadable, printable, aesthetically imaginative versions worthy of hanging in your classroom or revising with your students to write your own rules for phenomenal storytelling. The first rule Coats offers is "You admire a character for trying more than for their successes" (2013). My favorite rule is #6: "What is your character good at? Comfortable with? Throw the polar opposite at them. Challenge them. How do they deal?" And I often need rule #17: "No work is ever wasted. If it's not working, let go and move on—it'll come back around to be useful later." Building stories in your classroom relies on your belief that stories matter, that we learn from our mistakes, and that writing is a place to rehearse ideas, take risks, and try on different parts of yourself. Film theory will tell you that we are all characters in the Pixar films we love. We all have qualities of Remi, Mater, and Mr. Incredible or Elastagirl. The stories work, in part, because we are reminded of ourselves in unusual ways.

Consider the stories your students love and the writing process that was undertaken to make them so compelling, so laugh-out-loud funny, so capable of bringing tears. What is it that these writers did that we ourselves can do? That's the beauty of approaching the teaching of writing from a mentor text perspective. There are many wonderful books in the field that explore mentor texts so well, including *The Writing Thief* by Ruth Culham (2014), *Mentor Texts* (2007) and *Nonfiction Mentor Texts* by Lynne Dorfman and Rose Cappelli (2009), and *Mentor Author, Mentor Texts* by Ralph Fletcher (2011). This chapter builds on their groundbreaking work and offers a new conceptual framework for helping students to see writers as architects building stories from the ground up. Writing, like architecture, after all is all about representation. We use letters in the shapes of squiggles, dots, and lines to represent a lived experience or an idea, much like the architect who builds a model of the building she is going to create. As writers, we construct. We build from letters to form words, sentences, and paragraphs that create the structures that hold up our ideas. When we revise we deconstruct, looking at our work again to find new angles and approaches. The foundations underneath those structures are our strong ideas and interpretations. The bricks and mortar that bind our ideas together are our language choices and the conventions that make our writing understandable and effective.

Writers as Architects

Do you find that you often use words like *structure* in your explanations of writing, your students nodding in agreement when really they are lost behind the terminology? Do you ask students to tell you more and include more details, and do they repeatedly struggle to know what you mean? If the answer is yes, then you're with me. When teaching writing I often used words like *structure* and *details* and made assumptions that my students would know what these abstract terms mean when it comes to writing effective, purposeful pieces. When we use an architectural framework to make sense of what writers do when they build stories, we support students with a concrete, lived metaphor to strengthen their writing and their sense of purpose as writers.

The architect Matteo Pericoli (2013) wrote an opinion piece in the *New York Times* entitled "Writers as Architects." He wrote, "Great architects build structures that can make us feel enclosed, liberated or suspended. They lead us through space, make us speed up or slow down to contemplate. Great writers, in devising literary structures, do the same."

Before I went into education, I studied architecture, so I was immediately pulled into the idea that when I was learning about design choices, space, and materials, I had been paralleling the writing process. However, one doesn't need to study architecture for the framework to apply. We all move in and out of spaces constructed by others to make us pause at a particular view, or to meet up with others to collaborate on an idea, or to find restful solace.

In Pericoli's graduate-level course at the Sculoa Holden in Turin, Italy, and at the MFA writing program at Columbia University School of the Arts, he pairs writing students with architecture students to interpret stories and then physically build the literary architecture of a text. As described in the *New York Times* article, students each first choose something they've read that impacted them—a novel, a short story, or an essay. He encourages them to "start with the plot, the subject or simply a feeling that the student has about a text. We break the piece of writing down into its most basic elements and analyze the relationship of each part to the structure" (Pericoli 2013). What drives the student projects is the similar reduction that one can make in architecture and in words: that when you remove the "language" of architecture—the walls and ceilings—or the "language" of writing—the words—what remains is space. The student projects are designed to help viewers consider questions such as Does the story hold up? Would this building hold up? Several projects look at story beyond beginning, middle, and end, and explore the emotions of a story through zigzags, staircases, reflecting pools, and piercing structures. Pericoli challenged his students to architecturally represent the stories they chose. In this way, he positioned his writing students as architects both when they were creating physical models that represented the themes and impact of the stories they chose, and when composing their own words on the page. Students of all ages benefit from thinking about how writers are like architects.

By nature, most people love boundaries. Most young children start to understand the space of the page as a set boundary. Their drawing or painting can be just so big because the space allows for it. Their words start out physically large, taking up swaths of space, and over time the space each letter fills becomes smaller. Their understanding of spacing between words becomes more conventional. As early writers they are exploring the space of the page just as they are exploring the spaces around them—climbing on playground structures, figuring out what to do with their bodies when they line up with their class, and learning how to sit without falling off the chair.

My oldest son studied architecture in his prekindergarten year. He created a model of our home out of shoeboxes, construction paper, and glue. He worked hard to get the paint color just the right shade of blue-gray. He added the front door, windows, and a chimney. As someone who studied architecture, it warmed my heart to see how proud he was of his masterpiece (see Figure 5.1). What he was doing at the prekindergarten level was really brilliantly conceived of by his teachers, because he was learning about representation through building the model of our home and by learning about how letters represent sounds and words, while drawings represent ideas. The word on the page is not the feeling you have. It represents it. In the same way, Jack's model isn't our home, but it captures his version of it. Our words are our best attempts at capturing an idea, a feeling, a moment, or a story on paper so others can experience it.

Figure 5.1 My son Jack with his architectural model of our home

The following sections provide some ways to encourage students to build stories from a writers-as-architects point of view: that we can build stories the same way we build works of architecture, starting with the foundation, thinking about structure, and finding the tools to bring it all together. This chapter concludes with some overarching philosophies that both great architects and storytellers value, including the idea that less is often more and how one's view (or point of view) matters.

Building a Story

Foundation: Our Ideas

We like to think our life experiences are unique, that we engage in actions of our own free will and that to write about those experiences is to offer something new. Most of the time, however, our life experiences are like those of many other people. We wake up to start a new day, talk with friends, learn something new, face a challenge, make mistakes, find help through others, and either grow or remain fixed in our resolve. A great challenge for us as teachers is to help students use those foundational daily experiences to tell compelling stories (see a sample story in Figures 5.2–5.4).

One of the oldest kinds of stories is the hero's journey explained by Joseph Campbell (2008) in his book and life's work, *The Hero with a Thousand Faces*. Campbell, a psychologist and researcher, studied hero myths across cultures and time, and named the basic stages that nearly every hero-quest

Chloe and Joey were always best friends. They did everything together. They especially loved making art works together. But, once our day became dark and dreary they found themselves in the midst of an argument.

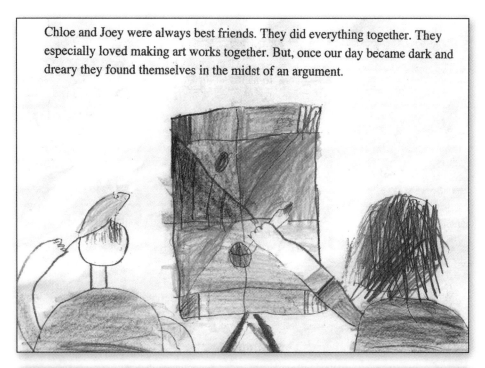

"I think my drawing is so much better than yours," said Joey. "I think they are equally good. See my colors and your colors...my lines and your lines...all of my shapes and your shapes. They're both great, do you see?" asked Chloe with a smile. "I still think mine is better!" exclaimed Joey.

Figure 5.2 (above) and 5.3 (below) Pages from a story cowritten by a small group of fourth graders who were experiencing friendship issues in their lives

Figure 5.4 Page from a story cowritten by a small group of fourth graders who were experiencing friendship issues in their lives

goes through. He refers to this as the monomyth. Matthew Winkler's (2012) interpretation of Campbell's theories can be found in his presentation "What Makes A Hero?" Winkler opens with the question, "What do Harry Potter, Katniss Everdeen, and Frodo all have in common with the heroes of ancient Greece?" It's a guiding question that immediately encourages viewers to wonder and theorize. Worthy of viewing closely and sharing with students, Winkler presents Campbell's theory in a way that lets students consider the foundations of great storytelling through common elements—ordinary worlds, calls to adventure, entering the unknown, helpers, tests, and rewards. One could argue that all great stories are built on this foundation. We can help our students to strengthen the foundations of their stories when they analyze the foundations of the stories they love. What are the central ideas of those Pixar movies we love? What are the bases of superhero comics? What do the characters we love have in common? Where do their paths mirror our own? Where do they depart?

When we immerse students in great stories and help them to find common ground across stories, we strengthen the ideas they have for their own writing, drawing, and dictation of stories. When they analyze and interpret great stories, they realize that story ideas are less about beginning, middle, and end than about the ways their stories fit into the plotline that most stories have and most humans experience in their own lives. Consider E. B. White's (1952) *Charlotte's Web*, often voted the best children's book of all time. Journalist Maureen Corrigan (2011) explained the story behind *Charlotte's Web*, saying that "one early fall morning in 1949, E. B. White walked into the barn of his farm in Maine and saw a spider web. That in itself was nothing new, but this web, with its elaborate loops and whorls that glistened with early morning dew, caught his attention." White woke up and paid attention to something he saw. He noticed that the spider spun an egg sac and that the spider didn't return. Thus, Charlotte was born. We can turn to *Charlotte's Web* as an example to help us understand how great stories work, much as we can turn to Homer's *Odyssey*, *Harry Potter*, or *The Lord of the Rings*. The following is my abridged interpretation of Campbell's work, simplified to apply both to the hero's journey as often seen in folk and fairytales, myths, legends, and fantasies, and to the stories of the everyday captured in other genres and forms.

- **We live in ordinary worlds.** So, how do we describe what we see and hear around us to explain that world? What colors do you see that tell you it's morning, noon, or night? What's happening around you? How do you know if it's cold or hot, inside or outside, city or country?

- **We experience something new or unknown or hard.** Stories are more compelling when something happens. So, what are the firsts, lasts, and significant moments you've had? Let's write about those times. Your first lost tooth. The day you rode a bike without training wheels. The last time you saw your parent or grandparent. The night you slept without a nightlight. The sled ride with your new rockin' tube. The time you were stung by a jellyfish. The letter that told you that you were loved. The piano recital where you flourished or didn't.

- **We are tested and wonder if we'll succeed.** A story usually isn't interesting if things work out right away. When we are confronted by something new, unknown, or hard we usually have to work at it. Here we can take a page from the work of positive psychologists, who continue to develop new frameworks for happiness and success, all of which are rooted in determination and the right levels of challenge. So, how did you know something was tough? Describe that feeling. What were your thoughts?

- **We have helpers in life.** Our journeys, be they great quests or small moments, are about others as much as they are about ourselves. Who are the people (or animals) that give you strength? What do they say or not say that moves you in some way or drives you through your challenges? What makes them so integral to your story?

- **We often succeed but not always.** One of the big hits of 2014 was the song "Happy" by Pharrell Williams. Everyone I know loves that song. And why not? It's okay to be happy. To succeed. And to celebrate that. It's also okay not to succeed every time in every story.

There are many different ways we can encourage students to explore their ideas or the foundations of their stories. We can read and interpret our read-alouds through these foundational lenses. We can track characters' journeys over time. We can create and display anchor charts and character journey time lines to guide our writers from interpretation to writing. We can engage students in brainstorming and mind mapping. We can create shared stories through shared and interactive writing techniques that follow these foundational principles. We can pull together small groups of writers to build their ideas together. We can confer with students about their foundational ideas, using these principles as conversation and teaching points. We can use print texts, and visual and multimedia stories, to explore the ideas behind stories.

To strengthen the ideas, or the foundations, of your students' stories, start by supporting them with the analysis and interpretation of stories they love. In addition, find overlap across stories. Great writers are inspired by writers who came before them. It's hard to imagine that Mo Willems wasn't familiar with Arnold Lobel's Frog and Toad when he envisioned the characters Elephant and Piggie. In the same way, Suzanne Collins's Hunger Games trilogy builds on the foundation of Lois Lowry's *The Giver,* as *The Lion King* is built on Shakespeare's *Hamlet.* Supporting students with the ideas that came before them makes them stronger builders of their own stories.

Walls and Ceilings: Our Structures

If walls and ceilings are the structures of buildings, words, sentences, and paragraphs are the structures we use as writers to make our stories stronger. To support students as they strengthen the structures of their own writing, we need to encourage them to slow down and notice the words, sentences, and paragraphs that grab them and begin to name how and why the authors used those structures. To do so means noticing these structures in our own reading. In this section, I describe two pieces of writing from literature, name the structures the authors used, and consider how the structures might align with their purposes.

The One and Only Ivan by Katherine Applegate (2012) was the 2013 Newbery Medal Winner. It's hard not to get emotional when reading this story based on a real gorilla living his life in a cage in a mall. The idea for the story is powerful and moving, but the writing structures Applegate chose make the meaning even more apparent for us as readers. Throughout the book, Applegate uses simple sentences and even fragments that are like short, staccato notes in music. Below are the lines that open the book:

> *I am Ivan. I am a gorilla.*
>
> *It's not as easy as it looks.*
>
> *People call me the Freeway Gorilla. The Ape at Exit 8.*
>
> *The One and Only Ivan, Mighty Silverback.* (2012, 1–2)

Applegate uses this simple sentence structure throughout the book to reveal the inner thoughts of the main character, Ivan, the gorilla trapped in the cage. As the story unfolds we see repetition of "I" to start many of the sentences. While we often tell students not to overuse "I," here Applegate uses this repetition to make concrete for us as readers that this is Ivan's story; these are his thoughts and words. The simple sentence structure mirrors how we might imagine gorillas would communicate through words. Like the sentences, the paragraphs are short, often only one or two lines long. This strays far from the five-sentence paragraph structure often taught as the rule of thumb. The author's structural choices are purposeful, and naming them helps students consider and explain their own use of simple sentences and paragraphs.

The Old Man and the Sea by Ernest Hemingway (1952), often taught in middle and high school as a canonical text, is sometimes a breakthrough book for students who have been lost with complex sentence structures. Hemingway, like Applegate, uses simple and compound sentences for effect. Hemingway uses them to portray the seemingly simple experiences and relationship among the old man, the boy, and the sea. Of course, it is often in the simple where complexity is revealed. The following paragraphs are from the opening of the book:

> *He was an old man who fished alone in a skiff in the Gulf Stream and he had gone eighty-four days now without taking a fish. In the first forty days a boy had been with him. But after forty days without a fish the boy's parents had told him that the old man was now definitely and finally* salao, *which is the worst form of unlucky, and the boy had gone at their orders in another boat which caught three good fish the first week. It made the boy sad to see the old man come in each day with his skiff empty and he always went down to help him carry either the coiled lines or the gaff and harpoon and the sail that was furled around the mast. The sail was patched with flour sacks and, furled, it looked like the flag of permanent defeat.*
>
> *The old man was thin and gaunt with deep wrinkles in the back of his neck. The brown blotches of the benevolent skin cancer the sun brings from its reflection on the tropic sea were on his cheeks. The blotches ran well down the sides of his face and his hands had*

> the deep-creased scars from handling heavy fish on the cords. But none of these scars were fresh. They were as old as erosions in a fishless desert.
>
> Everything about him was old except his eyes and they were the same color as the sea and were cheerful and undefeated.
>
> "Santiago," the boy said to him as they climbed the bank from where the skiff was hauled up. "I could go with you again. We've made some money."
>
> The old man had taught the boy to fish and the boy loved him. (1952, 1)

Virtually every page of *The Old Man and the Sea* (as well as countless other texts) can be used with students to notice and name the sentence types Hemingway uses, where he varies his sentences, and what effect his structural choices have on us as readers. In addition, the opening paragraphs use a descriptive text structure, so we can picture the old man and imagine ourselves next to him, eager to fish with and learn from him as the boy did. Through this thick description, we are brought into the story. We are invited to learn more about this man and what we might learn from him. As students learn about various paragraph structures, they can begin to notice and name their purposes, be it descriptive, comparative, chronological, or to explain a cause-and-effect relationship. Rather than teaching these structural concepts in isolation, we can turn to literature itself for mentor texts to strengthen our students' interpretive skills and the structural choices in their own writing.

When we teach students about text structures through a variety of mentor texts, we support them with models of what writers in different genres do. Writers carefully consider their words and how they put them together in sentences and paragraphs. Their choices reveal more about their characters, the events, and the themes of their work. Analysis of authors' structural choices supports whole-class understandings as well as small-group and individual conferences. In your own classroom, consider ways that conferences about structure can be enhanced by questions like, Based on your character, what types of sentences do you think could best mirror who he or she is? and Where can a (descriptive, compare-and-contrast, chronological, cause-and-effect) structure draw connections for your readers? Draw from your read-alouds for inspiration. When we do so, our students already know the story line and can focus on the structural choices the author made. They can read as writers. With structural support, the stories our students write have the necessary walls and ceilings they need to "stand up" and be better understood by readers.

I have found that it is less about finding the perfect text and more about navigating the texts you already use to find examples of various text structures that will resonate with students and provide a mentor for their own writing. At Sarah Noble Intermediate School in New Milford, Connecticut, the teachers and I recently worked for a year analyzing text structures across literature and informational texts. We used the books and texts they were already engaging students with as readers (Figure 5.5), including *Wonder* by R. J. Palacio (2012), *Walk Two Moons* by Sharon Creech (1994), *Frindle* by Andrew Clements (1996), and newsela.com, thinkcerca.com, and readworks.org for informational texts at various Lexile levels.

Figure 5.5 Texts and notes teachers used to plan lessons about text structure and language choices

Figure 5.6 is a lesson I conducted with fifth graders to encourage them to notice the sentence structures in select sections of *Wonder*. In debriefings, several teachers reported how lessons on text structures came to life in their classrooms using texts their students were interested in and identified with.

INTRODUCTION	
Connect previous teaching, capture students' attention and interest, or activate prior knowledge.	*I have heard from your teachers that you have just finished a unit on narrative texts or stories and that you read one of my all-time favorite books—*Wonder *by R. J. Palacio. There are so many things that I love about* Wonder. *I love the compelling characters and how R. J. writes from different points of view—August, Via, Summer, and Jack. Her choices as a writer really made me feel like I knew them as people and that I would want to get to know them more. I also really love how the story made me think about my own life differently. Anyone want to share something they loved about* Wonder *to help me get to know your class a little bit better?*
TEACH	
Teach one thing. Choose the way to teach. Try and model as much as you can.	Wonder *is one of those books you just can't put down because of all the things you shared. But what also makes us engaged as readers are the choices she made when composing her sentences. She varies her sentences, both in terms of the lengths of her sentences and in the types of sentence she uses.* *Let's take a look at some of the sentences from the first few chapters of* Wonder *and notice how R. J. Palacio varied her sentence types. What do you notice about these sample sentences?* **Simple** ***I know I'm not an ordinary ten-year-old kid. I eat ice cream. I ride my bike. I play ball. I have an Xbox.*** **Compound** ***The last surgery I had was eighteen months ago, and I probably won't have to have any more for another couple of years.*** **Complex** ***Since I've never been to a real school before, I am pretty much totally and completely petrified.*** *These sentences have special names for them: simple, compound, and complex. We're going to use these examples to help us define what that means.* *A simple sentence has to have two things: a subject and a predicate. In all of our simple sentence examples the subject is "I" and the predicate is what August (the narrator at this part) was doing: a person and what he was doing. A simple sentence is a complete thought.* *A compound sentence is similar to a compound word (butterfly, baseball). Compound words are two words that are put together to make a new word. A compound sentence is when two sentences that could stand alone are put together with the help of certain words called* coordinators: *for, and, nor, but, or, yet, so.* *A complex sentence is composed of a complete thought along with what is called a* dependent clause. *Complex sentences use special words called* subordinators— *because, since, after, although, or when (and many others).*

Figure 5.6 Mini-Lesson: Writers use a variety of sentence types to make their writing more engaging for the reader.

GUIDED PRACTICE	
Engage students with a quick opportunity to rehearse their ideas, such as through a turn and talk, stop and jot, stop and act, or brief discussion.	*Turn and talk about which types of sentences the following other examples are:* Simple *I know ordinary kids don't make other ordinary kids run away screaming in playgrounds. I know ordinary kids don't get stared at wherever they go.* Compound *Zach and Alex always invited me to their birthday parties when we were little, but Eamonn and Gabe never did.* Complex *So when I was in my mom's stomach, no one had any idea I would come out looking the way I look.* *When I came out of mom's stomach, she said the whole room got very quiet.*
CLOSURE	
Restate the teaching point, and connect it to ongoing student work.	*So today we looked at the variety of sentences R. J. Palacio used when she composed the sentences for* Wonder. *You are going to go off and analyze another page in* Wonder, *noticing the types of sentences R. J. Palacio used, and writing down your favorite simple, compound, and complex sentences to share.* OR *So today we looked at the variety of sentences R. J. Palacio used when she composed the sentences for* Wonder. *Today you are going to look back at your own stories you've written, noticing the sentence types you used. Do you tend to use the same sentence types as R. J. Palacio does? Do you notice a place where you think you could change the sentence type to make your writing more effective?*
INDEPENDENT PRACTICE	
Students will be reading, thinking about, and recording various sentence types in R. J. Palacio's *Wonder*.	
WRAP-UP	
The teacher shares what he or she noticed about student successes and challenges in identifying sentence types with their small groups.	

Figure 5.6 (*continued*)

Beyond print texts, consider encouraging your students to analyze the use of structures in digital stories, short two-to-five-minute narrated presentations using still and moving images, to create their own. Digital stories are used in classrooms for students to say more about themselves, as an alternative or companion to personal narratives or memoirs. They are also used as alternatives to summary writing or book reports as a means for students to respond to what they have read or viewed. While driven by compelling ideas or themes like all narrative stories, digital stories are composed of strong structures that often weave together visual, audio, and written texts. Design Lab (http://designlab.wisc.edu/digital-storytelling) offers several examples of digital stories that can be viewed with students to get them to notice and name the structural choices the writers used. For students to build their own digital stories, it is helpful to model and support the use of storyboards to consider the types and sequence of images, sounds, and printed text they want to use. Many digital stories begin with a single element such as a soundless image, a string of white text on a black background, or a sound devoid of image or text.

Tracking the structural choices of other digital storytellers will strengthen the structural choices your students make. In my New Technologies course, my graduate students create digital stories that explore their own metaphors for what it means to be a teacher. They start with an idea, the foundation of their stories. I've had students create digital stories based on the idea of teacher as pillar, teacher as book, and teacher as compass. The strongest stories are driven by a compelling idea and use the structural elements digital storytelling offers to help the audience better understand and interpret the story. The storytellers consider framing, close-ups and extreme close-ups, panoramic shots, the rate of their frames, slowing down and speeding up at pivotal moments, and increasing, decreasing, and delaying sound. Students need to notice and name the structures used in digital stories so they can build their own. Chart with students the visual, print, and audio elements they notice across several digital stories. Figure 5.7 is an example chart that could be used to notice and name some of the structural elements digital storytellers use.

Print	Frames where text appears Length of text Use of questions Color of font
Visual	Use or absence of color Framing Rate of frames
Sound	Use or absence of sound Speed of sound Use of multiple sounds

Figure 5.7 Structural Choices to Build Strong Digital Stories

Bricks and Mortar: Our Use of Language and Conventions

The structures of our buildings would not hold up well without bricks and mortar, nails or screws. As in architecture, cohesion in writing matters. To understand cohesion in writing is to understand language, conventions, and how our use or misuse of these elements affects the reader's experience. At Sarah Noble Intermediate School we dove into text structure alongside language. As we analyzed various texts for sentence types, sentence variety, and paragraphing, we also noticed how and why authors used particular words. We read for parts of speech and noticed how and why certain words were used, including conjunctions, prepositions, and interjections. We also read for literary devices, including similes and metaphors. We read, noticed, jotted, and shared. We moved from words to punctuation, noticing how authors use punctuation for effect. We found that some authors love ellipses, others the dash. (I know which punctuation I love—hmmm, what could it be?) We started to get excited about language and conventions, using our favorite authors as our guides. This excitement transferred to classroom teaching. We engaged in this process of reading like writers together, acknowledging that literacy is a social practice. Reading, rereading, analyzing, and interpreting the language and conventions authors chose would not have been nearly as professionally engaging if we had done so in isolation. At Sarah Noble, we were making a radical shift away from workbooks to "cover" grammar, usage, and punctuation. Instead, we started with stories students knew and loved, using them as the vehicles to help students understand language and conventions and as models for cohesion in their own writing. Teaching these topics in isolation was not working, and neither was a workbook-based approach. It was time for a new approach—one that was purposeful, joyful, and rooted in reading experiences students already had. The bricks and mortar of writing do not need to be taught as stand-alones. After all, a pile of bricks and some cement don't make a building.

To encourage students as wordsmiths, that is, to use the bricks and mortar of writing more effectively, we ourselves needed to notice the words that grabbed us in texts, the various parts of speech used, and how language helped us to more vividly picture scenes in our minds or allowed us to make stronger personal connections to texts. So what did we do? We circled, named, and sorted. We then turned to punctuation and followed the same process of noticing, naming, and sorting. Figure 5.8 is a lesson I conducted with fourth graders to encourage them to consider the power of punctuation during their study of traditional literature. I turned to one of my favorite traditional texts, Arnold Lobel's (1980) *Fables*. I wanted students to notice the variety of ways Lobel used quotation marks with various dialogue tags. For guided practice, I used Jerry Pinkney's (2013) nearly wordless picture book *The Tortoise and the Hare* to support students as they drafted their own lines of dialogue for the characters at the start of the race, using the images and speech bubbles to guide them. This was one lesson in a series of lessons on language and conventions the teachers were giving in their own classrooms, using children's literature as the blueprint. These lessons gave the students a growing interest in and awareness of punctuation with purpose. They noticed more about punctuation in reading and became more thoughtful about their use of punctuation in writing.

INTRODUCTION	
Connect previous teaching, capture students' attention and interest, or activate prior knowledge.	*I have heard from your teachers that you have just started a study of traditional texts. These are stories that have been told for generations and are often told all over the world. These are some of my favorite stories because of the ways the characters talk to one another. They often reveal the message of the stories in their dialogue, so I always read those lines of talk very closely.* *One of my favorite writers is Arnold Lobel. He wrote a book of fables just like Aesop did and in these stories are great words of wisdom—especially when we read closely the words the characters say to one another.* *I'm going to read a short fable to you today, and then we're going to look together at the lines of dialogue, noticing how the author used punctuation so that it is clear to the reader who is speaking.* Read aloud "The Mouse at the Seashore." Discuss how the lines of dialogue between the mouse and his mother and father are some of the most important lines in the story.
TEACH	
Teach one thing. Choose the way to teach. Try to model as much as you can.	*Today we're going to closely read for how Arnold Lobel used punctuation to make it clear who was speaking. When writers properly use punctuation, it allows us as readers to focus on the message of the story.* Display lines of dialogue: **"We are very alarmed!" they cried.** **"I have made my decision," said the Mouse firmly.** **"Then we cannot stop you," said Mother and Father Mouse, "but do be careful!"** Highlight the ways quotation marks are used along with commas and end punctuation inside the quotation marks to signal a complete thought or a continuing thought.
GUIDED PRACTICE	
Engage students with a quick opportunity to rehearse their ideas, such as through a turn and talk, stop and jot, stop and act, or brief discussion.	Have students work with a partner to insert proper punctuation into another fable where the dialogue has already been written. Review for accuracy.

Figure 5.8 Mini-Lesson: Writers use commas and quotation marks to signal dialogue.

CLOSURE	
Restate the teaching point and connect it to ongoing student work.	*Today we have focused on how to properly add quotation marks, commas, and end punctuation to signal to a reader when characters are speaking. For independent practice today you are going to generate a few lines of dialogue for an illustrated fable. It's a story you probably know well—"The Tortoise and the Hare." In this version of the story, the author has written the story without many words. You are going to imagine what the characters might be saying to one another for one of the pages of the story. Think about both what you want them to say and how to properly add quotation marks, commas, and end punctuation to signal to your reader that characters are speaking.*
INDEPENDENT PRACTICE	
Students write for ten to fifteen minutes, starting with *The Tortoise and the Hare* and moving to their own stories.	
WRAP-UP	
Students share their lines of dialogue with the class. Collect student work to analyze for accuracy with punctuation.	

Figure 5.8 (*continued*)

More of What Architects and Storytellers Know

Strong ideas rooted in how great stories work, structures to guide readers, and language and conventions to build cohesion are fundamental as we help students to build strong stories in their writing. There are also other things we can learn from architects that apply to how our students write. Architects, like writers, often know that less is more. Less ornamentation allows you to notice the amazing windows. Sometimes an all-white room is more peaceful than a swirl of colors. Architects, like writers, also know that the view matters. If you've ever lived in an apartment where your view is an airshaft or alley and then lived somewhere where you see the sky every day, you know that view matters. In writing, the point of view, or who's telling the story, is critical. When our students are writing, we want them to consider from the outset who is telling the story. Is it the student? Is it a fictional character? Why does the voice matter? How will it be revealed? The following sections are designed to further your students' thinking about the power they have as writers to tell stories in new ways.

Less Is More

Thomas Jefferson is said to have stated, "The most valuable of all talents is that of never using two words when one will do." What a contrast with most classrooms, which advocate for long and strong, which for some students translates into writing as much as they can without consideration of structure or purpose. To challenge students to say more with less is a fundamental shift for many workshop-based classrooms, but one that aligns with our current culture as much as it does with Jefferson's stance. Consider your own use of sites like Facebook and Twitter. I never read or wrote so much in my everyday life before using these social media. These sites are founded on the principle of saying more with less.

In my New Technologies course, I have all of my graduate students create Twitter accounts (increasingly, they already have accounts), and we tweet out short summaries, reactions, and questions, and our class conversation builds in person and online. I have found that some of my students are skilled users of hashtags. Hashtags were created by Twitter users to organize content, and are now used across several social media platforms including Tumblr, Instagram, and Google+. Several hashtags have caught the attention of the public, from the popular Throwback Thursday hashtag #tbt, to politically charged hashtags including #yesallwomen, #heforshe, #bringbackourgirls, and literacy's leading hashtag #weneeddiversebooks. All of these succinctly state their messages, and the tag lasts. Setting boundaries—be they character limits, word limits, sentence limits, or sentence frames—gives writers the freedom to focus on word choice. Boundaries give us a safety net to try.

We have the power of the sticky note as a boundary. I learned from a brilliant colleague to call sticky notes "thinking squares." Limited by the boundary of the 3-by-3-inch square, we are liberated to jot down a word, a phrase, or a series of bullets. The sticky note is our greatest low-tech boundary setter. It mirrors the tweet experience, to say the most you can in the fewest words. This is the challenge that drives the six-word memoir movement, based on the legend that Ernest Hemingway was challenged to write a short story in only six words and answered with "For sale: baby shoes, never worn." *SMITH* magazine created the "Say It in Six" campaign and provides an online space for writers to record their six-word memoirs and share them with the world. To date there are over 800,000 six-word memoirs on *SMITH*'s site www.sixwordmemoirs.com. You can search by topic, including love, advice, happiness, pain, war, and death. You can follow the Six in Schools project and even share your students' work with a global audience.

The "Say It in Six" concept is rooted in the idea that boundaries are freeing. In our classrooms, there are countless ways to encourage students to strengthen their writing by using boundaries to say more with less, including the following.

Character and word limits: *"Say it in six" (or one or ten).*

Sentence limits: *Say it in a sentence (or two or three).*

Paragraph limits: *Say it in a single paragraph.*

Word inclusion: *Use the word(s) _____ in your response.*

Sentence frames: *Use "I agree _____ because*
_____ *."*

Paper boundaries: *sticky note/thinking square, notecard, single sheet, or poster size*

Saying more with less is a concept that bridges print, visual, and multimedia texts. If you know Mark Rothko's paintings, you know what I mean. Shades of a single color on canvas—minimalism at its best. Advertising has long caught on to the power of less is more. In 2013, during the Superbowl blackout, Oreo sent out a Tweet that went viral almost instantaneously, a black-and-white photo of an Oreo cookie against a spotlit background with seven words in block, all-caps text: "YOU CAN STILL DUNK IN THE DARK." The ad has been retweeted more than 14,000 times. In the world of multimedia, pop music videos have long been flashy and overly stimulating, whereas recent artists have taken a more minimalist and less-complicated approach to their music videos. Examples of this approach include Lorde, the White Stripes, and Radiohead. Supporting students as visual and multimedia text creators is as important today as supporting them as wordsmiths. Many of our students will excel at the creation of these texts, using the codes and conventions described in Chapter 3 to create their own less-is-more works. Notice with students the visual and multimedia texts that say more with less on book covers, in advertisements, in works of art, and in music videos. This will strengthen their understanding of a less-is-more approach.

View Matters

When we experience physical space, our bodies move and our eyes take things in. Think of a time when you were at a place where the view took your breath away. I can picture the Macy's Thanksgiving Day parade from a New York rooftop. I can picture the ocean seen from a cliff. I can picture the view outside my son's classroom looking out into the woods. Architects know that views matter. They build structures that let in light and capitalize on access to nature. In writing, what we see in a story depends on who's telling the story. We see what the narrator sees, and as such, the narrator gives us our eyes. He or she guides our view and our interpretations of the characters, the events, and the themes we draw from them. Asking students to read with the initial question "Who's telling the story?" can propel them to consider the impact of point of view in their own work. One of my favorite stories to use with students in upper elementary grades is Anthony Browne's (1998) *Voices in the Park*, which tells the story of an afternoon at the park from four different points of view. In this book, we see how class and gender play out in the prejudices of characters as each character's voice prompts us to reflect on our own views of other people. With middle school students and beyond, I often use the short film *Scared Is Scared* (Giaever 2013) to explore the complexity of point of view.

Who's telling the story is complex in this engaging and moving work. Filmmaker Bianca Giaever weaves her own voice together with the voice of the six-year-old boy who she partnered with to tell his story. The story is both hers and his as well as that of the main characters, Asa Bear and Toby Mouse. Every time I watch *Scared Is Scared*, I laugh and I cry. I am reminded of the great beauty, complexity, and wonder of life. When my students write, I want them to think about point of view in this way. I want them to consider who's telling the story and what that voice has to share with us—what do we get to see that we may never have seen before thanks to that voice? I learn from the voices of Asa Bear and Toby Mouse. I learn from Remi in *Ratatouille,* Mater in *Cars,* and Baymax in *Big Hero Six.*

I learn from the stories my students write and the ways they share their own points of view, not only through personal narratives but through the characters they create. When I read with students, I often pause after the first few pages and ask "So, who's telling this story? Why is that important? What is this character or voice trying to tell us so far?" Likewise, when I teach about theme, I teach about how the author is whispering to us throughout the story. We need to listen to those whispers. A theme is whispered, never shouted. In the same way, point of view is almost never simple.

Every text shares the point of view of the author alongside the narrator alongside the other characters. To play with the concept of point of view, I have students write short quick-write stories from unexpected points of view—write a story from the point of view of your pet or the sun, wind, or moon. Borrowing from Pixar's Emma Coats (2013), I have students take their own stories and flip them by writing the same story from a different character's point of view. These quick-writes help students realize that view matters. The view shapes our experience as readers much as it does when we look out a window. Who's telling the story gives us our eyes as readers, showing us what to see and where to look.

Final Thoughts

Jerome Bruner (as cited in Campbell, Martin, and Fabos 2013) stated, "We are storytelling creatures, and as children we acquire language to tell those stories we have inside us" (13). No author explores this central concept better than Peter Reynolds. His books *Ish* (2002) and *The Dot* (2003) have convinced countless students that their stories matter and that they are, in fact, storytelling creatures. In *Ish*, the main character, Ramon, loved to draw but becomes filled with self-doubt after his big brother laughs over his shoulder and asks of his latest work, "What is THAT?" He reclaims the courage to draw and write thanks to his little sister's encouragement. By saying his drawing looked "vase-ish," his sister freed him to try again. As readers, we witness the power of how an "ish" mind-set empowers Ramon to see himself as an artist, writer, and storyteller. Like Ramon, all of our students are storytelling creatures. They take bold, courageous moves each day when those models make their marks through words, pictures, and sounds. They all have models in their lives for writing, whether they are characters in books, television shows, movies, or the stories of their classmates and teachers. They all have everyday experiences where they are faced with a challenge and engage in a hero's journey. They all have doubts and sometimes hesitate to make their own marks on the page. They all have the capacity to build stories with compelling ideas based on human experience, using structures that guide us, and language and conventions that hold the story together. They are builders, architects of their own stories.

 TOOLKIT Write Your Own Phenomenal Storytelling Rules

This chapter began with a reference to Emma Coats's "22 Rules of Storytelling" based on her work as a story artist for Pixar. Investigate her rules as a class and then use the following guiding questions as well as your own to compose your own Phenomenal Storytelling Rules as a class or encourage students to write their own.

1. What kind of worlds do memorable characters usually live in?
2. What do we love about our favorite characters?
3. What kinds of trouble do characters we love get into? What makes for a great adventure?
4. How can writers help characters to get out of trouble?
5. Why are "helper" characters important? What is their job in a story?
6. Why is it important that stories leave us with surprises or things unknown?
7. How do we know if our story or writing feels right?
8. What should we do if something doesn't feel right in our story?
9. How do we know when to pull back or try a new angle?
10. How will we know when to say "It looks phenomenal!"?

Chapter 6

How Do We Talk About Stories?

If stories come to you, care for them. And learn to give them away
where they are needed.

—Barry Lopez, *Crow and Weasel*

These days I often ask myself, When we talk about stories, what are we really talking about and how are we talking about it? I live in a house of boys, and lately there is a lot of talk about video games. Through these animated discussions, I learn about video game characters, their powers, moves, attacks, and symbols, and the intricate fantasy world they live in. Recently, my six-year-old figured out how to find YouTube videos of other people playing and explaining his favorite games so that he could learn from others. As a parent, I had to draw on my courage to realize what he had really done. He was using YouTube the same way my husband had when he wanted to learn the guitar. He was finding ways to teach himself. He was embodying the how-to genre, and I had to tread lightly to avoid language that villainized his interests or demeaned the story world he identified with just then. When we talk about video games, I'm lead learner—modeling what it is like to be interested in someone else's story world. "Tell me more about 'leveling up.'" "Who do you like more, Stealth Elf or Crusher? Why?" "Hmmm . . . it sounds like you know a lot of ways to become a better player." Through my words, my body language, and my eye contact I strive to let my son know that, at that moment, what he is saying is the most interesting thing we could be talking about. I strive for the same level of mindfulness and commitment in my classroom by being wholly present with my students during discussions. In those moments, I am lead learner more than I am expert.

The best discussions I have with my students are ones where I can't predict everything. I have my purposefully planned lessons. I anticipate where comprehension will break down. Yet, I know I cannot anticipate everything. This is sometimes hard for the color-coding, label-loving teacher in me. As a second-grade teacher, I read the My Father's Dragon (Gannett 1948) series aloud with my students, and at times we read it in text clubs. In the final book of this early fantasy trilogy by Ruth Stiles Gannett, we meet a character named Mr. Wagonwheel, a man who demeans his wife and barks orders at her. I initiated a conversation about whether Mr. Wagonwheel was a good man and how we knew if he was or wasn't "good." As expected, most students declared that Mr. Wagonwheel was not a good man, and they provided text evidence for their thinking, using the illustrations and words in the book. Unexpectedly, one of my students said that Mr. Wagonwheel reminded him of his father and then shared some stories that revealed his thinking about the Mr. Wagonwheel in his own life.

I've found over my years in the classroom that I no longer fear conversation and where it may take us. Rather, I worry about silence. Not every discussion in my classroom is rich. We all sometimes find ourselves repeating our classroom equivalent of "Bueller. Bueller." In these moments when I find myself hearing crickets, I turn inward. What could I have done differently to generate a spark? Could I have used a different text? Could I have asked a different question? Could I have initiated more? Stepped back and spoken less?

In the book *Antifragile: Things That Gain from Disorder,* by the contemporary philosopher Nassim Nicholas Taleb (2012), the introduction reads:

> *Wind extinguishes a candle and energizes fire. Likewise with randomness, uncertainty, chaos: you want to use them, not hide from them. You want to be the fire and wish for the wind.* (3)

When we open up our classrooms to talk, we invite randomness, uncertainty, and potentially chaos. We don't know what our students will say or how they will react to one another or the topic at hand. Ask yourself, in your own classroom, what are your discussion goals? In my classrooms, both at the elementary and higher education levels, I hope for students to share their connections, disconnections, concerns, noticings, and wonderings. I hope to be the fire and wish for the wind. I hope my students speak to each other more than to me. I hope that they look at and listen to whomever is speaking. I hope their hearts are open and they are willing to change. I hope they surprise themselves.

This chapter explores how we talk about stories. It is designed to give you some concrete suggestions about how to encourage students to share their stories, to give them away, and to care for the stories of others. In this way, we regard stories as sacred objects, valuable treasures in our classrooms. In this chapter, I use the term *story* liberally because, as the rest of the chapters have expressed, every opinion we have has a story behind it, as does every photo we are in, every image we create, every utterance we make.

So, how do we talk about stories? In this chapter, I encourage you to consider moving beyond an I-R-E (Initiate-Respond-Evaluate) model of instruction. I-R-E involves dialogues between a teacher and students in which the teacher initiates a line of questioning, expects students to respond, and then evaluates students' ideas, ready to move on to a new question. In the book *Interactive Comprehension Strategies: Fostering Meaningful Talk about Text*, Frank Serafini (2009) calls this "instructional ping pong." This is a model known to most of us and one that can be hard to move away from. After all, we plan great and inspiring questions and we want to use them. However, our students need more than these methods, which can invite passivity.

To move away from an I-R-E discourse pattern and take a different approach, think about the best conversations you have with people in your own life. Usually someone shares a story, an idea, or a question and invites a response from others. No one raises their hands. These kinds of conversations happen in my own life at the dinner table, and I refer to them in my classroom as "dinner-table" conversations. When we are having a dinner-table conversation we look at and listen to each speaker. We ask questions of the original speaker. We add on by referring to previous ideas. We feel free to agree or disagree or to provide a counterpoint. There is no right answer. We are all philosophers and storytellers. No matter what, we respect the stories and ideas of those who were willing to share them.

As Lois Bridges (2013) explains in her blog post "The Having of Grand Conversations," when we rethink the I-R-E pattern, we can imagine other patterns, such as I-R-R-R (Initiate-Respond-Respond-Respond). We can imagine students as initiators. We rethink who serves as evaluator. We move away from a coverage approach and instead foster intellectual inquiry driven by students' questions, wonderings, and noticings. And we can do this while encouraging students to attend to the text before them. These collaborative conversations, referred to by Maryann Eeds and Ralph Peterson (1989) as "grand conversations," are not "anything goes." The speaking and listening Anchor Standards of the Common Core offer some guidance as you consider the conversational goals you have for students:

- Participate in a range of conversations and collaborations with diverse partners.
- Build on others' ideas and express their own clearly and persuasively.
- Evaluate information presented in diverse media and formats.
- Evaluate a speaker's point of view, reasoning, and use of evidence and rhetoric.
- Make strategic use of digital media and visual displays of data to express information.
- Adapt speech to a variety of contexts.

Whatever your political stance on the Common Core, these may align with goals you have for your students as conversation participants. The question remains, How do we encourage students to engage in these collaborative ways? The following sections are designed to help you consider what methods will work in your classroom to talk about stories, to care for them, and to give them away where they are needed.

Dinner-Table Conversations: Building Respect and Trust

My husband and friends know that I like to host dinner parties. When we were first living in New York City we had a 500-square-foot apartment and would cram in as many of our friends as we could. Despite my best attempts I know I'm not Ina Garten or Rachael Ray. Luckily, those dinner parties were never really about the food. They were all about the company and the conversation. Sometimes, those conversations were heated. We do not all agree on issues of politics, media, or even sports. As the evenings went on, our voices got louder and our opinions got stronger. No matter the topic or the dispute, respect and trust were central to our interactions with one another. Of course, some of us may recall conversations in our own lives that were less than respectful or trusting. These are conversations that can break friendships and families. These are conversations where at least one participant digs in his or her heels, unwilling to listen to the ideas of others. Unwilling to say, "I hear what you are saying, I can respect your thinking, but . . ." When we ask students to talk about stories, with full knowledge that it may be difficult and even discomforting, we encourage them to engage in respectful dialogue and build trusting relationships. This will serve them far beyond their time with us within the four walls of our classrooms.

Therefore, I'm not sure the term "grand conversations" is appropriate. Are conversations where students engage with one another and wrestle with ideas really grand? Shouldn't they be simply what we expect when we think about talk in our classrooms? I would rather think about these kinds of conversations, where there is no single answer or solution, as family-style gatherings or "dinner-table conversations." If we are in loco parentis (Latin for "in place of the parent") when our students' parents are not there, isn't our classroom talk at its best when it feels like a dinner-table conversation? My conditions for dinner-table conversation include the following:

- Look at and listen to whomever is speaking.
- Ask a question when you have one.
- Use respectful language such as "I like when you said _____ because _____";
  "I, too, feel that _____ because _____"; "I disagree when you said _____ because
  _____"; "I agree with _____ because _____."

- Trust in each other to care for our stories.
- Feel free to simply take in today, and share tomorrow.

I refer to these as conditions rather than rules because I don't really think that dinner-table conversations have rules per se. Yet, they do have conditions that can encourage respect and trust; when these conditions are not met, we run the risk of potentially destructive moments, disrespectful language and tone, and distrust of sharing. Therefore, I've never implemented "cold-call" techniques when it comes to talking about stories. There is so much invisible student thinking, so many personal connections, disconnections, and moments with the potential for shaking someone's beliefs. Likewise, rather than insist each student share an idea or question, I encourage students to listen and simply breathe in stories and ideas today and come prepared after a night of thinking to share a thought tomorrow. This way, I can lean in to a particular student and have a one-on-one conversation about a story that someone shared. I want them to know that I am ready to listen when they are ready to share. I also encourage students to rehearse their thinking by stopping and jotting or turning and talking to a partner. Gaining comfort with speaking up at the dinner table can be intimidating. In five years as a faculty member at a college, I have never spoken at a full faculty assembly. Yet, in smaller committee meetings I am an avid speaker, willing to share my thoughts and questions without much rehearsal of my thinking.

In addition to creating conditions for "dinner-table" conversations, consider the range of conversations and diverse partnerships that will encourage more students to share stories and listen to the stories of others. Consider how often your students engage in the following:

- Whole-class conversations
- Small-group conversations
- Text clubs
- Partnerships

In my classes, conversations often start in partnerships. When partnerships are comfortable and trust and rapport have been established, two partnerships may join together to become a small group or text club. In your classroom, notice how and when your students share their thinking and their stories, and in what group dynamic they are most comfortable sharing their dinner-table thinking.

For conversation to start, someone has to spark an idea, pose a question, or share a story. At the start of the year, that person may often be us, as our classes are building community. When we initiate conversation, we provide important modeling. When we initiate conversation by interpreting a text, we model multiple ways of thinking about text complexity. When we initiate conversation by sharing a story and posing relevant questions, we model how to encourage multiple perspectives and voices. Wait time is our friend in these moments. We can apply a gradual release of responsibility model (Pearson and Gallagher 1983) to our conversation building and can expect that, at the start of the school year, we will be the lead speaker, gradually nudging students to take the lead, pose questions, share stories, and form more nuanced interpretations as we shift from leader to facilitator.

When I visited Sam and Mike's first-grade classroom they were reading aloud *The Librarian of Basra* (Winter 2005), a picture book based on a true story about a librarian in Iraq who saved hundreds of books from being burned during the Iraq War. Sam and Mike welcomed complexity into their classroom, and they nudged their first-graders to wonder and become more aware of social issues.

Jim: *Is the war in Iraq still going on?*

Sam: *Can anyone respond to this comment? He said "Is the war in Iraq still going on?" I see hands but would like to give people who didn't speak yet a chance to respond.*

Freddy: *The war in Iraq is not still going on, but they are fighting because everybody is mad about oil all the time. That still happens.*

Sam: *So you are saying, everyone is mad. Everyone is fighting for oil. Can anyone respond to what he said?*

Ronnie: *An army came and attacked some place.*

Sam: *Can you please call on the next person, Ronnie?*

Jane: *I think her face is showing that she sees the other houses and doesn't want her house to be like those.*

Sam: *So you think she's looking at the damaged houses and worried about her own house?*

George: *It looks like she's a scaredy-cat. So who would mind if their house got damaged? I wouldn't.*

Sam: *Can you say more about that?*

George: *If your house is damaged you can go down to the store and buy some more things to fix your house and then it will be all done.*

Sam: *This is interesting because we've been talking about homes and homelessness, and you are saying that if your house is damaged you can just go to the store to get stuff to repair your house and it's all done. Does someone have a response to that?*

Amy: *Maybe you wouldn't have any money so you couldn't get stuff to repair your house.*

Freddy: *It's kind of like food. Like now in Africa and other places food is getting very expensive. It's like that but they don't have enough money to go to get something because you are going to have to live with what you have.*

Sam: *So you're making the connection we talked about yesterday. You're right, there is a food crisis. Food got expensive and there are people in the world who don't have enough money for food, and you are looking at this and saying in the war people don't have enough money to get things to repair things.*

When we analyze Sam's comments, we notice that he often rephrases student thinking and asks for clarification or further response to encourage the talk to keep going. The conversation went in many different directions, all of which are centered by student connections to the topic, to the text itself, and to other related topics beyond the story that they knew something about. Sam models the process of accountable talk, and he very purposefully directs his first graders to think, wonder, question, and listen to one another's thinking about very complex social topics. He could not predict exactly what his students would share, but he has teaching moves to fall back on that encourage wide-awakeness. As Sam said to me afterward:

> *They've got to say what they're going to say and think what they're going to think. It's our job to make sure they are listened to. There is this urge to be like the school counselor on South Park. "War is bad children, okay. Okay. War is bad. Okay. Killing is bad. Okay." And we're just not going to say that. You know. It's not our role. And these books that we've chosen spring from our own politics, but we've learned to bite our own tongues.*

Supporting students as they engage in purposeful dialogue that is both text-centered and socially conscious means that at times we step back. We trust them to care for each other's ideas and to listen with interest and curiosity. We know when to bite our own tongues.

Noticing Our Own Conversational Moves: Striving for Balance

As Sam and Mike demonstrate, part of achieving balance in teaching is knowing when to take the lead and initiate discussion and when to step back. In our lessons, we engage in all kinds of talk. Among other things, we are giving information, complimenting students, giving directions, asking questions, answering our own questions, sharing our opinions, annotating, revoicing, and perhaps even correcting or redirecting. We are also using nonverbal cues through our body language and gestures to communicate our ideas about the conversation.

One of the best opportunities I had as a classroom teacher was to invite a teacher leader in to observe me. I needed to know more about my own talk, so that I could better support my students' talk. I decided that the observation would focus on the ways I was talking throughout the lesson, so I would know more about how I responded to students. Mostly, I knew I wanted to balance the kinds of questions I was asking to encourage both text-dependent responses and open-ended complex thinking. In his first visit, my supportive teacher leader simply tracked my talking and calculated quantitatively what I was doing. I found out that 25% of the time I asked questions. I answered my own question three times during the lesson, or 4% of the time. I gave directions and information equally often, 28% of the time. This quantitative data let me know that, while I was devoting time to posing questions, I would strengthen the conversations in my class if I asked questions more often and gave less information and fewer directions. The next time my teacher leader came in, he moved from a quantitative analysis to a qualitative one. I wanted to know what my conversational moves were. Here's what I found out:

- Most of my questions were text-based, using language such as, "Why would the characters do or say _____? How do you know?" or "How do you think the characters felt about _____? What makes you say so?"
- Occasionally, I asked a question that asked students to take a stance, such as, "Do you agree with _____? / disagree with _____? Why?"
- Even less often, I asked questions that were more open-ended and were directed at ways someone could change, such as, "How will you treat others differently now?"

Once I had some data on my own conversation, it helped me to find more of a balanced position. After all, what I said was modeling the ways I wanted my students to talk and to raise questions. The questions I asked determined the initial direction of the conversation. The toolkit at the end of this chapter offers several ways of thinking about your own conversational moves as well as the ways your students are engaging in talk.

Turning Talk into Action

When stories matter, we are changed. We ask new questions. We offer small acts of kindness to strangers and friends alike. We give more of ourselves. For stories to take root in our classrooms, we must be open to the ways our students will be changed by the stories we read to them, that we view together, and that they willingly share with the class. As teachers, we play a pivotal role in inspiring students to turn talk into action. As a classroom teacher, I saw students change in all kinds of ways over the school year. Of course, they physically grew. They lost teeth. They lost pets. They made new friends. They also engaged in small acts of bravery every single day. If we want the stories in our classrooms to mean more than good conversation, we need to help students to draw connections between the bravery of the characters they read about, both real and fictional, and the ways in which they themselves are brave.

Turning talk into action can start with noticing and naming the ways characters take action. As co-author of the blog *The Classroom Bookshelf*, I seem to have a pattern of blogging about books with children as heroes, including Jeanette Winter's (2014) two-story biography *Malala: A Brave Girl from Pakistan/Iqbal: A Brave Boy from Pakistan* and the picture book biography *Brave Girl: Clara and the Shirtwaist Makers' Strike of 1909* by Michelle Markel (2013). Both of these picture books tell stories based on real children who strove for justice in their homelands. Malala Yousafzai has become a household name and rightfully so. As I write in my book review, "Attacked on her way to school and shot in the head, Malala has been fighting for the rights of girls to an education before she was in her teens and continues to do so today." With our students we can read about Malala, and we can watch her speeches at the United Nations and at the Nobel Peace Prize award ceremony. We can watch her on *The Daily Show.* And we can discuss what she stood up for, her acts of bravery, and why she took such risks for all children in the face of danger.

Iqbal is a boy I didn't know of until I read Winter's book. After years of bonded slavery, Iqbal became an international advocate for the freedom of children. In 1995, when he was only twelve, Iqbal was shot and killed while out riding his bike. His story can be shared more widely thanks to Winter's representation, and we can research who he was and the international community's praise of this brave boy who is no longer with us. We can read about Clara Lemlich and her protests as a girl working in factories. With older students, we can pair our reading about these brave children with clips from Howard Zinn's (2009) documentary, *The People Speak,* to notice the ways people have come together throughout human history to stand up for what they believe in. When we read across these stories, we find models who remind us to think for ourselves and live our own lives. I've spent my whole life trying to figure out what I stand up for, what I believe in, and what defines my best life. Maybe you are like me. With our students we can start small.

Small acts of bravery are just as valuable as grand events. One of my favorite videos to watch with students is Sara Bareilles's music video for the song "Brave." In the song she sings the rallying cry "Show how big your brave is." A simple way to document actions in your classroom is to start your own "Look How Big Our Brave Is" campaign. My colleagues at LitWorld have an event each year on October 11, the International Day of the Girl, called Stand Up for Girls. On this day, children and adults alike all over the world hold up "Stand Up for _____" signs. Join in the movement with your students on October 11, and throughout the year, by encouraging them to jot, draw, or say what they stand up for, that day and every day.

Final Thoughts

When we talk about stories we have the great power to either lift up or tear down. We have the chance to validate and affirm that our students' own stories and the stories they love matter. We also have the responsibility to care for stories and to model giving them away with our whole hearts. In the final chapter, I explain why centering stories in your classroom takes courage. Like your students who take to the page or share their stories every day, you are brave. Like me, you stand up for the rights of all children to read widely and share stories freely.

 TOOLKIT Noticing and Naming Talk

Reflect on your own teaching moves and consider what you think your strengths are as a teacher using the categories below as a guide. Then, invite someone to observe you in action, not as a required evaluation but to give you a better understanding of the ways you support student talk about stories.

To start, a simple tally system works well to have someone else notice how often you engage in particular lines of talk. Use that data to consider ways you could further emphasize specific kinds of talk, such as questioning and posing problems.

Noticing More About Ourselves: Striving for Openness

What kinds of talk do you use to engage students in whole-group, small-group, or partnered discussion?

KINDS OF TALK USED TO ENGAGE STUDENTS	TALLY
Modeling/Thinking Aloud	
Questioning	
Complimenting	
Giving Information	
Giving Directions	
Revoicing	
Recapping	
Posing Problems	

What kinds of questions do you ask to further student talk about stories?

KINDS OF QUESTIONS ASKED TO FURTHER STUDENT TALK	TALLY
What does the author want us to think about this topic?	
Why would the characters do or say _____?	
How do you think the characters feel?	
What are your thoughts about _____?	
Do you agree with _____? / disagree with _____?	
How has your attitude or actions changed about this topic?	
What can you do to change an attitude or condition that is unjust?	
How will you treat others differently now?	

Noticing More About Our Students: Striving for Engagement

Think about each of your students and the ways they participate in discussions of texts as well as the ways they bravely share their own stories. This tool can be used to take a closer look at students and their talk, to honor what they are doing well, and to support them as they set speaking and listening goals.

THINGS TO NOTICE . . .	QUESTIONS AND COMMENTS
Students are engaged in talk about stories when they do the following: • Share their thinking in a variety of classroom situations (whole class, small group, partnership) • Share stories from their own lives • Reflect on stories across text types • Share connections and disconnections • Independently share within a "dinner-table" context • Make comments that refer back to other students' ideas • Introduce new but related issues	

THINGS TO NOTICE . . .	QUESTIONS AND COMMENTS
Students are listening and caring for others' stories when they do the following: • Make eye contact with the speaker • Refer to a previous speaker • Connect comments to previous ideas • Compliment as well as offer critique	
Students work through confusion or misunderstanding about stories when they do the following: • Revoice, summarize, or synthesize another student's ideas • Ask someone to repeat, restate, or elaborate on a comment. • Express puzzlement or confusion	

Chapter 7

Why This Work Takes Courage

Do you wanna leave soon?

No, I want enough time to be in love with everything...

And I cry because everything is so beautiful and so short.

—Marina Keegan, "Bygones"

Day and night he moved up and down, up and down, on waves as big as mountains, and he was full of wonder, full of enterprise, and full of love for life. —William Steig, *Amos and Boris*

As a young girl, I was the kind of kid who would sneak off to the living room and pull old photo albums off the shelves. I would pore over fading photos of my parents in their twenties (Mom, what are you doing with that cigarette!). I wanted to jump into those photos and turn back time to be a part of it all. I imagined the stories that filled the pages. Stories of the people that mattered most to me. Stories of people I had never met and would never meet. Stories of who I was in years past. I still sit with albums and remember the stories that each photo represents. Lots of firsts and a lot of lasts. There's a lot of whole-hearted feeling on every page. Back then and still today, I tend to tear up when viewing these albums. Over the years I have come to realize that wearing my heart on my sleeve is not the deficit I thought it was, but might be one of my greatest strengths as a teacher. My students have always known that I soak it all in, feel things completely, and empathize with their struggles, and that I will be there to leap out of my seat at their triumphs and joys. I love the work I do and the people in my life whole-heartedly. I believe this kind of engagement takes risk. It takes courage to live and teach this way.

I had the great fortune of leading a professional development session for teachers on visual storytelling with Aaron Mace, a colleague of mine from the Jacob Burns Film Center. In this session, we focused on the power of storytelling through basic moviemaking. We knew better than to just ask teachers to start planning stories and making movies. Instead, we knew we needed to create some boundaries, what Aaron and the Jacob Burns team call "creative constraints." We asked teachers to develop a one- to two-minute movie that told a story with certain parameters around literacy, visual, oral, and structural components. Specifically, we said that their stories had to include homophone confusion (always hilarious—thank you, *Amelia Bedelia*), at least one close-up shot, and one sound effect, and had to end with cliffhangers. We asked teachers to be courageous—to take to their storyboards, the stage, and some iPads, ready to mess around. We knew it would be uncomfortable for some and liberating for others. After a moment or two of awkward silence, the room was abuzz. Small groups of teachers were gathered together, heads in a huddle, crafting stories. From the onset, we tried to instill confidence that their stories would be worthy of creating and sharing and that we would be there to support them in this messy process—all the while recognizing the great vulnerability this level of engagement took. We asked everyone in the room to call on their courage.

We asked this of teachers because we ask this of young people every day—to create. To take to the page and share their thinking with the world. This is no easy feat. We see how hard this is when we teach five-year-olds who are still trying to figure out how to hold a pencil correctly, eyeing their neighbor's paper and comparing their self-portraits to a friend's. We see it in middle schoolers who have ideas to share but hesitate to say or write something that could equal social suicide. And we see it in fellow teachers who may not see themselves as storytellers and are being asked to create. We are all vulnerable.

Creating Space for Vulnerability

Recently, I decided to give yoga a try. Far from a yogi, I do my best to attend a weekly class because I like how I feel during and after class, but more importantly because my instructor is all about progress, not perfection. In her class, I am able to actively embrace the vulnerability that comes with trying to hold tree pose with my eyes closed. I can try and fail some days, and try again and succeed on others. In her class, we are encouraged to practice vulnerability in the face of safety.

One of the schools that I have the great pleasure of working in is Saint Joseph's School for the Deaf. I am privileged to work with and learn from teachers who bring literacy to life for children who are deaf, many of whom are also English language learners, newcomers to America, and from low-income homes. In every grade at Saint Joseph's, students read, write, draw, act out, and sign their own narratives. At school, they are rooted in story and community, knowing they are in a safe space. Every day I am there, I am humbled by the triumphs of a student taking to the page, asking a question, and taking a risk. On my most recent visit, teachers were creating a unit on American Sign Language poems. The unit was designed to support students in performing their poems for live audiences, and to film them so they can be shared with other students year after year, building a bank of mentor texts for future poets. What a model of powerful, community-based practices that encourages students to embrace their own vulnerability and move beyond it in the face of safety! The staff at Saint Joseph's recognize that vulnerability just is. It isn't dwelled upon or limiting. Vulnerability is accepted as something integral to what it means to be human.

Here's what I've learned through my own teaching, through my observations of great teachers, and through deep reflection—vulnerability is not a bad thing. It just is what it is. Recognizing one another's vulnerability is arguably an essential component of a classroom that fosters happiness alongside achievement, particularly a classroom whose focus is on developing readers, writers, speakers, listeners, and thinkers.

Brené Brown, author of *Daring Greatly: How the Courage to Be Vulnerable Transforms the Way We Live, Love, Parent, and Lead* (2012) and *The Gifts of Imperfection* (2010b), studies human connection—that is, how we empathize, belong, and see ourselves as worthy of love. If we as teachers adopt her philosophy that vulnerability is a good thing, we can free our students (and ourselves) from feeling shame, unworthiness, and a lack of belonging. Instead, we can instill courage, care, and connection. Brown (2010a) spoke of "calling deep on her courage" and explained that, for her as a researcher, "stories are data with a soul." These are essential philosophical underpinnings to framing your class as a community where story matters. Specifically, Brown describes how people who live whole-heartedly and embrace vulnerability as a given have "the courage to be imperfect, compassion to be kind to themselves first and to others, and connection as a result of authenticity" (2010). Teaching with story as the heart of your classroom instruction means embracing vulnerability—doing something where there are no guarantees.

According to Brown's research, vulnerability is the birthplace of joy and creativity. When we ask students to turn off certain stories from their own life, or let them know that their reading and writing interests have no place in our classrooms, we ask them to numb parts of themselves. Since we cannot selectively numb emotion, we unintentionally end up numbing joy, gratitude, and happiness. As Brown advocates, we can instead create space for vulnerability. This starts by recognizing that, although children are hard-wired for struggle, we can let them know every day that they are worthy of love and belonging. That their stories matter. We can share our own stories. In doing so, we let ourselves be seen. We teach with our whole hearts, and we model practicing gratitude and joy.

Ultimately, a pedagogy of vulnerability is story-centered. It allows stories to enter and flourish even if they are discomforting. In the documentary film *Children Full of Life* (Kaetsu 2003), we meet Toshiro Kanamori, a fourth-grade teacher who recognizes the need for uncomfortable emotions to exist if happiness is the ultimate goal. If you have not seen this film yet, put this book down immediately and take forty minutes to watch it from start to finish. Watching Mr. Kanamori may have had more professional impact on my own thinking about teaching and learning than any graduate course or professional development session. To begin, Kanamori asks his students, "Why are we here?" They respond, "To be happy!" They know that their experience together is about happiness more than achievement. One structure he uses to explore all shades of happiness is letter writing. At the start of each school day, three students read their letters to the class. These letters reveal their ten-year-old selves. They share stories of happiness as well as stories of irritation, loss, and anger. Memories bubble to the surface. Sometimes they share things—like the loss of a loved one—so painful that the rest of the class weeps. Kanamori embraces compassion, and purposefully creates this space for vulnerability. He knows that he must if he is to help his students to live happy lives and care for others.

To embrace vulnerability as a teacher involves several things:

- Recognizing your own imperfection
- Asking for help when you need it
- Being comfortable with what you do and don't know
- Being wide awake to the ways your own story may be very different from your students' stories
- Recognizing that your story affects your work with students
- An appreciation for the preciousness of life
- Daily expressions of gratitude
- Allowing yourself and your students to feel

As a fourth-grade teacher, I had a student who had lost his mother to cancer when he was an infant. He did not remember her, but he knew many stories about her. Sean had just come to New York City from Taiwan, and began the school year without any English. In May, he asked me if he could read a letter to the class written in English by his mother. On the day he shared the letter, Sam read every word his mother had written. He stood at the front of the room beaming with pride. I wept at my chair witnessing his courage. We all felt so many emotions that day, including happiness, despite the tears that ran down our faces.

So, what is at stake if we dismiss vulnerability? In short, happiness. More specifically, based on what I see in schools across sociocultural contexts, when we dismiss vulnerability we create passivity and disconnection. In classrooms where vulnerability is present and even modeled, students know they are worthy as readers, writers, speakers, listeners, thinkers, creators . . . anythingers.

So, what might it mean to integrate feelings with instruction? One of the ways you can embrace a pedagogy of vulnerability is to craft classroom rituals that let students' stories be heard. Consider having an open letter time at the start of each day, as in Kanamori's fourth-grade class, where any student can sign up to share a letter he or she has written to the class. Be open to what their letters may contain. Students may write about an amazing accomplishment, the death of a loved one, an unanswerable question, a struggle they are facing, what they love, or something they fear. Consider ways you can spotlight students' hidden talents and give them the floor to share their passions through invitations rather than requirements. I will never forget Alex's presentation on how to draw comics or Dominic's guitar sessions. Share student interests through a class newsletter, with a rotating weekly editor, who can seek out ways to spotlight students and their interests in each issue. Share moments of student success through class-composed tweets that are shared with families that follow your Twitter feed. Turn to characters who recognize their own vulnerability, including Jeremy in *Those Shoes* (Boelts 2007), Unhei in *The Name Jar* (Choi 2003), and Parvana in *The Breadwinner* (Ellis 2000). Read essays by figures who recognize their own vulnerability, like Muhammad Ali's (2009) *This I Believe* essay "I Am Still the Greatest." Read poems that explore themes of humanness and vulnerability, such as Maya Angelou's (1975) "Alone" and Billy Collins's (1995) "On Turning Ten." The sample thematic text sets in Chapter 2 give many examples of texts in different genres and mediums that explore themes associated with vulnerability, including friendship, belonging, conflict, courage, empathy, and resilience.

As much as we want to spotlight the good, consider ways to encourage a culture of revision, brilliantly explained in depth by Doug Lemov (2014) in *Teach Like a Champion, 2.0*. Invite students to share their attempts along with their polished pieces. Hang student drafts on bulletin boards alongside the final pieces of writing. Embrace your own errors. I had plenty of typos and what I call "write-os." Rather than recoil, I tried to embrace these moments to model my own humanness.

A pedagogy of vulnerability is a mind-set or a way of thinking about your own practice and about each student in your care. The work of positive psychologists like Carol Dweck (2007) has influenced the field of education in important ways in the last few years. Dweck explains how we can encourage a growth mind-set in our students and in ourselves, and the need to be aware of times when we have a fixed mind-set. Having a growth mind-set means being open and willing to try things that may be hard and to engage with something new, and recognizing that you may not get it right. Having a fixed mind-set is just the opposite. When you have a fixed mind-set you hesitate to try things that may be hard or new, and you risk missing opportunities for growth. A pedagogy of vulnerability is aligned with the idea of a growth mind-set in the recognition that there are no certainties in the classroom or in life. As a teacher who embraces vulnerability, you become more open and willing to embrace what might be new, challenging, or even discomforting.

Be the Story

The writer Edith Wharton said, "There are two ways of spreading light: to be the candle or the mirror that reflects it." My hope for teachers is that you will be both the candle lighting the path of learning and the mirror helping your students to see themselves for who they are and who they want to be.

In my New Technologies course, I encourage my graduate students to create digital stories that define who they are as teachers. As part of our writing process, I push them to find metaphors that will help drive their stories and help us connect with their identities as teachers. Over the years, I have had students anchor their stories with metaphors such as the teacher as a gardener growing learners, or as a compass guiding the students on their journeys. One of my students grounded her story in a metaphor that spoke to me more than any other: teacher as storybook. In her digital story, Chelsea explained that stories are for anyone. Stories stand the test of time. Stories are always there for you. Stories are right there on your bookshelf where you expect to find them. Our most cherished storybooks have jottings in the margins. Stories are changed by their readers, and in turn, their readers are changed. As a new teacher, Chelsea embraced her role of teacher as storybook, and the ways her story would be changed by the students who filled her classroom.

LitWorld is a nonprofit literacy advocacy group. The tagline that explains their mission is *Be the Story*. In their work with teachers and students in some of the world's most vulnerable communities, story drives everything they do. The group advocates for every child's human right to tell stories and for those stories to be heard, shared, and loved. This book is my call to action to the field. My hope is that each teacher who reads it finds the courage to be the story.

This book is framed by questions about stories and the roles they play in teaching and learning. However, there are many more questions to be posed about the role of story in today's classrooms. Most formidably, what is the future of story? I wholeheartedly believe that this is up to teachers to decide. Reforms will come and go, but in my experience the teachers who have the greatest impact on students' lives ground their work in the power of story. Like Robin Williams's character in *Dead Poets Society* (Weir 1989), these teachers encourage students to seize the day. In the film, Williams plays Mr. Keating, who draws from Walt Whitman to encourage his students to be their own stories. He embodies the teacher as story when he says, "We don't read and write poetry because it's cute. We read and write poetry because we are members of the human race. And the human race is filled with passion. And medicine, law, business, engineering, these are noble pursuits and necessary to sustain life. But poetry, beauty, romance, love, these are what we stay alive for." To help you draw on your own courage, I leave you with Walt Whitman's (1867) poem that celebrates the gift of life, in the hopes that as you finish reading and reflecting on my words, you will turn to his as a reminder of why we do this work. Contribute a verse. Be the story.

O Me! O Life!

Oh me! Oh life! of the questions of these recurring,

Of the endless trains of the faithless, of cities fill'd with the foolish,

*Of myself forever reproaching myself, (for who more foolish than I, and who
more faithless?)*

*Of eyes that vainly crave the light, of the objects mean, of the struggle ever
renew'd,*

Of the poor results of all, of the plodding and sordid crowds I see around me,

Of the empty and useless years of the rest, with the rest me intertwined,

The question, O me! so sad, recurring—What good amid these, O me, O life?

Answer.

That you are here—that life exists and identity,

That the powerful play goes on, and you may contribute a verse.

Appendix: Annotated Bibliography of Suggested Resources

My wonderful brother- and sister-in-law, Will and Laura, gave me a copy of *The Flavor Thesaurus: Pairings, Recipes, and Ideas for the Creative Cook* by Niki Segnit (2010) as a Christmas gift. Far from a traditional cookbook, *The Flavor Thesaurus* does not give you recipes to prescriptively follow. Rather, it is a collection of suggestions—a reference for aspiring foodies. Leeks, bacon, and risotto. Delicious. Why hadn't I thought of that before? The book is described by the author as a "patchwork of facts, connections, impressions and recollections, designed less to tell you exactly what to do than to provide the spark for your own recipe or adaptation" (2010, 15). Think of the annotations that follow as a patchwork of my impressions and recollections of texts that have had an impact on my thinking and the ways I teach. Consider which texts can support you and your students in new ways. What are the pairings and ideas that you notice? These entries elaborate on the ways they are incorporated across the book, drawing in many ways on my personal prejudice about what texts support students to lean in to stories and know that their story is heard.

Children's Literature

Alborough, Jez. 2009. *Hug*. Cambridge, MA: Candlewick Press.
Hug is often one of the first books I use at the start of the school year in a pre-K or kindergarten classroom to help all of the students see themselves as readers. I let the students know that, when they are reading the heartwarming illustrations about hugs, they are readers. Plus, who doesn't love a monkey?

Alcott, Louisa May. 1880. *Little Women*. Boston: Roberts Brothers.
Jo, Amy, Meg, and Beth. The March sisters had a huge influence on my life, and I continue to wonder which girl I most resemble. Do I have the steadfast strength of Jo? Am I motherly like Meg? Louisa May Alcott's short stories are also worth reading, including "What Love Can Do" and "Kate's Choice."

Alexander, Kwame. 2014. *The Crossover*. Boston: HMH Books for Young Readers.

Simply "slammerific." The 2015 Newbery winner *The Crossover* had my heart pounding as I feverishly read to find out what happened on and off the basketball court to the protagonist, JB, and his family. Written in verse, this novel masterfully serves as a reminder of the power of format. I sat down to read it in our local library and didn't get up until I was done. It helped that I was seated in a cushy chair right by a fireplace.

Boelts, Maribeth. 2007. *Those Shoes*. Somerville, MA: Candlewick Press.

Me + this book = tears. Jeremy is a boy who has his heart set on *those shoes*: black high-tops with two white stripes. With limited finances available, Jeremy and his grandmother set off in search of a pair. Finally, at a thrift store, Jeremy pays with his own money for those shoes. Those too-small shoes on his too-big feet. The ending will leave you humbled by the power of friendship and the human capacity to put others before oneself.

Browne, Anthony. 1998. *Voices in the Park*. London: DK Publishing.

A master at evocative storytelling, Anthony Browne tells four versions of an afternoon in the park. Told from four different points of view, this captivating book nudges readers to consider issues of class, race, and gender and is a powerful text for exploring power, positioning, and perspective. The text also positions readers to think like writers, inviting us to create our own four-part stories that tell of everyday events where each character's voice gives a different version of the story.

Bulla, Clyde Robert. 1987. *The Chalkbox Kid*. New York: Random House Books for Young Readers.

This gem of a book remains one of my favorite first chapter books to read with second and third graders. The main character, Gregory, represents many children who experience sudden change and family uprooting. When his father loses his job, Gregory moves to a new town and a new school. He finds he has an affinity for art after realizing that his family has moved next door to an abandoned chalk factory. The story offers an authentic representation of the courage of children in the face of adversity. Full of arts-based applications, the story inspires readers to create their own chalk drawings and even take their work to the streets as Gregory does in the chalk factory.

Choi, Yangsook. 2003. *The Name Jar*. Decorah, IA: Dragonfly Books.

The Name Jar has become my go-to text for exploring cause and effect, conflict, and the power of characters who face personal troubles with social implications. Thanks to Yangsook Choi's lyrical language, when I read *The Name Jar*, I feel Unhei's angry tears and embarrassment when she is teased for her name on the bus even if her experience isn't one that I share.

Creech, Sharon. 2001. *Love That Dog*. New York: HarperCollins.

A novel told in verse, *Love That Dog* is a captivating read-aloud during a poetry unit or at any time of year. The story models the power of writing poetry in tribute to an existing poem. Walter Dean Myers's "Love That Boy" becomes the inspiration for the main character, Jack's, poem, "Love That Dog." The story weaves the poems of William Carlos Williams, Robert Frost, William Blake, Valerie Worth, and others into the narrative, inviting students to notice themes and patterns across the poems and to be inspired to take to the page themselves.

Cronin, Doreen. 2000. *Click, Clack, Moo: Cows That Type*. New York: Atheneum.

At its core, *Click, Clack, Moo: Cows That Type* is about workers' rights. It's about protest. It's about standing up for what you believe in. And, yes, it's cleverly written. It's a crowd pleaser at any age and has more implications for teaching toward social justice than meets the eye.

dePaola, Tomie. 1978. *Pancakes for Breakfast*. Boston: Houghton Mifflin Harcourt.

Given to me as a gift by my dear friend Suzanne when I was pregnant with my first son, *Pancakes for Breakfast* remains one of my favorite wordless picture books. Living in the woods in Connecticut, my boys and I identify with the New England setting represented by dePaola. The stone walls, snowy fields, and barren trees feel like home. I often use this story to support preschoolers and early readers to think about craft technique through the close reading of illustrations. We zoom in on facial expressions and notice subtle actions. It's a wonderful initial text to support students as storytellers, charging each student to be an expert on a two-page spread by annotating what's happening, what dialogue may be used, and what thoughts the character may have. Capture your students' expertise through audiorecording devices and weave them together into a class-compiled oral retelling.

Ellis, Deborah. 2000. *The Breadwinner*. Toronto, Ontario: Groundwood Books.

The Breadwinner is Deborah Ellis's first story in a trilogy about Parvana, a girl growing up in Afghanistan when the Taliban came into power. Parvana is a strong female protagonist, and Ellis has written for middle school audiences a compelling, heartfelt story that serves as a true page-turner as well as a critical introduction to the realities some girls face in parts of the world where their rights are compromised and their educational opportunities limited. I often pair *The Breadwinner* with nonfiction texts Ellis has written, including *Kids of Kabul: Living Bravely Through a Never-Ending War* (2012), that highlight the voices of boys and girls in the Middle East sharing their lived experiences.

Fleischman, Paul. 1997. *Seedfolks*. New York: Joanna Cotler Books.

Seedfolks is a story written as individual vignettes, each told from the point of view of a character living in the same city neighborhood. When an empty lot is repositioned as a neighborhood garden, race, class, ethnic, and language barriers are eroded. *Seedfolks* is a wonderful story for introducing point of view and the power and purpose of setting. It serves as an anchor text for students to write stories of their own, mirroring Fleischman's vignettes. I often read *Seedfolks* in the springtime as the earth renews itself and we all come out from our winter hibernation. When I taught in New York City, I was privileged to have access to a school plot at a neighborhood garden where my students and I spent time each week tending to our plants, sketching, writing, and imagining. Any access to greenery makes this reading that much more powerful.

Idle, Molly. 2013. *Flora and the Flamingo*. San Francisco: Chronicle Books.

The Flora books by Molly Idle are nothing short of cinematic. *Flora and the Flamingo* and *Flora and the Penguin* are wordless picture books that feature a girl exploring the world through movement and animal mimicry. Molly Idle's brilliant use of flaps makes this an interactive text that the youngest of learners will want to participate in.

Jeffers, Oliver. 2012. *This Moose Belongs to Me*. New York: HarperCollins.

What does it mean to own something? How does ownership intersect with belonging? Can we "own" any parts of nature, including animals? *This Moose Belongs to Me* is classic Oliver Jeffers—quirky, amusing, and imaginative. The art that serves as the background are from paintings Jeffers found on the street in his Brooklyn neighborhood; his drawings are overlaid on top. Used as a mentor text, the book provides an opportunity to help students find images, paintings, or graphics that they want to weave together to tell their own story.

Konigsburg, E. L. 1967. *From the Mixed-Up Files of Mrs. Basil E. Frankweiler*. New York: Atheneum Books.

As a museum lover, I relished this Konigsburg classic as a child, and my New York City fourth graders devoured this book the same way I did. What would it be like to sneak into a museum and sleep there overnight? What mysteries would lie within the halls? Konigsburg capitalizes on the newfound independence many nine- and ten-year-olds are experiencing in life and takes that freedom to a whole new level. I love reading this book and asking my students about the ways they see themselves as independent and in what ways they would like to be more independent.

Lehman, Barbara. 2004. *The Red Book.* **Boston: HMH Books for Young Readers.**
The Red Book is a postmodern take on how we define story. This wordless picture book can be used with young learners, but I find it is best used with upper elementary students to rethink what's possible in illustration. In this story, a red book serves as a gateway from one setting to another as characters jump into the book to find themselves in the settings of the pages. I have found great success using this book with English learners, as each page begs to be studied more closely than the previous one. Without words, Lehman frees us to focus on the illustrations alone. This book is a great story to teach rereading because as you move forward in the story, you are often looking back to check your own understanding of what just happened.

Lester, Julius. 2005. *Let's Talk About Race.* **New York: HarperCollins.**
I was first introduced to *Let's Talk About Race* by one of my wonderful graduate students, Francesca DeLio, whose work serves as a sample in the Chapter 4 toolkit. In *Let's Talk About Race*, famed writer and illustrator Julius Lester offers us a way to talk about race by first considering the power and importance of our own stories. Counter to colorblind approaches, Lester foregrounds race as central to our own stories and the way we make our way through the world. A must-have for all classrooms.

Lionni, Leo.1995. *Matthew's Dream.* **Decorah, IA: Dragonfly Books.**
My son Matthew is named after several close friends of ours named Matthew, but in my mind he is also named after this brilliant character created by Leo Lionni. *Matthew's Dream* serves as a mentor text for life. To be Matthew is to find what you love in life and actively pursue it despite the obstacles before you. To be Matthew is to love colors, shapes, and texture. To be Matthew is to see everything as a new site of possibility. Dusty old attic corners become colorful abstract landscapes. Dreams become reality.

Lobel, Arnold. 1980. *Fables.* **New York: HarperCollins.**
Arnold Lobel is the author of the beloved Frog and Toad series, but less known is his collection of fables. Beautifully illustrated and chock full of sophisticated language, each story is grounded by a life lesson worth considering. I use Lobel's *Fables* to help bring stories to life in my classroom. We draw the fables using simple shapes to focus on what happened. We act out the fables in partnerships. We retell the fables in our own words. We write our own fables inspired by Lobel's anthropomorphized animals.

Markel, Michelle. 2013. *Brave Girl: Clara and the Shirtwaist Makers' Strike of 1909.* **New York: HarperCollins.**
I am always looking for stories about fierce and fearless females. This fictionalized biography of Clara Lemlich is one of those stories that should be shared widely. As a girl working in a New York City

sweatshop at the turn of the twentieth century, Clara protested for workers' rights and transformed the garment industry that kept many young girls from an education and a fair living. Acclaimed author Michelle Markel and Caldecott Honor artist Melissa Sweet often collaborate as a writer-illustrator team and take to the page again in *Brave Girl*. Their collective books provide a text set that can center social justice conversations and offer readers real stories of social action and possibility.

Mochizuki, Ken. 1993. *Baseball Saved Us*. New York: Lee and Low Books.

Baseball Saved Us is one of my son Matthew's favorite books. The era of Japanese internment camps during World War II featured in the book is a chapter of US history often overlooked in elementary school classrooms. Yet, it is critical for young learners to begin to recognize the complexity of history and the ways groups of people have been systematically marginalized. *Baseball Saved Us* details this historical injustice, but it does so through a compelling story about a boy's struggle to belong and the power of collective action to make change for the better.

Palacio, R. J. 2012. *Wonder*. New York: Random House.

I don't know of a more powerful book than *Wonder* for teaching about understanding, empathy, forgiveness, and the power of the human spirit. Told in vignettes, *Wonder* focuses on the story of August, a boy born with a facial deformity that impacts every facet of his life and the lives of his family members. After years of homeschooling, August transitions to a school where he is met with friendship by some and deeply rooted prejudice by others. Masterfully told, *Wonder* is a powerful read-aloud, text club selection, or independent reading book for upper elementary and middle school students. But, I have to say it should be required reading at any age.

Reynolds, Peter. 2003. *The Dot*. Cambridge, MA: Candlewick Press.

I love the work of Peter Reynolds. He captures the struggles many of us face to feel like confident, capable learners. How often do we stare at a blank page wondering if we are worthy enough to make a mark? All of his books serve as guideposts for breaking through, believing in yourself, and taking small steps in your own life. *The Dot* is my favorite. I have been delighted to be a part of schools on Dot Day, where students all make their own marks and celebrate the power of the dot as a symbol of individualism and risk-taking.

Richardson, Justin, and Peter Parnell. 2005. *And Tango Makes Three*. New York: Simon and Schuster.

This beautiful story based on true events at the Central Park Zoo amazes me. It amazes me that Roy and Silo, two male penguins, found each other and together cared for an abandoned egg, saving the life of what would have been an unborn baby penguin. It amazes me that this book is still so controversial today. It amazes me that school is not always a safe place for conversations about family. Yet, I hope that more teachers will take up *And Tango Makes Three* as my friend Anna-Bain did, knowing that this is a story that must be told.

Willems, Mo. 2010. *Knuffle Bunny Free: An Unexpected Diversion*. New York: Hyperion Books for Children.

I love the Knuffle Bunny trilogy. I love how it captures the great love young people have for their lovies. I love how playful the text and illustrations are in every book. I love that I lived along the blocks of Brooklyn captured in the photographs and that my son Jack played in the very sandpit and swung on the very swings that Trixie's Knuffle Bunny does in *Knuffle Bunny Too*. Of all of the books, *Knuffle Bunny Free* is my favorite because I love how we watch Trixie find the inner strength to know that she is safe and secure even without her Knuffle Bunny in her arms. The surprising ending reminds us of the power of young children to put others before themselves.

Winter, Jeanette. 2004. *September Roses*. New York: Farrar, Straus and Giroux.

Jeanette Winter's *September Roses* is a book I read aloud every year on September 11. Winter reminds us of the soulful power of coming together in times of great tragedy. Living and working in New York City on September 11, 2001, I will always remember the constant stream of parents—many of whom had walked from Wall Street, miles away—arriving for their children. I will remember the empty streets as I made my way home. I will remember my students' drawings of planes and darkened skies the rest of the year and how we as a school understood that this was the way our students were processing. *September Roses* commemorates the day by centering hope, care, and the power of creating something beautiful in a time of great pain.

Woodson, Jacqueline. 2014. *Brown Girl Dreaming*. New York: Nancy Paulsen Books.

A memoir told in verse, *Brown Girl Dreaming* is a lyrical text. Every page is a masterpiece and begs us to read and reread to find new meaning. *Brown Girl Dreaming* explores topics of identity, race, belonging, family, and civil rights, among others. A wonderful read-aloud, text club selection, or independent reading book, *Brown Girl Dreaming* offers all readers opportunities to notice where their story intersects with Woodson's and where their own story departs.

Poetry

Ahlberg, Allan. 1991. *Heard It in the Playground*. New York: Puffin Books.

Want to make a crowd of students or adults smile instantly? Read, in a choral fashion, the eponymous poem of this collection. The repetition, alliteration, and sheer clever turns of phrase are sure to keep you chanting "Heard/Heard it/Heard it in/Heard it in the/Heard it in the playground/The play/The play." The video of Class 4SA of Sheen Mount Primary School performing the poem is a must-see: https://vimeo.com/13766287.

Collins, Billy. 1995. "On Turning Ten." *The Art of Drowning*. Pittsburgh, PA: University of Pittsburgh Press.

Turning double-digits was a big deal in my fourth-grade classroom. It's a time to be celebrated but also a time of recognition that any coming of age is full of complexity, fear, and its own set of challenges. "On Turning Ten" is a complex poem with sophisticated language, but its message is completely comprehensible to students who themselves are experiencing the array of emotions about what it means to turn ten.

Fleischman, Paul. 1988. *Joyful Noise: Poems for Two Voices*. New York: HarperTrophy.

Joyful noise, joyful noise! Don't we all want classrooms full of joyful noise? Here we have Fleischman doing it again—playing with genre to release our imaginations. I often use *Joyful Noise* as part of our celebration of poetry, either early in the school year or in a unit of study dedicated to poetry. Hearing your own voice reading alongside another is a joyful experience that students relish. In this collection, Fleishman offers a mentor text for taking poetry to a new structural level for many students.

Hughes, Langston. (1945) 2004. "I, Too." *The Collected Poems of Langston Hughes*. New York: Knopf/Vintage Books.

I often begin to model what it means to be a close reader with "I, Too." I ask students to read the poem, noting words that have the most impact on them. I ask them to consider Hughes's position and how he positions us to take action as readers. I use this poem with all age groups, and I am always amazed at how young people understand the pain Hughes expresses but also the power of his voice to write for social change.

Mora, Pat. 1996. *Confetti: Poems for Children*. New York: Lee and Low Books.

Pat Mora is a master of poetry, and in this collection she has composed a series of poems that celebrate language, colors, and life. I love reading her poems with students who speak Spanish and become the experts in the room, teaching me how to pronounce and enunciate words to greater express the joy Mora writes about. *Confetti* is a collection to be read all year long to celebrate words and the simple possibilities of the everyday.

Whitman, Walt. (1867) 2007. "O Me! O Life!" *Leaves of Grass*. New York: Dover.

The late Robin Williams quotes from Whitman's "O Me! O Life!" as he urges his students in *Dead Poet's Society* to seize the day. Carpe diem: to seize life and take it all in. This is a poem to photocopy and put on your clipboard. To hang in your classroom. To come back to again and again. We all need reminders of the gratitude of simply being alive.

Videos

Radiolab. 2009. *16: Moments* (*Short film*). New York: WNYC Radio. Available at http://www.radiolab.org/story/91918-16-moments/.

Before you start a unit on narrative writing, watch *16: Moments*. While it contains a handful of small moments not suited for young audiences, it will remind you of why we write stories from our own lives. It will remind you that there is a story in every seemingly small action we take. Every footstep. Every utterance. Every interaction. Use this as inspiration as you set out to support your students as memoirists, six-word storywriters, and storytellers.

Jesse Filimon. 2012. *Belonging—A Short Film*. Available at https://www. youtube.com/watch?v=oeB6uxu57ss.

Do you ever feel like a red pyramid in a green-cube world? This short film so eloquently captures what it feels like to be stigmatized, to feel alone, searching for a space of belonging. Written and produced by a student, this film is nothing short of visionary. It is one I share widely with teachers and students of all ages.

Akira Kurosawa, dir. 1990. *Dreams* (*Motion picture*). Burbank, CA: Warner Brothers.

I often think about the power of dreams—that is, the stories of our night worlds and the stories we are lost in when we are supposed to be doing something else. Yet, I also think about dreams we have for ourselves and how some dreams are realized and others are forgotten. What dreamlike narratives live inside our students? What are their hopes for themselves and the world, and what do they imagine that they know is impossible? Sometimes the greatest and most affecting stories are those that represent a different kind of reality. Kurosawa's *Dreams* is a series of short stories—glimpses into dream worlds and interpretations of what we might hope is possible. Though I recommend viewing the full-length film, powerful clips are available on YouTube.

Bianca Giaever. 2013. *Scared Is Scared* **(***Short film***). Available at https://vimeo. com/58659769.**

Bianca Giaever is a filmmaker redefining the genre. Interweaving video, still images, text, and song, each of her pieces captivates me. Yet, "Scared Is Scared" remains my favorite. The short film captures what I find so fascinating about childhood—a time in our lives where we tell stories with heartfelt characters and imaginary plots with simple messages of hope, friendship, and love. Asa Bear and Toby Mouse have a place in my heart, and I often listen to young children talking, playing, scribbling, and writing, eager to hear about their versions of Asa and Toby.

Howard Zinn, Chris Moore, and Anthony Arnove, dirs. 2009. *The People Speak* **(***Motion picture***). Hollywood, CA: Artfire Films.**

The work of Howard Zinn has had a large influence on the way I view American history as the story of collective action and uprising. In his film *The People Speak*, we watch historical figures come to life through the voices of known actors. Any teacher of social studies needs to view this film (clips are available on YouTube). Watch with students to notice the power of words and the use of each actor's voice and body to portray struggle as well as hope. Use this as a mentor text to encourage students to portray historical figures that they have researched. How can they embody their words to make history come to life?

TED Talks

Adichie, Chimamanda Ngozi. 2009. "Chimamanda Ngozi Adichie: The Danger of a Single Story." Available at http://www.ted.com/talks/chimamanda_ adichie_the_danger_of_a_single_story.

As a young white girl, I was privileged to see myself in stories over and over again. To see myself on book covers. In movies. In advertisements. Chimamanda Ngozi Adichie powerfully reminds us of the danger of a single narrative and the underrepresentation of characters of color in the literary landscape. For every child who sees herself, there are countless others looking and wondering whether their story counts.

Brown, Brené. 2010a. "Brené Brown: The Power of Vulnerability." Available at http://www.ted.com/talks/brene_brown_on_vulnerability?language=en.

Profoundly affecting—I don't know if there is any other lecture I've watched that has fueled me as much as Brené Brown's. "The Power of Vulnerability" has helped me think about my own life and the impact of social and cultural forces on how we live. Brown reminds us of the gift that vulnerability brings to us as humans. As teachers, we can interpret her talk in our own context and think about the need for a pedagogy of vulnerability for ourselves and, more important, for our students.

Carr-Chellman, Ali. 2010. "Ali Carr-Chellman: Gaming to Reengage Boys in Learning." Available at http://www.ted.com/talks/ali_carr_chellman_gaming_to_re_engage_boys_in_learning?language=en.

Ali Carr-Chellman convincingly examines the systematic and systemic culture in schools that tells boys again and again that school is not a place for them. As our early childhood spaces become more academicized, we continuously position school as a place for girls. If you are a boy, you know what I mean. If you are a mother or father of boys, you know what I mean. Active, imaginative, often game-based play as a way to learn is often "othered" in school—if not outright demonized. Watch this talk and consider the times you might have told a boy he couldn't play, write, or draw something that was in all likelihood a simple part of what it means to be a boy. In what ways do we turn off readers and writers by privileging realistic fiction over fantasy or science fiction? In what ways do we limit boys' participation when we say Pokemon, sports, or video games aren't part of the classroom discourse? Carr-Chellman's findings from the 100 Girl Project are startling. A must-see for all teachers.

Winkler, Matthew. 2012. "What Makes a Hero?" Available at http://ed.ted.com/lessons/what-makes-a-hero-matthew-winkler.

What makes a hero? In this TED-Ed video, Matthew Winkler analyzes Joseph Campbell's work on the hero's journey. Using graphics alongside his powerful voice, Winkler considers the universal themes and sequential and predictable nature of stories both ancient and contemporary. This is a video that should be watched again and again with students as they interpret complex narratives and write their own.

This I Believe Essays

Ali, Muhammad. 2009. "I Am Still the Greatest." *This I Believe*, April 6. Available at http://www.npr.org/templates/story/story.php?storyId=102649267.

I think of Muhammad Ali in two ways: as a champion and as a survivor. His *This I Believe* essay complicates this duality and encourages us to rethink how we position other people and even ourselves. What we believe is possible in our own lives can be either limiting or liberating.

Allen, Phyllis. 2005. "Leaving Identity Issues to Other Folks." *This I Believe*, July 11. Available at http://www.npr.org/templates/story/story.php?storyId=4738649.

Is identity about who we think we are or how others view us? Phyllis Allen focuses inward and offers a definition of identity that can help students see identity issues as other people's problems. The mental stress that society can inflict on people is powerful and sometimes debilitating for young people. Allen's essay offers inspiration for talking back to "other folks" in empowering ways.

Yu, Ying Ying. 2006. "A Duty to Family, Heritage, and Culture." *This I Believe*, **July 17. Available at http://www.npr.org/templates/story/story. php?storyId=5552257.**

Our families' influence on the way we live and the responsibilities we have is formative. I turn to Ying Ying Yu's essay to explore with students how our beliefs are shaped by the beliefs of those in our own lives. As a result, our beliefs are deeply personal and culturally and socially rooted.

Songs

Bareilles, Sara. 2013. "Brave." *The Blessed Unrest.*

Even better than Sara Bareilles's song "Brave" is the music video. The lyrics celebrate the small acts of bravery we perform each day, and the video joyfully shows people of all backgrounds dancing in the streets and embracing their own vulnerability in the process. Why not begin to support students as close readers with texts like "Brave"? Use this song as an anchor text for noticing bravery in other texts of increasing complexity as well as celebrating small acts of everyday bravery.

Beatles. 1968. "Blackbird." *The White Album.*

My husband taught himself to play the guitar, and this is one of the first songs he learned. So, this song has made an impression on me, but I also love to watch it make an impression on young people learning about symbolism for the first time. Are they a blackbird flying? In what ways? Meant to be played slowly to enunciate each sound and syllable, this song reminds us to tend to ourselves. It's a song of hope and wide-awakeness.

Graphics and Paintings

Coats, Emma. "Pixar's 22 Rules of Storytelling." *Story Shots* **(Blog). Available at http://storyshots.tumblr.com/post/25032057278/22-storybasics-ive-picked-up-in-my-time-at-pixar.**

The rules themselves are incredibly powerful, but graphic artists across the digital landscape have taken up Emma Coats's words and added memorable graphics. Search them and find your favorite to hang in your classroom. Use them as a springboard for writing your own rules for storytelling. Which is your favorite rule? Which are your students' favorite rules? Why?

Goya, Francisco. 1814. *El Tres de Mayo de 1808 en Madrid* **(Painting).**

Revolution is a human phenomena. As people who inherently want justice, we historically gather to enact change. I often pair Goya's painting with Paul Revere's (1770) etching *The Bloody Massacre in*

King Street. Together, they serve as an overview of the ways revolution has stayed the same as well as how it has changed over time. Notice the central figures in each artwork and the way Goya uses light to frame the Revolutionary leader.

Lange, Dorothea. 1936. *Migrant Mother* (Photograph).

When I teach units on character development, I use Dorothea Lange's famed photograph of the migrant mother to explore internal thinking. What do we see in her face? What do we notice about her hands? Her eyes? Her clothing? How does she make us feel? What is her story and the story of her children? How do we know?

Leger, Fernand. 1919. *The City* (Painting).

When I teach about setting, I look to both realism and the abstract. Leger's city has a rhythmic palette, angular lines, and repetition that parallels life in the city. Often, I find that paintings serve as a visual prompt to encourage writers to say more about the place where their characters live. Paintings such as Leger's also help whole classes of students to quickly take to the page and say something about what they see. The abstract nature of the work allows many possibilities to unfold.

Picasso, Pablo. 1937. *Guernica* (Painting).

Aesthetics are often personal. I like to use Picasso's *Guernica* to discuss struggle, power, and positioning. The stark black-and-white palette lets us focus on the human emotion captured on the canvas.

Van Gogh, Vincent. 1890. *Wheat Field with Crows* (Painting).

Used as a companion piece with Kurosawa's (1990) *Dreams*, I use Van Gogh's work to help students imagine what's happening in the scene. Who might be there? What might they be thinking? How would we describe the day as it appears before us? I also often use Van Gogh's landscapes as a springboard for student poetry. Students focus on what they see and—before they know it—they have a list poem.

Websites

Harris, Jonathan. 2015. Cowbird. www.cowbird.com.

Cowbird offers teachers an endless supply of storytelling tools. The photographs and written texts can serve as mentor texts and inspire us to join the dialogue unfolding in real time, all the time.

Harris, Jonathan, and Sep Kamvar. 2015. We Feel Fine. www.wefeelfine.org.

How do you feel at this moment? How do others feel? Want to find out? In their exploratory site,

Jon Harris and Sep Kamvar have built a digital representation of human feeling, constantly updated according to the feelings projected in the blogosphere. They've redefined data. A source of wonder and inspiration, We Feel Fine lets us know that we are not alone, that our feelings are valid, and that they are worthy of writing about and exploring in new ways.

SMITH. Say It in Six. www.sixwordmemoirs.com.

SMITH magazine's Say It in Six site is an ever-evolving collection of six-word stories organized by theme. Use this as an inspiration for six-word student memoirs, six-word character memoirs, and six-word synthesis statements. The framework can serve as a methodology for embracing boundaries as sites for creativity. What about four-word stories, eight-word stories, twenty-word stories?

Stanton, Brandon. 2015. _Humans of New York_. www.humansofnewyork.com.

Humans of New York is a photoblog that documents stories told by everyday New Yorkers, catalogued and curated by Brandon Stanton. Follow the blog. Follow the Facebook page. Consider using it as inspiration for Humans of Our Classroom or Humans of Our School. Consider what the photos and statements reveal about the repertoire of human emotion. Consider what the photos and statements reveal about the identities of the individuals and about our collective experience.

References

Children's and Young Adult Literature

Ahlberg, Allan. 1991. *Heard It in the Playground*. New York: Puffin Books.

Alborough, Jez. 2009. *Hug*. Cambridge, MA: Candlewick.

Alcott, Louisa May. 1880. *Little Women*. Boston: Roberts Brothers.

Alexander, Kwame. 2014. *The Crossover*. Boston: HMH Books for Young Readers.

Anderson, Laurie Halse. 2011. *Chains*. New York: Atheneum.

Applegate, Katherine. 2012. *The One and Only Ivan*. New York: HarperCollins.

Atwood, Margaret. 1985. *The Handmaid's Tale*. Toronto, Ontario: McClelland and Stewart.

Avi. 2002. *Crispin: The Cross of Lead*. New York: Hyperion Books.

Bartoletti, Susan Campbell. 2008. *The Boy Who Dared*. New York: Scholastic.

Baylor, Byrd. 1985. *Everybody Needs a Rock*. New York: Aladdin.

Berne, Jennifer. 2013. *On a Beam of Light: A Story of Albert Einstein*. San Francisco: Chronicle Books.

Boelts, Maribeth. 2007. *Those Shoes*. Somerville, MA: Candlewick.

Browne, Anthony. 1998. *Voices in the Park*. London: DK.

Bulla, Clyde Robert. 1987. *The Chalkbox Kid*. New York: Random House Books for Young Readers.

Bunting, Eve. 1999. *Smoky Night*. New York: HMH Books for Young Readers.

Burdett, Lois. 1996. *Macbeth for Kids* (Shakespeare Can Be Fun! series). Ontario, Canada: Firefly Books.

———. 1999. *The Tempest for Kids* (Shakespeare Can Be Fun! series). Ontario, Canada: Firefly Books.

Carroll, Lewis. 1865. *Alice in Wonderland*. New York: MacMillan.

Choi, Yangsook. 2003. *The Name Jar*. Decorah, IA: Dragonfly Books.

Clements, Andrew. 1996. *Frindle*. New York: Simon and Schuster.

———. 2001. *The Janitor's Boy*. New York: Simon and Schuster.

Collier, Christopher, and James Lincoln Collier. 1974. *My Brother Sam Is Dead*. New York: Scholastic.

Collins, Suzanne. 2008. The *Hunger Games*. New York: Scholastic.

Creech, Sharon. 1994. *Walk Two Moons*. New York: HarperCollins.

———. 2001. *Love That Dog*. New York: HarperCollins.

Cronin, Doreen. 2000. *Click, Clack, Moo: Cows That Type*. New York: Atheneum.

dePaola, Tomie. 1978. *Pancakes for Breakfast*. Boston: Houghton Mifflin Harcourt.

Elliot, Zetta. 2008. *Bird*. New York: Lee and Low Books.

Ellis, Deborah. 2000. *The Breadwinner*. Toronto, Ontario: Groundwood Books.

———. 2012. *Kids of Kabul: Living Bravely Through a Never-Ending War*. Ontario: Groundwood Books.

Erskine, Kathryn. 2010. *Mockingbird*. New York: Penguin Young Readers Group.

Fleischman, Paul. 1988. *Joyful Noise: Poems for Two Voices*. New York: Harper Trophy.

———. 1997. *Seedfolks*. New York: Joanna Cotler Books.

Fletcher, Ralph. 2012. *Marshfield Dreams: When I Was a Kid*. New York: Square Fish.

Forbes, Esther. 1943. *Johnny Tremain*. Boston: Houghton Mifflin Harcourt.

Gannett, Ruth Stiles. 1948. My Father's Dragon series. New York: Random House.

Gonzalez, Maya Christina. 2007. *My Colors, My World/Mis Colores, Mi Mundo*. San Francisco: Children's Book Press.

Grimes, Nikki. 2002. *Bronx Masquerade*. New York: Penguin Young Readers Group.

Hoffman, Mary. 1991. *Amazing Grace*. New York: Dial Books for Young Readers.

Idle, Molly. 2013. *Flora and the Flamingo*. San Francisco: Chronicle Books.

Jeffers, Oliver. 2012. *This Moose Belongs to Me*. New York: HarperCollins.

Jiménez, Francisco. 1997. *The Circuit: Stories from the Life of a Migrant Child*. Albuquerque: University of New Mexico Press.

Khan, Rukhsana. 2014. *King for a Day*. New York: Lee and Low Books.

Konigsburg, E. L. 1967. *From the Mixed-Up Files of Mrs. Basil E. Frankweiler*. New York: Atheneum Books.

Lehman, Barbara. 2004. *The Red Book*. Boston: HMH Books for Young Readers.

Lester, Julius. 2005. *Let's Talk About Race*. New York: HarperCollins.

Lewis, C. S. 1950. *The Lion, the Witch and the Wardrobe*. London: Geoffrey Bles.

Lionni, Leo. 1995. *Matthew's Dream*. Decorah, IA: Dragonfly Books.

Lobel, Arnold. 1970. *Frog and Toad Are Friends*. New York: HarperCollins.

———. 1980. *Fables*. New York: HarperCollins.

Lopez, Barry. 1998. *Crow and Weasel*. New York: zinnSquare Fish.

Lowry, Lois. 1993. *The Giver*. Boston: Houghton Mifflin Harcourt.

Markel, Michelle. 2013. *Brave Girl: Clara and the Shirtwaist Makers' Strike of 1909*. New York: HarperCollins.

Mead, Alice. 1995. *Junebug*. New York: Yearling.

Merriam, Eve. 1964. "How to Eat a Poem." *It Doesn't Always Have to Rhyme*. New York: Atheneum Books.

Meyer, Stephenie. 2005. *Twilight*. New York: Little, Brown.

Mochizuki, Ken. 1993. *Baseball Saved Us*. New York: Lee and Low Books.

Montgomery, L. M. 1908. *Anne of Green Gables*. Boston: L. C. Page and Co.

Mora, Pat. 1996. *Confetti: Poems for Children*. New York: Lee and Low Books.

Munson, Derek. 2000. *Enemy Pie*. San Francisco: Chronicle Books.

Myers, Walter Dean. 2002. *Bad Boy: A Memoir*. New York: Amistad.

———. 2004. *Monster*. New York: HarperCollins.

Palacio, R. J. 2012. *Wonder*. New York: Random House.

Philbrick, Rodman. 1993. *Freak the Mighty*. New York: Scholastic.

Pinkney, Jerry. 2013. *The Tortoise and the Hare*. New York: Little, Brown Books for Young Readers.

Polacco, Patricia. 1994. *Pink and Say*. New York: Philomel Books.

Pullman, Philip. 1995. *Northern Lights*. New York: Scholastic.

Rathmann, Peggy. 1996. *Good Night, Gorilla*. New York: G. P. Putnam's Sons.

Reynolds, Peter. 2002. *Ish*. Cambridge, MA: Candlewick.

———. 2003. *The Dot*. Cambridge, MA: Candlewick.

Richardson, Justin, and Peter Parnell. 2005. *And Tango Makes Three*. New York: Simon and Schuster.

Rowling, J. K. 2001. *Harry Potter and the Sorcerer's Stone*. New York: Scholastic.

Schroeder, Alan. 2012. *Baby Flo: Florence Mills Lights Up the Stage*. New York: Lee and Low Books.

Selden, George. 1960. *The Cricket in Times Square*. New York: Yearling Books.

Sendak, Maurice. 1963. *Where the Wild Things Are*. New York: HarperCollins.

Snicket, Lemony. 1999. *The Bad Beginning*. New York: HarperCollins.

Spinelli, Jerry. 1997. *Wringer*. New York: HarperCollins.

———. 1998. *Knots in My Yo-Yo String*. New York: Ember.

Steig, William. 1971. *Amos and Boris*. New York: Farrar, Straus and Giroux.

Stone, Tanya Lee. 2013. *Who Says Women Can't Be Doctors? The Story of Elizabeth Blackwell*. New York: Henry Holt.

Tan, Shaun. 2007. *The Arrival*. New York: Arthur A. Levine Books.

———. 2014. *Rules of Summer*. New York: Arthur A. Levine Books.

Weston, Mark. 2014. *Honda: The Boy Who Dreamed of Cars*. New York: Lee and Low Books.

Whelan, Gloria. 2000. *Homeless Bird*. New York: HarperCollins.

White, E. B. 1945. *Stuart Little*. New York: Harper and Brothers.

——. 1952. *Charlotte's Web*. New York: Harper and Brothers.

Wiesner, David. 2006. *Flotsam*. Boston: Houghton Mifflin Harcourt.

——. 2011. *Tuesday*. Boston: Houghton Mifflin Harcourt.

Willems, Mo. 2004. *Knuffle Bunny: A Cautionary Tale*. New York: Hyperion.

——. 2007. *Knuffle Bunny Too: A Case of Mistaken Identity*. New York: Hyperion.

——. 2010. *Knuffle Bunny Free: An Unexpected Diversion*. New York: Hyperion.

Winter, Jeanette. 2004. *September Roses*. New York: Farrar, Straus and Giroux.

——. 2005. *The Librarian of Basra*. Boston: Houghton Mifflin Harcourt.

——. 2014. *Malala: A Brave Girl from Pakistan/Iqbal: A Brave Boy from Pakistan*. San Diego: Beach Lane Books.

Wise, Bill, and Adam Gustavson. 2012. *Silent Star: The Story of Deaf Major Leaguer William Hoy*. New York: Lee and Low Books.

Woodson, Jacqueline. 2014. *Brown Girl Dreaming*. New York: Nancy Paulsen Books.

Worth, Valerie. 1996. *All the Small Poems and Fourteen More*. New York: Square Fish.

Yang, Gene Luen. 2008. *American Born Chinese*. New York: First Second Books.

Yoo, Paula. 2005. *Sixteen Years in Sixteen Seconds: The Sammy Lee Story*. New York: Lee and Low Books.

Young, Ed. 1996. *Lon Po Po: A Red-Riding Hood Story from China*. New York: Penguin Putnam.

Professional Literature

Abate, Michelle Ann. 2014. "Children's Books Should Offer a Political Primer." *New York Times*, June 10. http://www.nytimes.com/roomfordebate/2014/07/09/should-books-for-childrens-be-political/childrens-books-should-offer-a-political-primer.

Allyn, Pam. 2015. "Diversity Is the Heartbeat of Our Humanity." edu@scholastic. http://edublog.scholastic.com/post/diversity-heartbeat-our-humanity.

Asian American Performers Action Coalition. 2012. "Ethnic Make-Up of Casts from Broadway and Non Profit Theaters." http://www.aapacnyc.org/stats-2011-2012.html.

Banyan Global Learning. 2015. *Big Dayta Project*. Banyan Global Learning. http://bigdayta.weebly.com/.

Barnhouse, Dorothy. 2014. *Readers Front and Center: Helping All Students Engage with Complex Texts*. Portland, ME: Stenhouse.

Beers, Kylene, and Robert Probst. 2012. *Notice and Note: Strategies for Close Reading*. Portsmouth, NH: Heinemann.

Bishop, Rudine Sims. 1990. "Mirrors, Windows, and Sliding Glass Doors." *Perspectives: Choosing and Using Books for the Classroom* 6(3): ix-xi.

Bomer, Randy, and Katherine Bomer. 2001. *For a Better World: Reading and Writing for Social Action*. Portsmouth, NH: Heinemann.

Bosman, J. 2010. "Picture Books No Longer a Staple for Children." *New York Times*, October 7.

Bridges, Lois. 2013. "The Having of Grand Conversations." edu@scholastic. edublog.scholastic.com/post/having-grand-conversations.

Campbell, Richard, Christopher R. Martin, and Bettina Fabos. 2013. *Media and Culture: Mass Communication in a Digital Age*. 9th ed. New York: Bedford/St. Martin's.

Cappiello, Mary Ann, and Erika Thulin Dawes. 2013. *Teaching with Text Sets*. Huntington Beach, CA: Shell Education.

Cappiello, Mary Ann, Erika Thulin Dawes, Grace Enriquez, and Katherine Cunningham. 2010-2015. *The Classroom Bookshelf* (Blog). www.classroombookshelf.blogspot.com.

Cooperative Children's Book Center. "2014 Multicultural Literature Statistics from the Cooperative Children's Book Center." http://www.cbcbooks.org/2014-multicultural-literature-statistics-from-the-cooperative-childrens-book-center/.

Costa, Arthur, and Bena Kallick. 2009. *Habits of Mind Across the Curriculum: Practical and Creative Strategies for Teachers*. Alexandria, VA: Association for Supervision and Curriculum Development.

Council of the Great City Schools. 2010. "Urban School Statistics." Council of the Great City Schools. http://www.cgcs.org/Page/75.

Culham, Ruth. 2014. *The Writing Thief*. Newark, DE: International Reading Association.

Cunningham, Katherine Egan, and Suzanne Farrell Smith. 2013. "Creativity Matters: The 7/6 Project and the Edges that Expand Writing." *The English Record* 63(1): 132-142.

Dorfman, Lynne, and Rose Cappelli. 2007. *Mentor Texts: Teaching Writing Through Children's Literature, K–6*. Portland, ME: Stenhouse.

———. 2009. *Nonfiction Mentor Texts: Teaching Informational Writing Through Children's Literature, K–8*. Portland, ME: Stenhouse.

Eeds, Maryann, and Ralph Peterson. 1989. *Grand Conversation: Literature Groups in Action*. New York: Scholastic.

Fletcher, Ralph. 2011. *Mentor Author, Mentor Texts*. Portsmouth, NH: Heinemann.

Frey, Nancy, and Douglas Fisher. 2012. *Text Complexity: Raising Rigor in Reading*. Newark, DE: International Reading Association.

Gallagher, Kelly. 2009. *Readicide: How Schools Are Killing Reading and What You Can Do About It*. Portland, ME: Stenhouse.

Gangi, Jane. 2008. "The Unbearable Whiteness of Literacy Instruction: Realizing the Implications of the Proficient Reader Research." *Multicultural Review* 17(2): 30-35.

Goldstone, Bette P. 2004. "The Postmodern Picture Book: A New Subgenre." *Language Arts* 81(3): 196-204.

Gottschall, Jonathan. 2013. *The Storytelling Animal: How Stories Make Us Human*. Thornwood, NY: Mariner Books.

Greene, Maxine. 1998. "Introduction: Teaching for Social Justice." In *Teaching for Social Justice*, ed. William Ayers, Jean Ann Hunt, and Therese Quinn. New York: The New Press.

Holdaway, Donald. 1979. *The Foundations of Literacy*. New York: Scholastic.

Heard, Georgia. 1998. *Awakening the Heart: Exploring Poetry in Elementary and Middle School*. Portsmouth, NH: Heinemann.

Jacob Burns Film Center. 2014. "Visual Glossary." Jacob Burns Film Center. https://education.burnsfilmcenter.org/education/visual-glossary/featured.

Lee and Low Books. 2015. "The Diversity Gap in Children's Books." http://blog.leeandlow.com/2015/03/05/the-diversity-gap-in-childrens-publishing-2015/.

Lehman, Chris, and Kathleen Roberts. 2013. *Falling in Love with Close Reading: Lessons for Analyzing Texts—and Life*. Portsmouth, NH: Heinemann.

Lemov, Doug. 2014. *Teach Like a Champion, 2.0: 62 Techniques That Put Students on the Path Toward College*. San Francisco: Jossey-Bass.

Madden, Mary, Amanda Lenhart, Maeve Duggan, Sandra Cortesi, and Urs Gasser. 2013. *Teens and Technology* 2013. Washington, DC: Pew Research Center. http://www.pewinternet.org/2013/03/13/teens-and-technology-2013/.

Miller, Brenda. 2011. "A Case Against Courage in Creative Nonfiction." *Writer's Chronicle* 2 (October/November): 80-92.

Mills, Claudia. 2014. "Children's Books Should Avoid Propaganda." *New York Times*, July 9. http://www.nytimes.com/roomfordebate/2014/07/09/should-books-for-childrens-be-political/childrens-books-should-avoid-propaganda.

Myers, Christopher. 2014. "The Apartheid of Children's Literature." *New York Times*, March 15.

Myers, Walter Dean. 2014. "Where Are the People of Color in Children's Books?" *New York Times*, March 15.

National Center for Education Statistics. 2014. "The Condition of Education." National Center for Education Statistics. nces.ed.gov/pubs2014/2014083.pdf.

Newkirk, Thomas. 2014. *Minds Made for Stories: How We Really Read and Write Informational and Persuasive Texts*. Portsmouth, NH: Heinemann.

Nieto, Sonia, Stephen Gordon, and Junia Yearwood. 2002. "Teachers' Experiences in a Critical Inquiry Group: A Conversation in Three Voices." *Teaching Education* 13(3): 341-355.

Paley, Vivian. 2014. *Boys and Girls: Superheroes in the Doll Corner*. Chicago: University of Chicago Press.

Pearson, P. David, and Margaret C. Gallagher. 1983. "The Gradual Release of Responsibility Model of Instruction." *Contemporary Educational Psychology* 8: 112–123.

Rideout, Victoria. 2012. *Social Media, Social Life: How Teens View Their Digital Lives*. New York: Common Sense Media. https://www.commonsensemedia.org/research/social-media-social-life-how-teens-view-their-digital-lives.

Schneider, Veronica. 2014. "Is TV Getting More Diverse? Not by the Look of This Year's Emmys." *The Open Book* (Blog). http://blog.leeandlow.com/2014/08/29/is-tv-getting-more-diverse-not-by-the-look-of-this-years-emmys/.

Schumacher, John. 2015. "Newbery Medalist Kwame Alexander." *Mr. Schu Reads* (Blog). February 6. http://mrschureads.blogspot.com/2015/02/newbery-medalist-kwame-alexander.html.

Serafini, Frank. 2009. *Interactive Comprehension Strategies: Fostering Meaningful Talk about Text*. New York: Scholastic.

Short, Kathy. 2013. Story as the Landscape of Knowing. Call for Proposals. National Council of Teachers of English. http://www.ncte.org/annual/call.

Trelease, Jim. 2009. "Why Read Aloud to Children?" Retrieved from http://www.trelease-on-reading.com/read-aloud-brochure.pdf.

——. 2013. *The Read-Aloud Handbook*. 7th ed. New York: Penguin.

Additional Influential Texts

Achenbach, Shane. 2012. "A Teen Confronts Her iPhone Addiction." *Washington Post*, October 22.

Adichie, Chimamanda Ngozi. 2009. "Chimamanda Ngozi Adichie: The Danger of a Single Story." http://www.ted.com/talks/chimamanda_adichie_the_danger_of_a_single_story.

Ali, Muhammad. 2009. "I Am Still the Greatest." *This I Believe*. April 6. http://www.npr.org/templates/story/story.php?storyId=102649267.

Allen, Phyllis. 2005. "Leaving Identity Issues to Other Folks." *This I Believe*. July 11. http://www.npr.org/templates/story/story.php?storyId=4738649.

Alter, Adam. 2013. "Where We Are Shapes Who We Are." *New York Times*, June 16.

Angelou, Maya. 1975. "Alone." In *Oh Pray My Wings Are Gonna Fit Me Well*. New York: Random House.

——. 1983. "Caged Bird." In *Shaker, Why Don't You Sing?* New York: Random House.

Baker, Russell. 1982. *Growing Up*. East Rutherford, NJ: Signet.

Bareilles, Sara. 2013. "Brave." *The Blessed Unrest*. Epic Records.

The Beatles. 1967. "When I'm Sixty Four." *Sgt. Pepper's Lonely Hearts Club Band*. Capitol Records.

———. 1968. "Blackbird." *The White Album*. Capitol Records.

Brand, Stewart. 2013. "The Case for Reviving Extinct Species." *National Geographic News*. March 12. http://news.nationalgeographic.com/news/2013/03/130311-deextinction-reviving-extinct-species-opinion-animals-science/.

Brown, Brené. 2010a. "Brené Brown: The Power of Vulnerability." http://www.ted.com/talks/brene_brown_on_vulnerability?language=en.

———. 2010b. *The Gifts of Imperfection*. Center City, MN: Hazelden.

———. 2012. *Daring Greatly: How the Courage to Be Vulnerable Transforms the Way We Live, Love, Parent, and Lead*. New York: Gotham.

Brown, Jeffrey. 2014. "From Author to Ambassador: Kate DiCamillo Approaches Reading with Celebration." *PBS Newshour*. http://www.pbs.org/newshour/bb/entertainment-jan-june14-literature_01-10/.

Burns, Catherine, and Jay Allison. 2015. *The Moth Radio Hour*. http://themoth.org/radio.

Campbell, Joseph. 2008. *The Hero with a Thousand Faces*. 3rd ed. Novato, CA: New World Library.

Carr-Chellman, Ali. 2010. "Ali Carr-Chellman: Gaming to Reengage Boys in Learning." http://www.ted.com/talks/ali_carr_chellman_gaming_to_re_engage_boys_in_learning?language=en.

Coats, Emma. 2013. "Pixar's 22 Rules of Storytelling." *Story Shots* (Blog). http://storyshots.tumblr.com/post/25032057278/22-storybasics-ive-picked-up-in-my-time-at-pixar.

Cohen, Adam. 2012. "A Back-to-School Fight Over the Right to Classroom Prayer." *Time*, August 28. http://ideas.time.com/2012/08/28/a-back-to-school-fight-over-the-right-to-classroom-prayer/.

Collins, Billy. 1995. "On Turning Ten." In *The Art of Drowning*. Pittsburgh, PA: University of Pittsburgh Press.

Collins, Phil. 1984. "Against All Odds." *Against All Odds: Music from the Original Motion Picture Soundtrack*. Atlantic Records.

Constantino, Bobby. 2013. "I Got Myself Arrested So I Could Look Inside the Justice System." *Atlantic*, December 17. http://www.theatlantic.com/national/archive/2013/12/i-got-myself-arrested-so-i-could-look-inside-the-justice-system/282360/.

Corrigan, Maureen. 2011. "How E. B. White Spun Charlotte's Web." *Fresh Air*. http://www.npr.org/2011/07/05/137452030/how-e-b-white-spun-charlottes-web.

Davis, Katy (dir.). 2013. *The Power of Empathy: Brené Brown on Empathy* (Short film). https://vimeo.com/81492863.

Dickinson, Emily. 1999. "They Shut Me Up in Prose." In *The Poems of Emily Dickinson*, ed. R. W. Franklin. Cambridge, MA: Harvard University Press.

DJ Danger Mouse. 2004. *The Grey Album*.

Dostoyevsky, Fyodor. (1866) 1956. *Crime and Punishment*. Reprint, New York: Random House.

Druckerman, Pamela. 2014. *Bringing Up Bebe: One American Mother Discovers the Wisdom of French Parenting*. New York: Penguin.

Dweck, Carol. 2007. *Mindset: The New Psychology of Success*. New York: Ballantine.

Dylan, Bob. 1973. "Forever Young." *Planet Waves*. Asylum Records.

Emerson, Ralph Waldo. (1841) 1981. "Self-Reliance." In *Emerson's Essays*. New York: HarperPerennial.

Filimon, Jesse. 2012. *Belonging—A Short Film*. https://www.youtube.com/watch?v=0eB6uxu57ss.

Frankston, Jay. 2013. "Speak Up." *This I Believe*. April 12. http://thisibelieve.org/essay/105932/.

Fritz, Thomas, Sebastian Jentschke, Nathalie Gosselin, Daniella Sammler, Robert Turner, Angela Friederici, and Stepen Koelsch. 2009. "Universal Recognition of Three Basic Emotions in Music." *Current Biology* 19(7): 573 576.

Gaiman, Neil. 1996. *Neverwhere*. London: BBC Books.

——. 2010. *Fragile Things: Short Fictions and Wonders*. New York: Harper.

Giaever, Bianca. 2013. *Scared Is Scared* (Short film). https://vimeo.com/58659769.

Gilbert, Elizabeth. 2014. "Elizabeth Gilbert: Success, Failure, and the Drive to Keep Creating." http://www.ted.com/talks/elizabeth_gilbert_success_failure_and_the_drive_to_keep_creating.

Gladwell, Malcolm. 2004. "Malcolm Gladwell: Choice, Happiness, and Spaghetti Sauce." http://www.ted.com/talks/malcolm_gladwell_on_spaghetti_sauce?language=en.

Glass, Ira. 2007. "339: Break-Up." *This American Life*. Chicago: Chicago Public Media.

Google. 2014. Doodle4Google. "If I Could Invent One Thing to Make the World a Better Place." http://www.google.com/doodle4google/.

Goya, Francisco. 1814. *El Tres de Mayo de 1808 en Madrid* (Painting).

Grant, Alice (prod.). 2011. TMB Panyee FC Short Film. https://www.youtube.com/watch?v=jU40A3kkAWU

Grazer, Brian. 2006. "Disrupting My Comfort Zone." *This I Believe*. January 6. http://www.npr.org/templates/story/story.php?storyId=5508283.

Grimaldi, Christine. 2013. "Can Hailing a Ride Really Be About Making Friends Again?" *Atlantic: CityLab*. November 18. http://www.citylab.com/commute/2013/11/can-hailing-ride-really-be-about-making-friends-again/7608/.

Harris, Jonathan. 2015. Cowbird (Website). www.cowbird.com.

Harris, Jonathan, and Sep Kamvar. 2015. We Feel Fine (Website). www.feelfine.org.

Hemingway, Ernest. 1952. *The Old Man and the Sea*. New York: Charles Scribner's Sons.

Hirsh, Lee. 2011. *Bully* (Documentary film). New York: The Weinstein Company.

Horgan, John. 2012. "A Network to Build a Dream On." *Wall Street Journal*, September 14. http://www.wsj.com/news/articles/SB10000872396390443819404577635344157787180.

Hughes, Langston. (1945) 2004. "I, Too." In *The Collected Poems of Langston Hughes*. New York: Knopf and Vintage Books.

———. (1951) 2004. "Theme for English B." In *The Collected Poems of Langston Hughes*. New York: Knopf and Vintage Books.

Jobs, Steve. 2005. "Steve Jobs: How to Live Before You Die." http://www.ted.com/talks/steve_jobs_how_to_live_before_you_die.

Kaetsu, Noboru (prod.). 2003. *Children Full of Life* (Documentary film). Japan Broadcasting Company.

Keegan, Marina. 2014. *The Opposite of Loneliness: Essays and Stories*. New York: Scribner.

Kid President. 2013. "I Think We All Need a Pep Talk." https://www.ted.com/talks/kid_president_i_think_we_all_need_a_pep_talk.

———. 2014. "Letter to a Person on Their First Day Here." https://www.youtube.com/watch?v=l5-EwrhsMzY.

Kiem, Brandon. 2013. "No More Night? The Meaning of the Loss of Darkness." *Wired*, September 12. http://www.wired.com/2013/09/bogard-end-of-night/.

King, Martin Luther, Jr. 1963. "I Have a Dream" (Speech). March on Washington for Jobs and Freedom, Washington, D.C., August 28.

Kipling, Rudyard. (1910) 1963. "If." In *A Choice of Kipling's Verse*. Essex, United Kingdom: Faber and Faber.

Kurosawa, Akira (dir.). 1990. *Dreams* (Motion picture). Burbank, CA: Warner Brothers.

Lange, Dorothea. 1936. *Migrant Mother* (Photograph).

Lawrence, Jacob. 1940/1941. *The Migration of the Negro* (Painting series).

Leger, Fernand. 1919. *The City* (Painting).

Low, Jason. 2013. "Where's the Diversity? The Tony Awards Looks in the Mirror." *The Open Book* (Blog). http://blog.leeandlow.com/2013/06/06/wheres-the-diversity-the-tony-awards-looks-in-the-mirror/.

The Lumineers. 2012. "Flowers in Your Hair." *The Lumineers*. Dualtone.

Mahanta, Siddhartha. 2013. "New York's Looming Food Disaster." *Atlantic: CityLab*. October 21. http://www.citylab.com/politics/2013/10/new-yorks-looming-food-disaster/7294/.

Majeed, Kamaal. 2007. "Being Content with Myself." *This I Believe*. May 7. http://www.npr.org/templates/story/story.php?storyId=10003803.

Mendelberg, Tali, and Christopher F. Karpowitz. 2012. "More Women, but Not Nearly Enough." *New York Times,* November 9.

Mott, Nicholas. 2012. "What Makes Us Human? Cooking, Study Says." *National Geographic News,* October 26. http://news.nationalgeographic.com/news/2012/10/121026-human-cooking-evolution-raw-food-health-science/.

Munch, Edvard. 1895. *The Scream* (Painting).

Nagle, Robin. 2013. "Material Remains: The Perpetual Challenge of Garbage." *Scientific American*, October 25. http://www.scientificamerican.com/article/material-remains-the-perpetual-challenge-of-garbage/.

Neruda. Pablo. 2013. *All the Odes: A Bilingual Edition*. New York: Farrar, Straus and Giroux.

Nye, Naomi Shihab. 1992. *The Same Sky: A Collection of Poems from Around the World*. New York: Simon and Schuster.

———. 1994. "So Much Happiness." In *Words Under the Words: Selected Poems*. Minneapolis, MN: Eighth Mountain Press.

Nyong'o, Lupita. 2014. "Black Women in Hollywood" Acceptance Speech. February 27. http://www.essence.com/2014/02/27/lupita-nyongo-delivers-moving-black-women-hollywood-acceptance-speech/.

Obama, Barack. 2010. University of Michigan Commencement Speech. http://www.huffingtonpost.com/2010/05/01/obama-michigan-graduation_n_559688.html.

———. 2013. Second Inaugural Address. January 21. https://www.whitehouse.gov/the-press-office/2013/01/21/inaugural-address-president-barack-obama.

Oliver, Jamie. 2010. "Jamie Oliver: Teach Every Child About Food." http://www.ted.com/talks/jamie_oliver?language=en.

Palmer, Brian. 2014. "Why Does China Not Have Famines Anymore?" *Slate.com*. April 2. http://www.slate.com/articles/health_and_science/feed_the_world/2014/04/why_does_china_not_have_famines_anymore_capitalist_and_socialist_reforms.html.

Parker-Pope, Tara. 2009. "What Are Friends For? A Longer Life." *New York Times*, April 20. http://www.nytimes.com/2009/04/21/health/21well.html?_r=0&adxnnl=1&adxnnlx=1427570277-Lv7M6LMSKr3HRKZIbsz9hw.

Parks, Rosa. 1996. "Standing Up to Injustice." *This I Believe*. http://thisibelieve.org/essay/530/.

Paul, Annie Murphy. 2012. "Lessons from the Lab: How to Make Group Projects Successful." *Ideas*: *Time.com*. May 16. http://ideas.time.com/2012/05/16/lessons-from-the-lab-how-to-make-group-projects-successful/.

Pericoli, Matteo. 2013. "Writers as Architects." *New York Times*, August 3. http://opinionator.blogs.nytimes.com/2013/08/03/writers-as-architects/?_r=0.

Picasso, Pablo. 1932. *Girl Before a Mirror* (Painting).

———. 1937. *Guernica* (Painting).

Radiolab. 2009. *16: Moments* (Short film). New York: WNYC Radio. http://www.radiolab.org/story/91918-16-moments/.

Revere, Paul. 1770. *The Bloody Massacre in King Street* (Engraving).

Riddle, Travis. 2013. "How Your Moral Decisions Are Shaped by a Bad Mood." *Scientific American*, March 12. http://www.scientificamerican.com/article/how-your-moral-decisions-shaped-by-mood/.

Rieland, Randy. 2013. "Science Can Help Us Live Longer, but How Long Is Too Long?" *Smithsonian*, August 12. http://www.smithsonianmag.com/innovation/science-can-help-us-live-longer-but-how-long-is-too-long-27677593/?no-ist.

Rodin, Auguste. 1902. *The Thinker* (Sculpture).

Rogers, Fred McFeely. 2002. Dartmouth College Commencement Address. http://www.dartmouth.edu/~news/releases/2002/june/060902c.html.

Rowling, J. K. 2008. Harvard Commencement Address. http://www.ted.com/talks/jk_rowling_the_fringe_benefits_of_failure.

Sandberg, Sheryl. 2010. "Sheryl Sandberg: Why We Have Too Few Women Leaders." http://www.ted.com/talks/sheryl_sandberg_why_we_have_too_few_women_leaders.

Schwartz, Barry. 2005. "Barry Schwartz: The Paradox of Choice." http://www.ted.com/talks/barry_schwartz_on_the_paradox_of_choice.

Segnit, Niki. 2010. *The Flavor Thesaurus: Pairings, Recipes, and Ideas for the Creative Cook*. New York: Bloomsbury.

Shakespeare, William. (1603) 1992. *Hamlet*. New York: Simon and Schuster.

——. (1605) 2004. *A Midsummer Night's Dream*. New York: Simon and Schuster.

——. (1623) 2004. *Twelfth Night*. New York: Simon and Schuster.

Sifferlin, Alexandra. 2013. "Does Your Diet Influence How Well You Sleep?" *Time*, February 7. http://healthland.time.com/2013/02/07/does-your-diet-influence-how-well-you-sleep/.

Sinek, Simon. 2009. "Simon Sinek: How Great Leaders Inspire Action." http://www.ted.com/talks/simon_sinek_how_great_leaders_inspire_action.

——. 2014. "Simon Sinek: Why Good Leaders Make You Feel Safe." http://www.ted.com/talks/simon_sinek_why_good_leaders_make_you_feel_safe.

Singer, Peter. 2013. "The Bitterness of Sugar." *Project Syndicate,* November 11. http://www.project-syndicate.org/commentary/peter-singer-on-corporate-food-giants—responsibility-for-their-suppliers—conduct.

SMITH. Say It in Six (Website). http://www.sixwordmemoirs.com/.

Stanton, Brandan. 2015. *Humans of New York* (Blog). www.humansofnewyork.com.

Stein, Garth. 2009. *The Art of Racing in the Rain*. New York: Harper.

Stevens, Cat. 1970. "Father and Son" and "Trouble." *Tea for the Tillerman*. Island Masters.

Stieglitz, Alfred. 1907. *The Steerage* (Painting).

StoryCorps (Podcast). http://storycorps.org/podcast.

Sullivan, Andrew. 2005. "Life, Liberty, and the Pursuit of Happiness." *This I Believe*. July 4. http://www.npr.org/templates/story/story.php?storyId=4723006.

Taleb, Nassim Nicholas. 2012. *Antifragile: Things That Gain from Disorder*. New York: Random House.

Tartt, Donna. 2013. *The Goldfinch*. New York: Little, Brown and Company.

This I Believe. http://thisibelieve.org/.

Thomas, Will. 2013. "The Birthright of Human Dignity." *This I Believe*. October 11. http://thisibelieve.org/essay/17047/.

Thompson, Helen. 2013. "Google and Twitter Help Track Influenza Outbreaks." *National Geographic Daily News*, January 10. http://news.nationalgeographic.com/news/2013/01/130110-google-twitter-track-flu-cases-health-science/.

Tortajada, Cecilia, and Asit K. Biswas. 2013. "Water Quality: An Ignored Global Crisis." *Business Week*, March 21. http://www.bloomberg.com/bw/articles/2013-03-21/water-quality-an-ignored-global-crisis.

United Nations Commission on Human Rights. 1959. Declaration of the Rights of the Child.

United States Bureau of the Census. 2000. "Language, School Enrollment, and Educational Attainment." http://factfinder.census.gov/faces/tableservices/jsf/pages/productview.xhtml?pid=DEC_00_SF3_GCTP11.US01PR&prodType=table.

Van Gogh, Vincent. 1887. *Bridge in the Rain* (Painting).

———. 1890. *Wheat Field with Crows* (Painting).

Vermeer, Johannes. 1657. *Girl Reading a Letter at an Open Window* (Painting).

———. 1665. *Girl with a Pearl Earring* (Painting).

von Garnier, Kaatja. 2004. *Iron Jawed Angels* (Motion picture). HBO Films.

Wakefield, Jane. 2013. "Tomorrow's Cities: How Big Data Is Changing the World." BBC News. http://www.bbc.com/news/technology-23253949.

Wallich, Paul. 2013. "Modern Families: Chips off the Old Block." *Economist*, January 12. http://www.economist.com/news/international/21569385-tracking-children-has-never-been-easier-nice-parents-not-privacy-chips.

Weir, Peter (dir.). 1989. *Dead Poets Society* (Motion picture). Burbank, CA: Touchstone Pictures.

Whitman, Walt. (1867) 2007. "O Me! O Life!" *Leaves of Grass*. New York: Dover.

———. (1885) 1983. "Song of Myself." *Leaves of Grass*. New York: Bantam Books.

Winkler, Matthew. 2012. "What Makes a Hero?" http://ed.ted.com/lessons/what-makes-a-hero-matthew-winkler.

Woolston, Chris. 2014. "These 5 Foods Will Be Harder to Grow in a Warmer World." *National Geographic*, April 7. http://news.nationalgeographic.com/news/2014/04/140406-climate-change-ipcc-report-foods-chipotle-guacamole/.

Yu, Ying Ying. 2006. "A Duty to Family, Heritage, and Culture." *This I Believe*. July 17. http://www.npr.org/templates/story/story.php?storyId=5552257.

Zinn, Howard, Chris Moore, and Anthony Arnove (dirs.). 2009. *The People Speak* (Motion picture). Hollywood, CA: Artfire Films.

Zuckerman, Mortimer B. 2013. "50 Feet from MLK." *U.S. News and World Report*, August 28. http://www.usnews.com/opinion/mzuckerman/articles/2013/08/28/50-feet-from-martin-luther-king-jrs-i-have-a-dream-speech.

Index

Page numbers followed by *f* indicate figures.

Numbers

16: Moments (film), 51, 157
"22 Rules of Storytelling" (Coats), 107, 127, 160
"50 Feet from MLK" (Zuckerman), 46 *f*
"339: Break-Up" (Glass), 63–64

A

Achenbach, Shane, 45 *f*
acting out stories, 86–87
actors, diversity, 98
Adichie, Chimamanda Ngozi, 45 *f*, 158
Adversity and Resilience text set, 44 *f*
Aesop's Fables, 97
African Americans
    children's literature, in, 24–25
    television shows, in, 98
"Against All Odds" (Collins, P.), 63–64
Ahlberg, Allan, 93–94, 155–156
Alborough, Jez, 94, 149
Alcott, Louisa May, 6, 149
Alexander, Kwame, 6–7, 55–56, 150
Ali, Muhammad, 43 *f*, 145, 159
Alice in Wonderland (Carroll), 93
Allen, Phyllis, 45 *f*, 159
All the Small Poems and Fourteen More (Worth), 59
"Alone" (Angelou), 46 *f*, 145
Alter, Adam, 42 *f*
Amazing Grace (Hoffman), 9
American Born Chinese (Yang), 36

American Indians in Children's Lit (blog), 27 *f*
American Indian Youth Literature Award, 28 *f*
American Library Association, 35, 92
Anderson, Laurie Halse, 46 *f*
Andrew Carnegie Medal, 28 *f*
And Tango Makes Three (Richardson and
    Parnell), 15, 154–155
Angelou, Maya, 46 *f*, 60, 145
Antifragile (Taleb), 130
Applegate, Katherine, 114–115
architects, writers as, 108–110
Arnove, Anthony, 158
Arrival, The (Tan), 44 *f*, 95
art. *See* visual arts
Art of Drowning, The (Collins, B.), 156
Art of Racing in the Rain, The (Stein), 34 *f*,
    57–58
Asian American Performers Action Coalition, 98
Asian Americans, representation in theater, 98
Asian/Pacific American Award for Literature, 28 *f*
audiobooks, 52, 69–70
authentic characters, 54–55
authenticity, 54
autobiographies, 37, 40 *f*
Avi, 43 *f*

B

Baby Flo (Schroeder), 37
"Back-to-School Fight Over the Right to
    Classroom Prayer, A" (Cohen), 46 *f*

Bad Boy (Myers, W. D.), 37
Baker, Russell, 47 *f*
Banyan Global Learning, 23
Barefoot Books, 27 *f*
Bareilles, Sara, 43 *f*, 64, 137, 160
Barnhouse, Dorothy, 84
Bartoletti, Susan Campbell, 43 *f*
Baseball Saved Us (Mochizuki), 9, 44 *f*, 154
Baylor, Byrd, 42 *f*
Beatles, 47 *f*, 66, 71, 160
BeBop Books, 92
Because of Winn-Dixie (DiCamillo), 2
Beers, Kylene, 88
"Being Content with Myself" (Majeed), 45 *f*
Belonging (film), 42 *f*, 70, 157
Berne, Jennifer, 37
Big Books, 87
big data, 23
BigDayta Project, 23
Big Hero 6 (film), 107, 126
bilingual literature, 31–32
billboards, 68
biographies, 37, 40 *f*
Bird (Elliot), 44 *f*
"Birthright of Human Dignity, The" (Thomas), 45 *f*
Bishop, Rudine Sims, 6–7
Biswas, Asit K., 42 *f*
"Bitterness of Sugar, The" (Singer), 47 *f*
Black Album (Jay Z), 71
"Blackbird" (Beatles), 66, 160
blogs, 27 *f*–28 *f*, 35
Bloody Massacre in King Street, The (Revere), 46 *f*
Boelts, Maribeth, 42 *f*, 145, 150
BookDragon (blog), 28 *f*
books
   multicultural content, 7, 8 *f*, 98
   race/ethnicity of characters, 6–7, 8 *f*, 9, 99
   stories and, 53
boundaries, 124–125
boys, imaginative play and, 73

Boys and Girls (Paley), 73
Boy Who Dared, The (Bartoletti), 43 *f*
Brand, Stewart, 42 *f*
"Brave" (Bareilles), 43 *f*, 64, 137, 160
Brave Girl (Markel), 37, 137, 153–154
Breadwinner, The (Ellis), 43 *f*, 145, 151
Bridge in the Rain (van Gogh), 61
Bridges, Lois, 131
Bringing Up Bébé (Druckerman), 6, 90
Bronx Masquerade (Grimes), 45 *f*
Brown, Brené, 44 *f*, 54, 143, 158
Brown Bookshelf, The (blog), 27 *f*
Browne, Anthony, 125, 150
Brown Girl Dreaming (Woodson), 7, 55, 155
Bruner, Jerome, 126
Bulla, Clyde Robert, 36, 54, 150
Bully (film), 44 *f*
Bunting, Eve, 43 *f*
Burdett, Lois, 86

C

"Caged Bird" (Angelou), 46 *f*
Caldecott Medal, 28 *f*
Campbell, Joseph, 110, 112–113
"Can Hailing a Ride Really Be About Making Friends Again?" (Grimaldi), 42 *f*
Cappelli, Rose, 108
Cappiello, Mary Ann, 33, 35
Carr-Chellman, Ali, 73, 159
Carroll, Lewis, 93
Cars (film), 69, 107, 126
"Case for Reviving Extinct Species, The" (Brand), 42 *f*
Chains (Anderson), 46 *f*
Chalkbox Kid, The (Bulla), 36, 54, 150
characters, authentic, 54–55
Charlotte's Web (White), 7, 9, 81, 113
Children Full of Life (film), 143–144
Children's Book Cooperative, The (blog), 28 *f*
children's literature
   awards, 28 *f*
   blogs, 27 *f*–28 *f*, 35

diversity in, 7, 8 *f*, 9, 24–26, 27 *f*, 36–37, 39, 48
formats, 35–36, 39
genre, 35–37, 39
Latino/a, 31–32
sociocultural backgrounds in, 36–37
themes, 35
whiteness of, 24–25, 36, 99
Children's Literature Diversity Festival, 26
Choi, Yoon, 42 *f*, 145, 150
"Choice, Happiness, and Spaghetti Sauce"
    (Gladwell), 45 *f*
choral reading, 93–94
Cinco Punto Press, 27 *f*
Circuit, The (Jiménez), 37
City, The (Leger), 42 *f*, 161
Classroom Bookshelf, The (blog), 27 *f*, 35, 137
classrooms
    diversity in, 6–7, 24, 48
    technological changes in, 23
    turning talk into action, 137
Clements, Andrew, 36, 117
Click, Clack, Moo (Cronin), 43 *f*, 151
close reading, 16–18
    complex texts, 91
    multimedia, 89–91
    poetry, 60–61, 89 *f*
    shared reading, 88, 90
    small-group instruction, 90
    songs, 89 *f*
    visual arts, 89, 89 *f*, 90
CNN news clips, 35, 41 *f*
Coats, Emma, 107, 126–127, 160
Cobb, Vicki, 37
Cohen, Adam, 46 *f*
cohesion, 121, 123
collaborative conversations, 131–132
Collected Poems of Langston Hughes, The
    (Hughes), 156
Collier, Christopher, 81
Collier, James Lincoln, 81
Collins, Billy, 47 *f*, 60, 145, 156
Collins, Phil, 63–64

Collins, Suzanne, 114
Colorin Colorado (blog), 27 *f*
comic books, 40 *f*
Coming of Age text set, 47 *f*
Common Core State Standards
    close reading, 16, 88
    conversational goals, 131–132
    teacher evaluations, 24
community, 19, 33
compelling events, 55–56
Confetti (Mora), 32, 156
Constantino, Bobby, 46 *f*
Cooperative Children's Book Center (website),
    35
Coretta Scott King Book Award, 28 *f*
Corrigan, Maureen, 113
Courage text set, 43 *f*
Cowbird (website), 52, 72, 161
creative constraints, 142
creative thinking, 80
Creech, Sharon, 42 *f*, 45 *f*, 117, 151
Crime and Punishment (Dostoyevsky), 93
Crispin (Avi), 43 *f*
critical thinking, 80
Cronin, Doreen, 43 *f*, 151
Crossover, The (Alexander), 6–7, 55–56, 150
Culham, Ruth, 108
curation, 72

D

"Danger of a Single Story, The" (Adichie), 45 *f*,
    158
Daring Greatly (Brown), 143
Dawes, Erika Thulin, 33, 35
Dead Poets Society (film), 146
Declaration of Independence, 46 *f*
Declaration of the Rights of the Child, 46 *f*
DeLio, Francesca, 101–105
dePaola, Tomie, 94–95, 151
Design Lab, 120
details, 108
dialogue, 134

DiCamillo, Kate, 2
Dickinson, Emily, 37, 44 *f*
digital stories, 41 *f*, 51–52, 120, 146
dinner-table conversations, 131–133
discussions
    balanced, 135–136
    collaborative conversations, 131–132
    conditions for, 132–135
    dinner-table conversations, 131–133
    Initiate-Respond-Evaluate (IRE) model, 131
    Initiate-Respond-Respond-Respond (IRRR)
        model, 131
    mindfulness, 129
    partnerships, 133
    purposeful dialogue, 134–135
    unpredictability of, 130, 135
"Disrupting My Comfort Zone" (Grazer), 44 *f*
diversity
    actors, of, 98
    children's literature, in, 7, 8 *f*, 9, 24–25, 27 *f*,
        36–37, 39
    classrooms, in, 6–7, 24, 48
    television shows, in, 98
    United States, 7
    young adult literature, in, 25
diversity gap studies, 7, 98
Diversity in YA (blog), 27 *f*
DJ Danger Mouse, 71
"Does Your Diet Influence How Well You
    Sleep?" (Sifferlin), 45 *f*
Doodle4Google 2014, 45 *f*
Dorfman, Lynne, 108
Dostoyevsky, Fyodor, 93
Dot, The (Reynolds), 13, 126, 154
dramatic interpretations, 97–98
dream mapping, 11–12
dreams, 79–80
Dreams (film), 79, 157
Druckerman, Pamela, 6, 90
"Duty to Family, Heritage, and Culture, A" (Yu),
    42 *f*, 160
Dweck, Carol, 145

Dylan, Bob, 47 *f*

E

early readers, 87, 92
Eeds, Maryann, 131
Elliot, Zetta, 44 *f*
Ellis, Deborah, 43 *f*, 145, 151
emerging readers, 87
Emerson, Ralph Waldo, 42 *f*
emotions, sounds and, 65–66
Empathy and Compassion text set, 44 *f*
Enemy Pie (Munson), 42 *f*
enlarged text, 87
Enriquez, Grace, 35
Erskine, Kathryn, 44 *f*
Everybody Needs a Rock (Baylor), 42 *f*

F

fables, 97
Fables (Lobel), 121, 153
Facebook, 23, 124
Falling in Love with Close Reading (Lehman and
    Roberts), 88
families, 33, 50
Family Survey Toolkit, 50
fantasy stories, 36, 40 *f*
"Father and Son" (Stevens), 47 *f*
    film. *See also* video
    language of, 71
    point of view, 126
    storytelling, 41 *f*, 52, 107
Fisher, Douglas, 88
Fitzgerald, F. Scott, 53
Flavor Thesaurus, The (Segnit), 149
Fleischauer, Seth, 23
Fleischman, Paul, 42 *f*, 81, 83, 94, 152, 156
Fletcher, Ralph, 42 *f*, 108
Flora and the Flamingo (Idle), 94, 152
Flotsam (Wiesner), 95
"Forever Young" (Dylan), 47 *f*
Frankston, Jay, 47 *f*
Freak the Mighty (Philbrick), 42 *f*

Freedom text set, 46 *f*

Frey, Nancy, 88

Friendship and Belonging text set, 42 *f*

Frindle (Clements), 117

Frog and Toad (Lobel), 114

From the Mixed-Up Files of Mrs. Basil E. Frankweiler (Konigsburg), 81, 152

Frost, Robert, 37

G

Gaiman, Neil, 83

"Gaming to Reengage Boys in Learning" (Carr-Chellman), 159

Gangi, Jane, 25

Gannett, Ruth Stiles, 130

genre, 35–37, 39

Giaever, Bianca, 126, 158

Gifts of Imperfection, The (Brown), 143

Gilbert, Elizabeth, 44 *f*

Girl Before a Mirror (Picasso), 45 *f*

Girl Reading a Letter at an Open Window (Vermeer), 45 *f*

Girl with a Pearl Earring (Vermeer), 45 *f*, 67

Giver, The (Lowry), 114

Gladwell, Malcolm, 45 *f*

Glass, Ira, 63–64

Goldfinch, The (Tartt), 90

Gonzalez, Maya Christina, 32

Good Night, Gorilla (Rathmann), 94–95

Google+, 124

"Google and Twitter Help Track Influenza Outbreaks" (Thompson), 42 *f*

Gottschall, Jonathan, 77

Goya, Francisco, 46 *f*, 160–161

graphic novels, 40 *f*

Grazer, Brian, 44 *f*

Greene, Maxine, 14

Grey Album, The (DJ Danger Mouse), 71

Grimaldi, Christine, 42 *f*

Grimes, Nikki, 45 *f*

Growing Up (Baker), 47 *f*

growth mind-sets, 145

Guernica (Picasso), 43 *f*, 161

Gustavson, Adam, 9

H

habits of mind, 18

Hamlet (Shakespeare), 56–57, 114

happiness, 144

"Happy" (Williams), 114

Harris, Jonathan, 51–52, 161

Harry Potter and the Sorcerer's Stone (Rowling), 69

Harry Potter series (Rowling), 36, 70, 113

hashtags, 124

Having of Great Conversations, The (blog), 131

Heard, Georgia, 11

Heard It in the Playground (Ahlberg), 93–94, 155–156

heart mapping, 11

Hemingway, Ernest, 115–116, 124

hero's journey stories, 110, 112–113

Hero with a Thousand Faces, The (Campbell), 110

historical fiction, 40 *f*

Hoffman, Mary, 9

Holdaway, Don, 87

Homeless Bird (Whelan), 43 *f*

Homer, 113

Honda (Weston), 37

Horgan, John, 46 *f*

"How to Eat a Poem" (Merriam), 60

"How to Live Before You Die" (Jobs), 47 *f*

"How Your Moral Decisions Are Shaped by a Bad Mood" (Riddle), 44 *f*

Hug (Alborough), 94, 149

Hughes, Langston, 37, 46 *f*–47 *f*, 60, 156

Humanity text set, 47 *f*

Humans of New York (photoblog), 21–22, 33, 47 *f*, 48, 162

Hunger Games, The (Collins, S.), 114

I

"I Am Still the Greatest" (Ali), 43 *f*, 145, 159

Identities text set, 45 *f*

Idle, Molly, 94, 152

"If" (Kipling), 46 *f*

"If I Could Invent One Thing to Make the World a Better Place" (Doodle4Google 2014), 45 *f*

"I Got Myself Arrested So I Could Look Inside the Justice System" (Constantino), 46 *f*

"I Have a Dream" (King), 46 *f*

imaginative play

 boys and, 73

 stories in, 73, 74 *f*–76 *f*, 77, 77 *f*, 78

Incredibles, The (film), 107

independent reading, 33, 93

informational reading, 37, 117

Initiate-Respond-Evaluate (IRE) model, 131

Initiate-Respond-Respond-Respond (IRRR) model, 131

Inkthinktank (website), 37

"inky courage," 5, 9–13

Instagram, 23, 124

Interactive Comprehension Strategies (Serafini), 131

interactive reading

 acting out a part, 86–87

 stop and jot, 86

 think-alouds, 84–85

 turn and talk, 85–86

Interesting Nonfiction for Kids (I.N.K.) (blog), 28 *f*, 37

Iron Jawed Angels (film), 97

Ish (Reynolds), 126

"I" statements, 10–11

"I Think We All Need a Pep Talk" (Kid President), 42 *f*

"I, Too" (Hughes), 46 *f*

J

Jacob Burns Film Center, 70–71, 141–142

Janitor's Boy, The (Clements), 36

Jay Z, 71

Jeffers, Oliver, 71, 152

Jiménez, Francisco, 37

Jobs, Steve, 47 *f*

John Newbery Medal, 28 *f*

Johnson, Christine Toy, 98

Joyful Noise (Fleischman), 94, 156

Junebug (Mead), 44 *f*

Just Us Books, 27 *f*

K

Kamvar, Sep, 51, 161

Karpowitz, Christopher F., 45 *f*

Keegan, Marina, 22

Keim, Brandon, 46 *f*

Khan, Rukhsana, 43 *f*

KidLitosphere (blog), 26, 35

Kid President, 42 *f*, 47 *f*

Kine, Starlee, 63–64

King, Martin Luther Jr., 46 *f*

King for a Day (Khan), 43 *f*

Kipling, Rudyard, 46 *f*

Knots in My Yo-Yo String (Spinelli), 44 *f*

Knuffle Bunny (Willems), 55

Knuffle Bunny Free (Willems), 55, 155

Knuffle Bunny Too (Willems), 55

Konigsburg, E. L., 81, 152

Kurosawa, Akira, 79–80, 157

L

Lange, Dorothea, 44 *f*, 161

language

 music and, 62–65

 poetry and, 59–60

Latino/a literature, 31–32

Latinos in KidLit (blog), 28 *f*

Lawrence, Jacob, 46 *f*

Leaves of Grass (Whitman), 157

"Leaving Identity Issues to Other Folks" (Allen), 45 *f*, 159

Lee and Low Books, 7, 25, 27 *f*, 36, 45 *f*, 92, 98

Leger, Fernand, 42 *f*, 161

Lehman, Barbara, 95, 153

Lehman, Chris, 88

Lemov, Doug, 145

lesson planning
 punctuation, 122, 123 *f*
 sentence structure, 117 *f*–119 *f*

"Lessons from the Lab" (Paul), 43 *f*

Lester, Julius, 87, 101–105, 153

Let's Talk About Race (Lester), 87, 101–105, 153

"Letter to a Person on Their First Day Here" (Kid President), 47 *f*

letter writing, 144–145

Lewis, C. S., 9

Librarian of Basra, The (Winter), 134

"Life, Liberty, and the Pursuit of Happiness" (Sullivan), 46 *f*

Lion, the Witch and the Wardrobe, The (Lewis), 9

Lion King, The (film), 114

Lionni, Leo, 79–80, 97, 153

literary devices, 121
 literature, 53, 78. *See also* books; children's literature; young adult literature
 African Americans in, 24–25
 bilingual, 31–32
 Latino/a, 31–32
 multicultural, 33, 39, 40 *f*–47 *f*, 48
 multigenre, 33, 39, 40 *f*–47 *f*, 48
 multimodal, 33, 35, 39, 40 *f*–47 *f*, 48
 nonfiction, 36–37

Little Women (Alcott), 6, 149

LitWorld (organization), 146

Living Barefoot (blog), 27 *f*

Lobel, Arnold, 97, 114, 121, 122 *f*, 153

Lon Po Po (film), 70

Lorde, 125

Lord of the Rings, The (Tolkien), 113

Louder Than a Bomb (film), 61

Love That Dog (Creech), 42 *f*, 151

Low, Jason, 25

Lowry, Lois, 114

M

Macbeth for Kids (Burdett), 86

Mace, Aaron, 141–142

Mahanta, Siddhartha, 42 *f*

Majeed, Kamaal, 45 *f*

Malala (Winter), 137

"Marbles" (Worth), 59–60

Markel, Michelle, 37, 137, 153–154

Marshfield Dreams (Fletcher), 42 *f*

mash-ups, 71–72

"Material Remains" (Nagle), 42 *f*

Matthew's Dream (Lionni), 79–80, 153

Mead, Alice, 44 *f*

Mendelberg, Tali, 45 *f*

Mentor Author, Mentor Texts (Fletcher), 108

mentor texts, 53, 72
 films as, 107
 poetry, 143
 teaching with, 108, 116–117
 writing and, 108, 114–117, 121

Mentor Texts (Dorfman and Cappelli), 108

Merriam, Eve, 60

metaphors, 121

Meyer, Stephenie, 36

Michael L. Printz Award, 28 *f*

Middle East Book Award, 28 *f*

Midsummer Night's Dream, A (Shakespeare), 43 *f*

Migrant Mother (Lange), 44 *f*, 161

Migration of the Negro, The (Lawrence), 46 *f*

Miller, Brenda, 9

mindfulness, 17–18, 129

Minds Are Made for Stories (Newkirk), 37

minimalism, 123, 125

mirrors
 race/ethnicity of characters, 6–7
 stories as, 5–7, 9

Mochizuki, Ken, 9, 44 *f*, 154

Mockingbird (Erskine), 44 *f*

"Modern Families" (Wallich), 47 *f*

monomyth, 112

Monster (Myers, W. D.), 36

Monsters, Inc. (film), 107

Moore, Chris, 158
Mora, Pat, 31–32, 37, 156
"More Women, but Not Nearly Enough"
    (Mendelberg and Karpowitz), 45 *f*
Moth, The (radio program), 35, 41 *f*, 70
Mott, Nicholas, 47 *f*
Mr. Schu Reads (blog), 6
multicultural literature, 8 *f*, 27 *f*
multigenre literature, 33, 39, 40 *f*–47 *f*, 48
multimedia
    close reading, 89–91
    minimalism, 125
    shared reading, 87–88
    stories in, 52–53, 68–69, 78
    teaching with, 41 *f*
multimodal literature, 33, 35, 39, 40 *f*–47 *f*, 48
Munch, Edward, 45 *f*
Munson, Derek, 42 *f*
music
    emotions in, 65–66
    language of, 62–65
    shared reading and, 89 *f*
    song structure, 66
    stories in, 62–63, 78
music videos, 125
My Brother Sam Is Dead (Collier and Collier), 81
Myers, Christopher, 25
Myers, Walter Dean, 24–25, 36–37
My Father's Dragon series (Gannett), 130

N
Nagle, Robin, 42 *f*
Name Jar, The (Choi), 42 *f*, 145, 150
narrative
    power of, 19
    writing and, 37
narrative reading, 37
National Public Radio (NPR), 51, 63, 69
Neruda, Pablo, 31, 37, 60
"Network to Build a Dream On, A" (Horgan), 46 *f*
Neverwhere (Gaiman), 83
Newbery Medal, 28 *f*

Newkirk, Thomas, 36
Newsela (website), 117
New York Knicks/Urban Word poetry slam, 61
"New York's Looming Food Disaster" (Mahanta),
    42 *f*
New York Times, 39, 108–109
"No More Night?" (Keim), 46 *f*
nonfiction literature, 36–37
Nonfiction Mentor Texts (Dorfman and Cappelli),
    108
Nonfiction Minute, 37
nonfiction writing, 37, 38 *f*
Northern Lights (Pullman), 93
Notable Books for a Global Society, 28 *f*
Notice and Note (Beers and Probst), 88
Noticing More About Ourselves Toolkit,
    138–140
NPR. *See* National Public Radio (NPR)
Nuyorican Poets' Café, 61
Nye, Naomi Shihab, 37, 47 *f*, 61
Nyong'o, Lupita, 45 *f*

O
Obama, Barack, 43 *f*
"Ode to a Sock" (Neruda), 60
"Ode to Fried Potatoes" (Neruda), 60
Odyssey (Homer), 113
Old Man and the Sea, The (Hemingway),
    115–116
Oliver, Jamie, 45 *f*
Oliver, Mary, 59
"O Me! O Life!" (Whitman), 147, 157
On a Beam of Light (Berne), 37
One and Only Ivan, The (Applegate), 114–115
"On Turning Ten" (Collins, B.), 47 *f*, 145, 156
Open Book, The (blog), 27 *f*
Opposite of Loneliness, The (Keegan), 22
oral reading, 97
oral storytelling, 96–97

P
Palacio, R. J., 9, 44 *f*, 83, 117, 118 *f*–119 *f*, 154

Paley, Vivian, 73
Palmer, Brian, 43 *f*
Pancakes for Breakfast (dePaola), 94–95, 151
"Paradox of Choice, The" (Schwartz), 45 *f*
paragraphs, 114–116, 121
Parker-Pope, Tara, 42 *f*
Parks, Rosa, 46 *f*
Parnell, Peter, 15, 154–155
partnerships, 133
Paul, Annie Murphy, 43 *f*
People Speak, The (film), 137, 158
performance-based assessment, 98
Pericoli, Matteo, 108–109
Peterson, Ralph, 131
Philbrick, Rodman, 42 *f*
Picasso, Pablo, 43 *f*, 45 *f*, 161
picture books, 37, 39, 40 *f*
    postmodern, 95
    wordless, 94–95, 99
Piñata Books, 27 *f*
Pink and Say (Polacco), 42 *f*
Pinkney, Jerry, 121, 123 *f*
Pinterest (website), 72
Pixar, 107–108, 126
play, imaginative. *See* imaginative play
plays, 97–98
podcasts, 41 *f*
poetry, 37, 40 *f*
    art and, 61
    close reading, 60–61, 89 *f*
    language of, 59–60
    performing, 142–143
    shared reading and, 89 *f*
    stories in, 58–62
    wide reading, 61
Poetry Foundation, 61
Poetry Out Loud (website), 40 *f*
poets
    performances, 59
    reading work, 61
point of view, 125–126
Polacco, Patricia, 42 *f*

postmodern picture books, 95
Power of Empathy, The (film), 44 *f*
"Power of Vulnerability, The" (Brown), 158
Probst, Robert, 88
Pullman, Philip, 93
punctuation, 121, 122 *f*–123 *f*
Pura Belpré Award, 28 *f*, 31
purposeful dialogue, 134–135

R

"racebent" characters, 99
race/ethnicity of characters, 6–7, 8 *f*, 9, 99
Radiohead (musical group), 125
Radiolab (NPR), 51, 57
Rainbow Project Reading List, 28 *f*
Randolph Caldecott Medal, 28 *f*
Ratatouille (film), 107, 126
Rathmann, Peggy, 94–95
Read-Aloud Handbook, The (Trelease), 83
Read-Aloud Planning Guide Toolkit, 99–105
read-alouds, 33
    oral storytelling, 96
    ritual, 81
    sample scaffold, 101–105
    student interactions, 84–87, 99
    thinking and, 84–85
    value of, 83–84
readers
    early, 92
    emerging, 87
    reflected in literature, 6–7, 8 *f*, 9
Readers Front and Center (Barnhouse), 84
reader's theater, 97–98
"readicide," 19
reading
    independent, 93
    pleasure and, 83–84
    preferences, 33, 34 *f*
    shared, 87, 90
    structure, 114–117, 120
    thinking and, 84–85

reading strategies
　choral reading, 93–94
　close reading, 88–91
　compelling stories, 91–92
　independent reading, 93
　shared reading, 87, 90
　small-group instruction, 91–92
　visualization, 91
　wordless picture books, 94–95, 99
Readworks (website), 117
realistic fiction, 36, 40 *f*
Red Book, The (Lehman), 95, 153
representation, 109
Resolving Conflicts text set, 43 *f*
Responsibility and Interdependency text set, 42 *f*
Revere, Paul, 46 *f*
Reynolds, Peter, 13, 126, 154
Richard, Randy, 45 *f*
Richardson, Justin, 15, 154–155
Rich in Color (blog), 27 *f*
Riddle, Travis, 44 *f*
ritual read-alouds, 81
Roadrunner Press, 27 *f*
Robert F. Sibert Informational Book Award, 28 *f*
Roberts, Kathleen, 88
Rodin, Auguste, 67
Rogers, Fred, 42 *f*, 96
Rowling, J. K., 44 *f*, 69–70, 113
Royal Society for the Encouragement of Arts, 44 *f*
Rules of Summer (Tan), 95

S

Sandberg, Sheryl, 43 *f*
Say It in Six (website), 124, 162
Scared Is Scared (film), 125–126, 158
Schneider Family Book Award, 28 *f*
Scholastic, 70
School Library Journal, 35
Schroeder, Alan, 37
Schwartz, Barry, 45 *f*
"Science Can Help Us Live Longer, But How
　Long Is Too Long?" (Richard), 45 *f*

science fiction stories, 36, 40 *f*
Scream, The (Munch), 45 *f*
Seedfolks (Fleischman), 42 *f*, 81, 83, 152
Segnit, Niki, 149
"Self-Reliance" (Emerson), 42 *f*
sentence structure, 121
　digital stories, 120
　lesson planning, 117 *f*–119 *f*
　mentor texts, 114–116
September Roses (Winter), 96, 155
Serafini, Frank, 131
Series of Unfortunate Events, A (Snicket), 69
Shakespeare, William, 43 *f*, 45 *f*, 56–57, 80, 114
Shakespeare Can Be Fun! series, 80, 86
shared reading, 33
　close reading, 90
　emerging readers, 87
　media and, 87–88, 99
　schedule for, 88 *f*
Sifferlin, Alexandra, 45 *f*
silence, 130
Silent Star (Wise and Gustavson), 9
Silverstein, Shel, 61
similes, 121
Singer, Peter, 47 *f*
Sixteen Years in Sixteen Seconds (Yoo), 9
six-word memoirs, 12, 124, 162
Siy, Alex, 37
small-group instruction, 33
　close reading, 90
　strategies for, 91–92
small scenes/big themes, 56–58
SMITH magazine, 124, 162
Smoky Night (Bunting), 43 *f*
Snapchat, 23
Snicket, Lemony, 69
social media, 22–23, 99, 124, 145
Social Structures and Institutions text set, 43 *f*
"So Much Happiness" (Nye), 47 *f*
Song of Myself (Whitman), 45 *f*
songs, close reading, 89 *f*

songwriters
   emotions, 65–66
   language of, 63–65
   song structure, 66
Songza (website), 65
sounds, emotions and, 65–66
South Asia Book Award, 28 *f*
"Speak Up" (Frankston), 47 *f*
Spinelli, Jerry, 43 *f*–44 *f*
"Standing Up to Injustice" (Parks), 46 *f*
Stanton, Brandon, 21, 33, 48, 162
Steerage, The (Stieglitz), 44 *f*
Stein, Garth, 34 *f*, 57–58
Stevens, Cat, 47 *f*, 65
sticky notes, 124
Stieglitz, Alfred, 44 *f*
Stone, Tanya Lee, 37
Stonewall Book Award, 28 *f*
stop and jot, 86
stories, 1–3
   art and, 67–68, 78
   audiobooks, 69–70
   authentic characters, 54–55
   bringing to life, 79–81, 83, 96–97
   centering, 16
   close reading of, 16–17, 88–91
   community building, 33
   compelling, 55–56, 91–92, 110, 111 *f*–112 *f*
   curation, 72
   digital, 51–52
   discussions, 131
   foundations of, 110, 112–114
   hero's journey, 110, 112–113
   imaginative play and, 73, 74 *f*–76 *f*, 77, 77 *f*, 78
   importance of, 4–5, 146
   "inky courage," 5, 9–13
   mash-ups, 71–72
   mentor texts, 53, 72, 107–108, 116–117, 121, 143
   mirrors, as, 5–7, 9
   multimedia and, 68–69, 78
   music and, 62–66, 78
   poetry and, 58–62, 78

   small scenes/big themes, 56–58
   threats to, 18–19
   traditional, 36
   turning talk into action, 136–137
   video and, 68–71
   voice and, 69–70
   wide-awakeness, 5, 14–15
   windows, as, 5–7, 9
stories, digital. *See* digital stories
StoryCorps (NPR), 69
story scripting, 98
Story Shots (blog), 160
storytelling
   moviemaking and, 141–142
   oral, 96–97
   physical actions, 97
   rules for, 107–108
   students, 126–127
   tools for, 51–53
   visual, 23, 67–68
   vulnerability, 142–145
Storytelling Animal, The (Gottschall), 77
structure. *See* sentence structure; text structure
Stuart Little (White), 80
student-created texts, 41 *f*
student podcasts, 41 *f*
students
   acting out a part, 86–87
   close reading of, 16–18
   discussions, 130–135
   gender, 26, 29
   happiness, 144
   identities, 26, 29–33
   interests, 33, 34 *f*, 35
   multimedia, 125
   partnerships, 133
   reading preferences, 33, 34 *f*
   response to reading, 80, 81 *f*–82 *f*, 84
   sharing, 10–12
   social media, 22
   sociocultural backgrounds, 36–37
   stop and jot, 86

storytelling, 126–127
think-alouds, 84–85
thinking strategies, 91
trust, 9–10
turn and talk, 85–86
visual storytelling, 23, 67–68, 125
writing preferences, 33
Student Survey Toolkit, 48–50
"Success, Failure, and the Drive to Keep Creating" (Gilbert), 44*f*
Sullivan, Andrew, 46*f*

T

Taleb, Nassim Nicholas, 130
Tan, Shaun, 44*f*, 95
Tartt, Donna, 90
"Teach Every Child About Food" (Oliver, J.), 45*f*
teaching
bringing stories to life, 83
centering stories, 16
digital stories, 146
discussions, 129–135
diversity, 25–26, 36
habits of mind, 18
mentor texts, with, 108, 116–117
mindfulness, 17–18
read-alouds, 81, 83–84
reading preferences, 34*f*
sharing, 33
silence, 130
text sets, 33, 35
vulnerability, 144–145
wide-awakeness, 14–15
Teaching Channel, 68
Teaching with Text Sets (Cappiello and Dawes), 33
Teach Like a Champion (Lemov), 145
TED Talks, 35, 43*f*–45*f*, 47*f*, 73, 158–159
"Teen Confronts Her iPhone Addition, A" (Achenbach), 45*f*
television shows, diversity in, 98

Tempest for Kids, The (Burdett), 86
Text Complexity (Frey and Fisher), 88
text sets
Adversity and Resilience, 44*f*
Coming of Age, 47*f*
core texts, 35
Courage, 43*f*
creating, 39
Empathy and Compassion, 44*f*
Freedom, 46*f*
Friendship and Belonging, 42*f*
Humanity, 47*f*
Identities, 45*f*
multigenre, 40*f*–47*f*
multimodal, 40*f*–47*f*
Resolving Conflicts, 43*f*
Responsibility and Interdependency, 42*f*
Social Structures and Institutions, 43*f*
student-created, 41*f*
thematic, 35, 39–41, 42*f*–47*f*, 48
Transitions, 46*f*
types of, 33
Wellness, 45*f*
text structure, 108, 114–117, 118*f*–119*f*, 120–121
theater, diversity in, 98
"Theme for English B" (Hughes), 47*f*
themes, 35, 126
"These 5 Foods Will Be Harder to Grow in a Warmer World" (Woolston), 46*f*
"They Shut Me Up in Prose" (Dickinson), 44*f*
think-alouds, 84–85
ThinkCERCA (website), 117
Thinker, The (Rodin), 67
"thinking squares," 124
thinking strategies, 87
This American Life (radio program), 63
This I Believe (radio program), 35, 41*f*–47*f*, 145, 159–160
This Moose Belongs to Me (Jeffers), 71, 152
Thomas, Will, 45*f*

Thompson, Helen, 42 *f*
Those Shoes (Boelts), 42 *f*, 145, 150
Tolkien, J. R. R., 113
toolkits
    Family Survey, 50
    Noticing More About Ourselves, 138–140
    Read-Aloud Planning Guide, 99–105
    Student Survey, 48–50
    Where to Find Stories, 78
    Write Your Own Phenomenal Storytelling
      Rules, 127
Tortajada, Cecilia, 42 *f*
Tortoise and the Hare, The (Pinkney), 121, 123 *f*
Toy Story (film), 107
traditional stories, 36, 40 *f*, 121, 122 *f*–123 *f*
Transitions text set, 46 *f*
Trelease, Jim, 83–84
Tres de Mayo de 1808 en Madrid, El (Goya), 46 *f*,
    160–161
"Trouble" (Stevens), 65
trust, 9–10
Tu Books, 36
Tuesday (Wiesner), 95
Tumblr, 99, 124
turn and talk, 85–86
Twelfth Night (Shakespeare), 45 *f*
Twilight series (Meyer), 36
Twitter, 124, 145

V

van Gogh, Vincent, 61, 67, 79, 161
Vermeer, Johannes, 45 *f*, 67
    video. *See also* film
    music videos, 125
    stories in, 68–71
Vimeo, 41 *f*, 68, 94
visual artists, storytelling, 68
visual arts
    close reading, 89, 89 *f*, 90–91
    poetry and, 61
    shared reading and, 89 *f*
    stories in, 67–68, 78

visual literacy, 23
visual storytelling, 23, 35, 41 *f*, 61, 67–68, 125,
    141–142
voice, 69–70
Voices in the Park (Browne), 125, 150
vulnerability, 142–145

W

Walk Two Moons (Creech), 45 *f*, 117
Wallich, Paul, 47 *f*
Warren, Andrea, 37
"Water Quality" (Tortajada and Biswas), 42 *f*
We Feel Fine (website), 51–52, 161
#weneeddiversebooks movement, 26
Wellness text set, 45 *f*
Weston, Mark, 37
"What Are Friends For?" (Parker-Pope), 42 *f*
"What Makes a Hero?" (Winkler), 159
"What Makes Us Human?" (Mott), 47 *f*
Wheat Field with Crows (van Gogh), 79, 161
Whelan, Gloria, 43 *f*
"When Has Reading Felt Good?" 34 *f*
"When I'm Sixty Four" (Beatles), 47 *f*
"Where Are the People of Color in Children's
    Books?" (Myers), 24
Where to Find Stories Toolkit, 78
"Where We Are Shapes Who We Are" (Alter),
    42 *f*
White, E. B., 7, 9, 80–81, 113
White Album (Beatles), 71
whiteness
    children's literature and, 24–25, 36, 99
    media and, 99
White Stripes (musical group), 125
Whitman, Walt, 45 *f*, 146, 157
wholehearted people, 54–55
Who Says Women Can't Be Doctors? (Stone), 37
"Why Does China Not Have Famines Anymore?"
    (Palmer), 43 *f*
"Why We Have Too Few Women Leaders"
    (Sandberg), 43 *f*
wide-awakeness, 5, 14–15

Wiesner, David, 95

Willems, Mo, 55, 71, 114, 155

Williams, Pharrell, 114

Williams, Robin, 146

windows, stories as, 5–7, 9

Winkler, Matthew, 112, 159

Winter, Jeanette, 96, 134, 137, 155

Wise, Bill, 9

Wonder (Palacio), 9, 44 *f*, 83, 117, 118 *f*–119 *f*, 154

Woodson, Jacqueline, 7, 55, 155

Woolston, Chris, 46 *f*

wordless picture books, 94–95, 99

Worth, Valerie, 59–60

Wringer (Spinelli), 43 *f*

"Writers as Architects" (Pericoli), 108–109

Write Your Own Phenomenal Storytelling Rules Toolkit, 127

writing

  architecture, as, 108–110

  boundaries, 124–125

  cohesion, 121, 123

  conventions, 121

  language, 121

  mentor texts, 108, 114–117, 121

  point of view, 125–126

  saying more with less, 123–125

  structure, 114–117, 118 *f*–119 *f*, 120

  teaching, 108, 110, 112–114

  themes, 126

Writing Thief, The (Culham), 108

Y

Yang, Gene Luen, 36

Yoo, Paula, 9

Young, Ed, 70

young adult literature

  blogs, 35

  community building, 33

  diversity in, 25, 48

  formats, 35–36, 39

  genre, 35–37, 39

  themes, 35

YouTube videos, 35, 41 *f*, 68, 70, 129

Yu, Ying Ying, 42 *f*, 160

Z

Zinn, Howard, 137, 158

Zuckerman, Mortimer B., 46 *f*